The Major

THE MAJOR

The Senior Officer in Charge: Commanding Fellow Prisoners of War

W. Thomas McDaniel Jr.
Colonel, US Air Force, Retired

Copyright © 2011 by W. Thomas McDaniel Jr.

Library of Congress Control Number: 2011911331
ISBN: Hardcover   978-1-4628-2985-9
           Softcover   978-1-4628-2984-2
           Ebook   978-1-4628-2986-6

All rights reserved. No part of this book may be reproduced or transmitted in any form or by any means, electronic or mechanical, including photocopying, recording, or by any information storage and retrieval system, without permission in writing from the copyright owner.

This book was printed in the United States of America.

To order additional copies of this book, contact:
Xlibris Corporation
1-888-795-4274
www.Xlibris.com
Orders@Xlibris.com
100197

Contents

Prologue 11

Chapter One—Land of the Free and Home of the Brave
   (1916 to 1950) 13

   The Major: Major William T. McDaniel 14
   The Fighter Pilot: Captain William D. Locke 21
   The Steadfast Adjutant:
      First Lieutenant James B. Smith 24
   The Indispensable Interpreter:
      Sergeant Takeshi Kumagai 26
   The Underage Privates: Allen J. Gifford, Edward
      G. Halcomb, Valdor W. John, Robert L. Sharpe,
      Edward N. Slater, and James Yeager 28

Chapter Two—First Blood: Men against Tanks
   (25 June to 20 July) 44

Chapter Three—Battle, Evasion, and Capture
   (20 July to August) 65

Chapter Four—Mr. Kim's School for Propaganda
   (August to 20 September) 98

Chapter Five—The Longest, Bleakest Trudge
   (20 September to 10 October) 122

Chapter Six—In the Enemy's Capital (10 to 14 October) ... 147

Chapter Seven—Train to Manchuria (14 to 20 October).... 163

Chapter Eight—Cavalry to the Rescue
 (20 to 24 October) 169

Chapter Nine—Home Not-So-Sweet Home
 (July 1950 to December 1953) 190

Chapter Ten—Judgment Day: Congressional Hearings
 (December 1953) 234

Chapter Eleven—Rites: Second and Last (1954 to 1955) 312

Epilogue 327

Appendices 333
 1. Silver Star Award Citation 333
 2. Timeline 334
 3. Basic Military Map Symbols 340
 4. POW Leadership 342
 5. North Korean Guards Who Executed
  the Sunchon Tunnel Massacre 345
 6. Distinguished Service Cross Award Citation 346

Acknowledgments and Sources 349

Endnotes 359

Index 369

Glossary 374

Map of Korea—1950 376

In Remembrance

To my father, William Thomas McDaniel, who promised me—at the age of four, on the day he departed for war—that upon his return he would bring me a gift. Little did the father know that "the gift" would continue to give ever more abundantly.

Cadet Fourth Class W. T. McDaniel, West Point (1937)

Caveat

Before turning the page, the reader needs to know that this book is historically accurate—as accurate as the memories of the people in it and the research competency and integrity of the author. Every consequential event has been corroborated by two or more people. Every character—good and/or bad—is a real person. Only some speech has been embellished to give voice to those who could not or would not tell their story. Moreover, that voice is expressed in the language of the 1950s with some words—such as *Negroes*, *Colored,* and *Orientals*—that are no longer politically or morally correct, but were not considered inappropriate by American mores at the time. In addition, the English spelling conventions of cities and towns in this book likewise conform to those used at midcentury.

The author has also identified all the graduates of the United States Military Academy (USMA) in this book when they are introduced. This designation follows their name in a parenthesis with the year of their graduation: for example (USMA 1941). The purpose is to show the influence of this venerable institution and the extensive role of its graduates in key command positions during the Korean War and its aftermath.

Although the author is not a disinterested party to how this tale is told, any sins of commission or omission are his alone. The author's intent is twofold: first, to honor his father and the men he directed and served and, second, to correct and expand the historical record of the events associated with one specific group of prisoners of war (POWs) and their families.

Many previous written accounts have often been inaccurate and too narrow in scope to convey the enormity of the events in which the POWs unwillingly participated. In short, with its publication, this book is meant to enhance the history of American POWs in the Korean War.

In sum, let the "truth will out."

Prologue

The most forgotten men in the "Forgotten War" were the American POWs, especially those who endured captivity during the early months of the Korean Conflict. Most were subjected to unspeakable horrors and extreme deprivations. Few survived.

This text tells the story of several hundred Americans who struggled to maintain their human dignity under brutal conditions while trying to make their way home to those they loved. Their story takes place before American servicemen were trained to cope with torture and brainwashing and prior to "The Code of Conduct" becoming the standard by which American POWs would be judged.

For many soldiers, gone were the memories of World War Two (WWII) and the viciousness of an Oriental enemy. Most soldiers were young and soft, living in occupied Japan where the Nipponese tended to junior enlisted men's needs: polishing their boots, shining their brass, and offering female "companionship." These American soldiers rarely trained for combat as virtually no suitable sites existed to conduct large-scale exercises in the country. And an apathetic and old officer corps did little to encourage and hone individual combat skills.

In short, by 1950 the Truman administration had wreaked havoc on the conventional military forces of the United States (US): slashing Pentagon budgets while the President boasted that "we are not alarmed by any sense of the word" with our cost-cutting initiatives. As a result, US Army Basic Training had been reduced to a scant eight weeks. The army numbered only 591,000 soldiers although its authorized strength was 677,000. The new Patton heavy tank consisted of a mere 310 vehicles, all located in the continental United States. And the 3.5-inch antitank bazooka, having superseded the ineffectual World War II 2.36-inch bazooka, had an inventory that was extremely small and none were deployed in the Far East.[1]

Nonetheless, then as now, when confronted with a global upheaval, the first to respond are usually those US military forces in closest proximity to a crisis area. So it was early Sunday morning, 25 June 1950, when the North Korea People's Army launched an invasion into South Korea. And the largest American community most immediately and catastrophically affected was the army units, individual soldiers and their families stationed in Japan. Thus, this narrative begins.

Chapter One

Land of the Free and Home of the Brave (1916 to 1950)

No man that warreth entangleth himself with the affairs of this life; that he may please him who hath chosen him to be a soldier.
—2 Timothy 2:4 (KJV)

Growing up in the United States during the twentieth century was like no other time in history. The freedoms enjoyed by most Americans were unprecedented in spite of economic displacement and depression. True, to preserve liberty much innocent blood had been shed; but the world's despots had largely been destroyed, defeated, or contained. And although the Communist menace loomed large, no one anticipated the attack from the North into southern Korea in the summer of 1950—particularly the young men who grew up in the twenties, thirties, and forties. Like their fathers before them, these young men were preoccupied with school, girls, family, and work. Never imagining a destiny as a POW, each man was living a unique life as his personal history reveals.

* * *

The Major

**William T. "Tom" McDaniel Receiving the
Legion of Merit in Burma (1944)**

A gentle child from birth, no family member could envisage the boy would someday grow into a courageous combat soldier. But William Thomas McDaniel knew—from second grade on—that he would follow the path of his ancestor General Robert E. Lee (USMA 1829) and become a professional soldier. Whether it was the family conversations about his hero or the spanking he got from "Mrs. Lee," Tom always understood who he was and what he would become.

Born in Union Springs, Alabama, on 20 February 1916, Tom spent his earliest years mainly in North Carolina—Raleigh and Henderson. Both Papa and he were surrounded in their household by women: five sisters, a mother, a grandmother, and a great-aunt. His two brothers were away at the University of North Carolina. George was playing football, and Everett was in graduate school preparing for a medical degree. For six years, Tom was the "baby" until the McDaniels had their last child: Beryl.

But Tom almost met the fate of his sister Margaret's twin, Mary, who died at age five. Returning from his first visit to the circus, the four-year-old was overcome with fever and became bedridden. Diagnosed with diphtheria, the family prayed and helplessly watched their baby fight the disease. Weeks later when he had beaten this dreaded illness, Tom was convinced the elephants had made him sick. Yet this flight of fantasy was rare, as he loved history with all its facts and personalities. This infatuation with history was, undoubtedly, instilled from the storytelling and readings of his ever-attentive mother Madge and his sisters Virginia and Anne.

Tom, however, did once get his facts wrong. He informed a schoolteacher that his "uncle" was none other than the revered Civil War icon Robert E. Lee. And while many Southerners made the claim of having a family connection to the Lees, this teacher was a Lee and she knew of no familial relationship with any McDaniel. Moreover, the general could not possibly be this seven-year-old's "uncle." Now Mrs. Lee may have let this brazen assertion slide, but Tom stood his ground—for him, it was a matter of honor. He did what his hero would do: he would not recant the truth. (At his age, he thought all male relatives outside the immediate family were uncles.)So the teacher did what any self-respecting teacher would do in those days to an unrepentant liar; she gave him a good "whuppin'." Of course, his mother had "words" with the teacher the next day and established Tom's lineage through the Dawsons, her side of the family.

A majority of Tom's formative years were spent in Albany, Georgia, where Papa found he could best feed his large family working as a life insurance salesman. Tom was considered a star athlete in football, track, tennis—you name it. And he was well respected for his character and was honored with the top "citizenship" award. Perhaps an example of his sense of service and compassion was best illustrated when, much to the consternation of his mother, he once gave his winter coat away to a classmate who had none. Moreover, the Albany High yearbook staff—when describing each senior under their individual photograph—chose to inscribe the word "Manly" under Tom's picture: especially fitting for him, given his favorite poem was Kipling's "If."

Although he hit the books hard in high school to get a congressional appointment to West Point, he failed to beat out other candidates who had better records, political pull, or both. So, after graduation, he headed off to the University of Georgia. There, he majored in journalism and lettered in track, excelling in the brutal 440-yard run. But he never gave up on his dream of attending the United States Military Academy (USMA). Finally, after three years at Georgia and having resolved an apparently erroneous heart condition identified during his West Point physical, he at last secured—with the help of Papa and his brother George—an appointment through Congressman E. E. Cox from the Second District of Georgia. Tom would become a member of the USMA Class of 1941—the class the stars fell upon.

At West Point, however, "Mac" struggled to survive academically. The amount and level of mathematics overwhelmed him. His grades in quantitative courses would drag him down in the Academy's "Order of Merit." At graduation, Tom finished fourteenth from the bottom in his class of 424 cadets. But academics aside, he flourished at being a soldier, and no cadet could love his new alma mater more. He played plebe (freshman) football, continued to compete in intercollegiate track, and even found time to sing "First Tenor" in the Cadet Choir.

Yet despite his age and former college experience, his roommates—who knew him best—thought of him as a "rover boy" (coined from a popular children's book series of the day). In other words, Tom was indeed valiant and principled, but often naïve and inexperienced in the ways of the world. As an upperclassman, he also had a hard time "crawling plebes"—applying harsh discipline to freshmen—as his Southern upbringing required he always be a gentleman when dealing with anyone. In sum, his journey from the "Deep South" to "old Hell on the Hudson" was for him analogous to traveling to another planet in both time and distance from his beloved Georgia.

In 1941 during his first class year, Tom toyed with going into the air corps as a pilot, but was pleased that he was ultimately given the opportunity to become an infantryman. His worst fear, given his position on the Order of Merit, was that he might not be allowed to serve in a combat arms branch. His new branch's motto, "Follow me," fully captured his intense willingness and desire to lead.

Equally significant to his future, the "firstie" had begun dating a Virginian, Helen Elizabeth Jordan (pronounced *Jer-don*). She would graduate from Peace College in Raleigh and was now living with Aunt Hallie and Uncle Ben in Bronxville, New York. In Carolina, this former debutante loved to dress up and go dancing to the big bands in floorless tobacco barns. At West Point her dance card was always full, and she was able to revive her passion in a more formal setting. This initial pairing of Tom and Helen would start slowly and finish strong.

After the Japanese attack on Pearl Harbor, Tom would not see combat for a while, but he felt its impact right away. His good friend, Alex R. "Sandy" Nininger Jr. (USMA 1941)—who had only months ago trained with him at the infantry school in Fort Benning—was killed in Bataan, 12 January 1942. Nininger would be the first classmate to die and the first Medal of Honor recipient in WWII. Like Tom,

Sandy was soft-spoken and temperate in manner as bespeaks an English whiz kid: the best student in his class according to the English Department. No one could have foreseen, however, how courageous and fierce Nininger was in combat, killing more than a dozen Japanese soldiers singlehandedly before succumbing to his multiple wounds.

But in spite of the obvious risks involved in wartime, the couple was ready to tie the knot. Tom and Helen married at Fort Jackson, South Carolina, on 7 March, two days before his promotion to first lieutenant. Fortunately, the newlyweds were to have a year together before Captain McDaniel—promoted again on 21 September 1942—shipped out to the China-Burma-India (CBI) Theater.

In the CBI, McDaniel served as a liaison officer to the Chinese in Burma while attached to the 2nd Battalion (Bn), 65th Infantry (Inf) Regiment (Regt) of the 22nd Infantry Division (ID), and with the Mars Task Force that had subsumed the remnants of "Merrill's Marauders." For his actions in Burma, the commander of the Northern Combat Area Command, Lieutenant General Daniel I. Sultan (USMA 1907), the replacement for General Joseph Stilwell (USMA 1904), pinned a Legion of Merit (LOM) on his chest after he had become a newly minted major on 15 April 1944.

In brief, this LOM recognized his contribution in achieving tactical successes that broke the Japanese lines and forced them to retreat in two engagements: at Warazup and Wakawng. Before leaving the theater, this LOM award would accompany the Combat Infantry Badge, a Bronze Star, and the Asiatic-Pacific Campaign Medal with two battle stars.

In Burma, Major McDaniel learned many lessons. When he met Lord Mountbatten, he discovered how well his British Allies could "look after" visitors in a combat zone: he had never been treated this royally in food and drink in the US Army. But one lesson became indelible in his mind which he recorded: "The Chinese are very good soldiers if they have the equipment to fight with. They have plenty of fortitude and can carry more on their backs than anyone in the world."

Perhaps, the most revealing of his attitudes and experiences as an infantry officer in WWII was captured in his letters to family. Besides grousing about how slow promotions were in his theater of operation as compared to stateside, one letter to his mother was especially telling of the man he had become via the crucible of ground combat. The Major wrote:

> Have you ever seen a picture of a strong man standing stiff and erect and looking unemotional and expressionless out into space while some woman or man is kneeling down in front of him begging for mercy or sympathy and still his expressions and feeling remain the same regardless of how much pleading the kneeling person does? Well, I hate to admit it in a way and yet it may be a good thing, but that is about the way I feel in combat. I have seen so many dead and wounded that I think my heart has turned to stone. I have no sentiment in my heart. Of course, I do everything in my power to help those in need, but that desire to aid comes from the mind and not the heart. However, I believe that is a good way to be for if a tactical decision was based on sentiment then I am afraid there would be no victory for a person with sentiment, and also if a man let his sentiments get the best of him I think he would crack within a few days of combat. Mama, do not get me wrong. I still have my Christian Spirit, but there is nothing Christian about any man's war. I always wondered how I would react in combat before I came over here. But I know now. In war there is no love of woman, no feeling of joy, sorrow, or sympathy that one encounters in civil life. There is nothing one can like or admire in war . . . .

At war's end and after twenty months in the CBI, the Major received orders to return to his home state where he began teaching—among other skills, bayonet—at the Infantry School. He also completed an "air transportability course," thereby earning his "gliderman" wings. So he did fulfill his wish to fly, even though it was nonpowered flight. More notably, while at Benning, both army brats Tom Jr. and John Douglas were not only born healthy, but they were born Georgians.

John's birth in 1947, regrettably, did provoke some family drama when a prevaricating aunt announced that John would be named after her husband. When this "promise" did not materialize, both Tom's family and Helen's got excessively involved, prompting Tom to put in writing—in a letter to the supposedly offended parties—what had always been his most fundamental credo: "In all my life, I have never promised anyone anything and . . . later decide to not fulfill the promise and then . . . deny that I had promised it in the first place. Maybe that is my failing . . . but I do not even tell a white lie when maybe that little lie may make things run smoothly."

The Major left his infantry instructorship in 1948 with his family after an early selection to attend Command and General Staff College (C&GSC) at Fort Leavenworth, Kansas. And then upon graduation from C&GSC, he preceded his family to Honshu, Japan, where he assumed the position of executive officer for the 2nd Bn, 32nd Inf Regt of the 7th ID in the fall of 1949.

Following a brief stint in Long Beach, California, Helen and the boys boarded an army transport ship, the *General E. D. Patrick*, and headed for Japan. With custom-made leather harnesses and leashes for Tom and John, Helen had some measure of control as the threesome spent a twelve-day "eternity" crossing the Pacific, including Christmas, in unrelenting rough winter seas: swells that occasioned numerous tumbles and contagious vomiting episodes among the four hundred passengers before arriving in Yokohama.

By the spring of 1950, the McDaniels left their temporary idyllic Japanese home in Morioka and moved into their permanent quarters at Camp Haugen near Hacchinohe. There they began to settle into a stable family routine, albeit in a very exotic country. For Helen, the word *foreign* nowadays would forever have more meaning.[1]

The Fighter Pilot

A combat-tested pilot before coming to the Far East, Captain William Davis Locke had already had an aerial "kill" downing a German plane during a dogfight in WWII. Bill was a stereotypical fighter pilot: "full of piss and vinegar." Although reared in North Carolina, he was no laid-back Southerner. He was always in the "ready position" for whatever came his way. These traits endeared him to many who flew with him, but it often exasperated those mere mortals who had to work with him on *terra firma*.

William "Bill" D. Locke

On 10 December 1919, Bill was born into a prosperous North Carolinian farming family. It was said by the locals that "the Lockes owned Halifax County." The family coop's main crops were cotton, tobacco, and soybeans. And the extent of their agricultural enterprise required Negro tenants housed on their land to efficiently work the fields.

Bill was the fourth boy and, as a toddler, always sat close to his father until finally usurped by his younger sister. He was considered very bright by his parents and actually proved it when he achieved the only 100 percent score on a statewide exam. This prompted his school to have him skip fifth grade. This advancement, coupled with his December birthdate, paired him with older, more mature contemporaries throughout his early life. Entering High Point College in his midteens, he was able to graduate from there at a mere nineteen years old.

His last year of college in 1939 was his most momentous, when he met the love of his life. Ronda was a freshman and worked in the college president's office. Although when he first met her he thought she was conceited, Bill was soon smitten. This romance would become his obsession. He would often sit in his dorm window and watch Ronda leave work and catch the bus home. If she missed her ride, he would scurry out to her and offer to walk her two miles to her home. Then, after what became a prolonged hand-holding session, he would catch a cab back to his dorm.

His father died while Locke was in college. So absent his father's counsel, upon graduation, he decided to interview with several big businesses but was told to come back when he was twenty-one. But for this hard-charging entrepreneur, this refrain was unacceptable. And with his family's wealth, Bill was able to go into business with a more seasoned local gentleman. In short, he secured a half interest in a small appliance store in Enfield.

But when the nation became embroiled in a world war, he went to Charlotte and enlisted in the army air corps. This act propelled him into officer and pilot training as he made his way from one air base to another: Maxwell to Shaw to Moody to Zephyrhills. Finishing in the top of his classes, he was finally anointed with pilot wings and joined the 10th Squadron flying P-51 Mustangs and preparing for deployment to Europe. For this "hotshot," everything was working to plan. The only hitch was his marriage to Ronda: she insisted they wait until his return. She was not going to raise a fatherless child.

During WWII Bill flew some eighty-three missions against the Nazis. His Mustang squadron converted to P-47 Thunderbolts. And his new fighter plane was soon embossed in bright red letters with his fiancée's name: "Ronda Belle." Many of his fellow pilots, depending on the combat aircraft they flew, rarely survived thirty missions. But the ones that did manage to stay alive and gain experience with each mission tended to prevail until the war's end.

Locke was more than a survivor. One day, in the skies over Cologne, Germany, Bill achieved the fighter pilot's perpetual quest: besting another aviator in a lethal dance above the earth's surface. In this singular moment of a flying career, Locke was at the top of a loop when the bullets from his Thunderbolt's eight guns—four .50-caliber guns per wing—found their target: an FW-109, considered the Luftwaffe's best fighter plane.

After the war, Bill left the army air corps and returned to North Carolina. Ronda said "yes" on his third and his preannounced "last" proposal. They married and moved in with her parents in High Point. Bill got a job with Sears, Roebuck, and Company, and the couple began to reestablish family roots where they both grew up.

But when the air corps broke away from the army in 1949 and became a separate Service, Bill received a letter from the air force with an offer he could not refuse. He essentially could come back in and accrue all the rights and privileges as if he had never left. So Captain Locke exchanged his civilian work clothes for brand-new blue uniforms. Yet, more jubilantly, he would no longer have to "fly" a desk. The fighter pilot would once again be "slipping the surly bonds of earth"—this time in the Far East from Yokota Air Base, Japan.[2]

The Steadfast Adjutant

A former Tuskegee Airman, James Bryant Smith was an "old" lieutenant by 1950. Jimmy was born in 1917 at Grant Hospital in Columbus, Ohio. By the time of the Korean War, JB's life experiences had been more diverse and richer than his fellow junior officers. And his journey to manhood was, undoubtedly, more torturous than for most lieutenants in a segregated army. Yet he had evolved into an ethical and trustworthy American military officer consistent with the teachings of his Christian Science heritage.

James B. "JB" Smith

Without question Jimmy's most traumatic and scarring childhood experience was his parents' divorce. Feeling abandoned by his mother, he often misbehaved in grade school and at home, as his dad and stepmother sought to retrieve normalcy for the boy. In time, however, they succeeded as he was able to channel his anger and a Mother Superior raved about his maturation and academic progress, plus his extraordinary work routine maintaining the school grounds.

At Cleveland East High School, he became a "Golden Gloves" boxer and ran track. Both endeavors demanded physical courage and stamina, not to mention mental toughness to withstand the intense competition. His tenaciousness carried over to his time at Ohio State University (OSU) where he had to bike 124 miles to attend school when he first started. He also had to work part time to pay for college as his folks had limited resources. And here at college he first met his future wife, Florence Evelyn Jordan.

JB did find some recreational time at OSU to run varsity track and also joined a fraternity—Alpha Phi Alpha, the first Negro Greek frat organization in America. There he was unmercifully hazed by a fraternity brother: Jesse Owens, the 1936 Olympian multi-gold medalist. JB did not know what was worse: the way Jesse humiliated him on the "cinders" or in the fraternity hazing.

Nonetheless, he managed to graduate in 1942 with a degree in education and was then accepted into the Tuskegee Institute—the army air corps' segregated pilot training program at Moton Field, Alabama. Close to graduation, the army decided to pare the class back from the current number of pilots. And JB was one of the unfortunate told to leave. But before his departure, the army found out that JB's father's sister was Fannie Norton Smith—the first wife of Booker T. Washington, Tuskegee Institute's inaugural school president. The army told JB that his name was mistakenly put on the list and he could graduate after all. But JB's pride and integrity were resolute: he did not make the first cut, so he should leave. And he did.

In the throes of WWII, the army decided to send JB to work at the Curtis Wright plant in Dayton, Ohio. So his love affair with aviation could continue, albeit on the ground. He became an electrician and repaired combat aircraft. He was also an inventor and devised an auto brake system as well as other ingenious devices for government use. Following WWII, he transferred to the infantry branch and was sent to Japan with his wife for peacetime occupation duty and placed in a segregated unit—the 24th Inf Regt of the 25th ID.[3]

The Indispensable Interpreter

A Nisei Hawaiian born in Olaa on 26 May 1922, Takeshi Kumagai was the prodigy of Buddhist parents, a minister, and schoolteacher. Growing up on Maui, "Tak" was taught compassion for his fellow man and allegiance to his country of birth. And above all, his parents instilled an inexhaustible work ethic to excel.

Takeshi "Tak" Kumagai

In 1930, his father, a Buddhist minister of the Shingon sect, moved the family and became a special on-call police officer on Maui. He assisted local law enforcement officials in their investigations involving the growing number of Japanese immigrants. As a youth on a small island, Tak was a precocious reader. But his interests expanded to fishing, motorcycling, firearms, and judo as he matured. He even had a passing fascination with professional wrestling.

The Depression, however, and the consequent need to finance a family of seven siblings forced Tak to abandon his formal education. He became, along with the older children, a breadwinner for the greater good of his kinfolk. Never completing his secondary education at Lahaina High School, he did go on, in 1938, to be technically certified from two schools based on the mainland—one focused on electrical power and the other, diesel power plants.

After the 1941 surprise attack on Pearl Harbor, Tak's father was detained and questioned by the Federal Bureau of Investigation (FBI) for days. Convinced of his loyalty, the father was released. And then Tak, at age nineteen, was also questioned and quickly released. These interrogations of the two Kumagai males helped enable Tak's follow-on employment on the highly secretive Red Hill Project on Oahu, begun in 1940. This project was to construct a mammoth underground fuel tankage and pipeline system for the navy. As an electrician on the project, Tak was draft-deferred for the duration of the war.

In April 1946, Tak, however, decided to enlist in the army. He went to infantry training at Schofield Barracks in Hawaii and then became a criminal investigation agent assigned to a military police (MP) company. He left his home islands in 1948 for the island of Kyushu, Japan. There, Sergeant Kumagai was on a Civil Affairs team before finally being assigned to the 34th Inf Regt.[4]

The Underage Privates

Like virtually all wars, much of the fighting is done by soldiers who have not reached their majority—twenty-one years old. Most are teenagers who have the strength, energy, and yes, recklessness to prevail in combat when led by competent superiors. They are usually ignorant of the violence and hardship they will endure if called upon to fight. But they are also more malleable and able to be molded into effective warriors before the pessimism and doubt of longevity take hold. These are the kind of "boys" that were fated to end up in the Far East when the war in Korea broke out.

* * *

The fourth boy, Allen James Gifford, was born into a farm family in Pemberton, New Jersey, on 13 January, 1930. His dad was a hard drinking man who valued his sons for the labor they provided. His mom was a devout Methodist who kept the boys in line by never sparing the "rod" of discipline. Strife was common between his mother and father and between the parents and the children. So from an early age on, Al looked for ways to put some "space" between himself and his family.

Al worked hard as a teenager, chopping wood and harvesting blueberries. And in the seventh and eighth grades, he even found some time for football. He had to walk four miles after practice to get home, and then he still was required to do his chores. But by age sixteen, Al dropped out of school. The demands of the farm were too great. And the only thing he would miss at school was the daily interaction with the girls, as he fashioned himself quite a "Casanova." And with his good looks, so did his potential girlfriends.

Allen "Al" James Gifford

It was no surprise, then, when in July of 1948, at age eighteen, Al enlisted in the army. He went to basic training at nearby Fort Dix and, from there, to Fort Worden in Washington State. Here he acquired his first skill: preparing food for large numbers of soldiers. He became especially adept at dressing chickens for cooking.

Al did not remain long in Washington as the army needed soldiers for occupation duty in Japan. On Honshu, he would learn a variety of skills before finding his niche as a medic. In the barracks, Al was well-known for his self-taught harmonica playing. This talent led to a stint in the drum and bugle corps where he played trumpet. He also learned to drive army vehicles of various sizes and capabilities. For recreation, he played catcher on a unit baseball team and had a Japanese girlfriend—or *koibito* as the GIs called them—whom he had met at the Oasis Club.[5]

* * *

A kid who instinctively knew how to gain the initiative, Edward Grady Halcomb sometimes viewed himself as somewhat of a "ladies' man," but he always was certain that he was "his own man." Born in Seville, Florida, in 1931, Grady hitch-hiked with his dad to Hamilton, Ohio. He was only four. His father was escaping the "fifty cents a day" salary he received working with his wife on a plantation of orange orchards. His dad's new job—initially sweeping floors—was in a Chevrolet garage where the owners would pay $12 per week and the family would be temporarily housed with his grandparents.

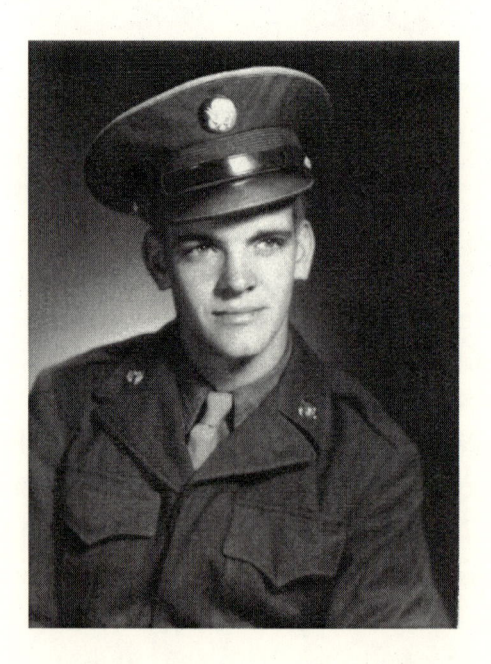

Edward G. "Grady" Halcomb

From the start, Grady learned the most valuable lessons in life, mainly, by trial and error. There was the time the toddler challenged his grandmother. Standing on a chair near a window with a match held high over his head, Grady announced, "Grandma, I am going to strike the match."

"If you strike the match, I'm going to spank you," promised the elderly woman.

"Grandma, I am going to strike the match," the child insisted and then grandmother repeated her threat. After his third dare and his granny's unwavering response, his hand sweep the window screen and the match ignited into flame.

The punishment was swift and prolonged as his grandmother's hand found his "behind" repeatedly. Never, again, did matches have the same allure, as Grady learned early on to modify behavior that failed to yield beneficial outcomes.

He was a "tumbler" and excellent wrestler in junior high. And Grady boxed until he took a horrific punch to the solar plexus from a larger boy, collapsing on the school stage. Quickly surrounded by his many female admirers, his pugilistic loss was not all that disappointing, given most of his ambitions had some connection to his goal of attracting the opposite sex.

By age sixteen, however, Grady's family had grown to nine. And he had developed some competency in doing automobile body work for a Lincoln/Mercury dealer. After school he would earn some money applying his father-taught skills. Though good grades were easy to come by when he applied himself, school itself had little appeal to Grady now that work replaced sports. So one day, without consulting his parents, he visited the local army recruiter.

"Yes, sir. I am seventeen and want to join the army," lied Grady.

"Son, we'll need your parents' permission since you're not eighteen," the recruiter insisted.

"But I'll be eighteen soon on September 20," Grady compounded his ruse.

"Great! Your swearing-in ceremony is on the twenty-third. So no permission needed," smiled the sergeant.

Traveling to Fort Knox and then to Ford Ord in California, Grady's leadership skills were evident early, and he quickly became a trainee platoon sergeant. But it was not long before the young lad got homesick and went AWOL (absent without leave). He spent seven days and six hours hitchhiking his way home to Hamilton. When he arrived, all the family was waiting. An officer from Fort Ord had called his parents, predicting the prodigal son's imminent return. The officer told them he could stay three days before they had to send him back. So when he disembarked from the bus in California, he had given himself a two-week unauthorized leave and also soon earned a $50 fine and a suspended thirty-day confinement. Unfortunately, in Halcomb's mind, the punishment was well worth the reward of being back in Ohio, however briefly.

Consequently, it was no surprise when Grady tried to replicate his first AWOL. This time he was stationed in San Antonio. Again, he was hitchhiking and made it to Miami, Oklahoma, before being arrested at 2 AM by a cop on patrol. The charge was vagrancy.

Next day before the judge, Grady told everyone he was no vagrant. In fact, he was in the army. This time, Halcomb was escorted back on a train with two army guards who were sent to retrieve him. And in addition to another $50 fine, a thirty-day imprisonment was enforced. But while in the stockade, he broke up a planned jailbreak by informing authorities of the impending attempt. For this action, his stay was reduced by five days for good behavior. But Grady was now fed up with the army. He called his mom who sent him his birth certificate, and the army expeditiously gave him a "general discharge under honorable conditions."

But it wasn't long back home in Ohio before he realized that the army wasn't so bad. Certainly, the prospects in Hamilton were meager. It seems he had grown up during those months away from his family and friends. Now, he knew what he wanted. His mom asked why he couldn't make up his mind before about being a soldier. Grady, however, knew he had when he reenlisted on 1 February 1949. His parting words were "Mom, see ya in twenty years."[6]

* * *

A Native American, Valdor W. John hailed from his tribe's namesake, Oneida, Wisconsin. The Oneida tribe was one of five founding nations of the Iroquois Confederacy originally from upstate New York. Born on 15 March 1931 not far from Green Bay, Valdor lived in Oneida until his father returned from his service in WWII. Then, the family moved to Milwaukee.

In his most formative years, his grandmother would teach Valdor the greatest lessons of life. Her counsel was largely confined to the spiritual realm where she believed the most important enduring principles resided. Foremost, she taught him how to be at peace with himself: that he had the power to control his reaction to the world around him, no matter what the world offered him. From his wise grandmother he would learn to try to influence those things within his capacity to change and accept those things over which he would never have dominion.

At age seventeen, Valdor quit school and joined the army. He needed some adventure in his perceived dull life. But as the only male child, his decision did not please his dad. Nonetheless, Valdor was inducted at Fort Sheridan, Illinois, and then moved on to Fort Knox for basic training. During training, his own words validated his decision to enlist: "I loved running up and down hills and crawling in the mud. It made me feel like a grown man."

Valdor W. John

After basic training Valdor shipped out to Japan, but he was forced to return to the States due to his age. After receiving a release from his dad, he returned to Japan and began working in Graves Registration. He was assigned to a recovery team retrieving bodies from WWII. By the start of the war, however, he had managed to secure an infantry position—his ultimate goal when he first entertained an army career.

* * *

His feat of pitching a no-hit baseball game typified Bob's young life: the right mix of physical ability, mental tenacity, and luck. Surrounded by a nurturing family, Bob was instilled with great wisdom, especially from his grandfather Julius Braxton Sharpe. The lessons he learned at Julius's knee would sustain him his whole life.

In Burlington, North Carolina, on 2 June 1932, Robert L. Sharpe entered the world. And his world was a happy one from the start. His parents were loving stewards and he had a grandfather who had the opportunity to spend generous amounts of time with him. The grandfather lived on a small farm and Bob would be dropped off before and retrieved after school, when his parents' workday was over.

Robert "Bob" L. Sharpe

An inquiring youngster Bob would incessantly accost Julius with a question that had the depth only a naïve child or a learned sage would pose. For example, Bob once asked, "Grandpa, why can't people get along?" As was typical, Julius, would respond with, "Son, can't you see I am busy." Then, after some reflection he would tell Bob to go down to the chicken coop and watch the chickens for a while and they would talk later.

Then when the chores were done, the two would come together in the shade of an oak tree and nibble some peanuts and drink some cool lemonade. Julius would sit Bob at his knee and nonchalantly ask, "Well, tell me, son, what you saw down at the chicken house?" And then Bob would relate—not necessarily chronologically—how some hens would try to eat all the corn. Other hens would then peck the gluttonous hens.

Next, the roosters got involved and there would be a big fight and on and on.

Then his grandfather—who was never "preachy"—would slowly and meticulously demonstrate to Bob how people are a lot like chickens: they want something, they take it, they don't share, they get mad, they hurt each other, and sometimes, they get their family or friends to help them get what they want or to help punish those who kept them from getting what they want. Yes, if the first five years are determinate, then Bob had no finer mentor than Julius.

In 1944, Bob and his family moved to High Point where his dad became a skilled furniture upholsterer. He would still see his grandfather, but now school and his peers would be his chief associations. The family lived in a large subsidized apartment complex supported by the philanthropist, Clara Cox. The two story apartments were constructed in a circle whose center was comprised of a building that housed a basketball court and athletic fields for baseball and football. In short, his living arrangement was every boy athlete's dream—walking out the door of your home and finding facilities for every sport and enough local kids to form, at least, two teams without prior planning.

At age twelve, Bob pitched his best game for the Exchange Club in the High Point city league. And his dad was there, behind the backstop, for the whole seven innings. It was hard enough for a preteen to concentrate getting the ball across the plate. And, of course, you had each batter to contend with; however, blotting out an overly excited father in your constant field of vision was a whole other matter. But Bob always had good ball control, especially his curve. As each inning concluded, the pressure mounted as a "no-hitter" seemed unexpectedly in the offering. Despite his father's highly visible antics, Bob, somehow, kept his poise, and more importantly, his accuracy, allowing only three walks before the potential last batter approached the plate. Then, with the count 2 and 2, Bob launched his best curve, a superb strike that everyone thought caught the corner of the plate—everyone but the umpire. Words were exchanged between the father and the ump while Bob, mortified, was forced to watch the verbal melee from the mound. Then gathering himself, he went back to the rubber and finished his quest when the batter whiffed his next pitch.

In 1945, Julius died at age eighty-four. Death ended one life, but could not extinguish Bob's relationship with his grandfather. The wisdom once imparted extended to his high school years, where Bob continued to acquire knowledge and character. At school, he especially liked math and English. But history held special sway, especially as related by his friend and fellow pitcher's four brothers who had recently returned from the battlefields of WWII. These brothers captivated the impressionable teen with their stories and good cheer. Consequently, when college was ruled unaffordable by the family, the army seemed for Bob a great way to start a life on your own.[8]

* * *

"You have a choice, son—either go to jail or join the army." Thus, a law enforcement officer helped Ed Slater embark on a new path where he ended up in Korea long before the invasion and his travail as a POW. But his story from the beginning was one of hard times. The year of his birth was 1930 in Quincy, Illinois. Depression rocked the nation and was having an especially cruel effect on his family. He was one mouth among a family of fifteen mouths to be fed: seven brothers and five sisters. His mother died when he was two years old. As a result, Ed spent two years in an orphanage before his dad remarried. His father was a plumber, and the family often survived on government subsistence. All told, Ed would eventually lose six brothers and two sisters to premature deaths before achieving manhood.

Edward "Ed" N. Slater

In short, Ed became a troubled youth in a troubling time. He had little interest in school, and his life was consumed with work. Odd jobs around town left him no opportunity for play or rest. Endless hours were spent scrapping for junk to sell, shining shoes for eight cents per customer with his brother Leo, and setting pins in a bowling alley. He would often dream of better places perched on a ledge above the tenpins. But his life, like the pins he reset, would keep being knocked down. And no matter how often he tried to right his life, he always found himself in the same old positions—waiting for someone or something to bowl him over.

Fourth grade was the high point in his life when Ed could contemplate being a high school basketball star like anyone of his three cousins: Frank, Harold, or Don. But he stopped attending school after the first month of sixth grade and, by age sixteen, had become, in his own words, a "hoodlum." He was stealing cars and burglarizing homes. He impregnated his girlfriend. No doubt, he was headed for the "big house" or an untimely death. So when the police, after his latest arrest, gave him an ultimatum—the army or "reform school"—he chose soldiering. His dad signed the waiver, and the seventeen-year-old headed off to Fort Ord for thirteen weeks of basic training.

Leaving a wife and child at home, Ed traveled to faraway South Korea on his very first assignment. The precise location was Haeundae in the coastal area of Pusan, where he guarded an ammunition dump. Later, his transfer to an infantry unit had him move around Korea, performing duties on the 38th Parallel and in Seoul. It was in the capital city that he got his first taste of "fire." Bored with guard duty, some of the soldiers were horsing around; and when one of them yelled, "Quick, draw!" another private drew his .45 pistol and inadvertently discharged the weapon, hitting Ed square in the gut.

Evacuated to Japan, Ed recovered and returned to Korea until all the American units withdrew permanently in 1949. He would now be stationed in Japan with the 3rd Bn, 21st Inf Regt, 24th ID until the outbreak of the war.[9]

* * *

Jim was groomed almost from birth to be a soldier. His father was devoted to instructing his firstborn son how to prepare for military service. Whether motivated by his own service and/or his failure to see combat in World War One (WWI), the father would ensure his boy would grow up with all the requisite martial skills needed to prevail over America's enemies.

It was 22 April 1930, in Wichita, that Clarence and Myrtle Yeager had their first child, James Yeager. Although ranching and farming during a lot of his life, Jim's father viewed himself first and foremost a soldier. He was a sergeant in the army, and he loved the camaraderie he shared with his brothers in arms. During the WWI, Clarence was hopeful he would accompany the 35th ID to France. But a spinal meningitis epidemic struck the division that was in the process of preparing to deploy from Fort Sill, Oklahoma. Jim's dad was one of the men stricken and was in the hospital in serious condition when the division departed for Europe. After being released back to active duty, he was sent to Fort Logan, Colorado and upon termination of his enlistment, he was discharged. Later, Clarence would reenlist in the Kansas National Guard.

James "Jim" Yeager

At age five, Jim fired his first rifle at Fort Riley as he accompanied his dad often when the father performed duties with the Guard. His grandfather had two years of college and was a schoolteacher. But the elder Yeager never encouraged Clarence to pursue education, which was just fine with him as "book learnin'" had never really taken hold. This soldier/rancher was a man of action who was an expert rifleman and could field strip a weapon in the dark.

Not surprisingly, Jim also had little interest in school and was content to learn through doing vice studying. He was active on the farm: milking cows and plowing the fields behind two horses. And he worked in his uncle's feed store, on occasion, delivering chickens to customers. From the money he earned from his uncle, he bought his own .22 rifle and learned to kill and dress game for food.

In 1944, his parents—with Jim age fourteen, Paul age eleven, and Caroline age six—moved to a ranch ten miles from Delta, Colorado. In Colorado, Jim grudgingly continued his schooling, but on his seventeenth birthday, he joined the Naval Reserve and stayed on with them for eighteen months. He also completed high school and toyed with junior college in the hope of securing a West Point appointment. But he soon realized the USMA competition was too keen, especially for a kid who only recently was willing to hit the books.

Therefore, Jim got the navy to release him on the proviso he would enlist in the National Guard, and so he did in October 1948. Then in the summer of 1949 Jim attended summer camp at Camp Carson, Colorado. Jim, by this time, had decided to join the army and try for OCS (Officer Candidate School). So he enlisted in October 1949, heading off to Fort Riley for basic training. Because of his reserve service and his weapons expertise, Jim was made a squad leader.

His assistant squad leader John Toney and he became fast friends. And when John became a squad leader on Jim's recommendation to the platoon sergeant, their relationship became cemented for life. They would both go on to Advanced Leadership Training together and then were sent to Okinawa for their first regular assignment with the 29th Regimental Combat Team (RCT).

But before their departure, Jim had a whirlwind romance with Barbara, whom he met in Kansas City through an army classmate. Together for less than two months, the two twenty-year-olds got married in a fever.

Arriving in Okinawa in May of 1950, Jim and John briefly guarded supply "dumps" that were being pilfered by black marketers and Communist infiltrators. Then, when the Korean War erupted, the 29th RCT had to make personnel adjustments because they were not up to combat strength. The 2nd Bn was broken up, and some of the men were placed in the 1st and 3rd Battalions. Moreover, the 29th RCT had recently received about four hundred new soldiers from the States who had only completed eight weeks of basic training. They also had to be integrated into the unit at this time.

Because the 29th RCT was short of soldiers in the S-2 Intelligence section, their first sergeant sent Jim and John to the Headquarters (Hq), 3rd Bn where they became scouts and observers. Jim and John had been begging the first sergeant ever since arriving on Okinawa to change their assignments: Jim still wanting to go to OCS and John, to cooking school. Now due to poor unit readiness, the 29th RCT was scheduled to go to Camp Drake for sixteen weeks of advanced infantry training. But en route to Drake, orders came down when their ship reached Sasebo, Japan, for the unit to proceed directly to Korea.[1]

* * *

Before the summer of 1950 would conclude, all the aforementioned Americans regardless of their background—officer or enlisted; Caucasian, Negro, Oriental, or Indian; upper, middle, or lower class; college, high school, or grade school educated; Northerner, Southerner, Midwesterner, or Westerner—would all acquire and share equal status: that of a POW. Moreover, these ten men, along with their larger POW group, would be the recipients of the worst treatment via an enemy ever experienced by Americans at war.

Chapter Two

First Blood: Men against Tanks (25 June to 20 July)

> . . . I came close to shame when I think about the men who did better jobs—some who died doing them—and did not get recognition. I wouldn't have awarded myself a wooden star for what I did as a commander . . .
> —**Major General William F. Dean,
> Medal of Honor recipient**

"What a great Sunday afternoon. Good friends, *tak-san* food, and interesting conversation—at least, from our ladies. We really are blessed here in Japan," Major McDaniel drawled.

"But just like Fort Benning, you never come home to dinner on time. He's always talking to his men, helping them with their problems," Helen McDaniel chided.

"Yeah, Helen, but you don't have to cook and do the dishes," quipped Lieutenant Colonel Don Carlos Faith Jr.

"No, Don, I don't have to do the cookin'. I never really learned how to cook. But I do miss the cleaning up. Something I know how to do," Helen responded.

"You are lucky to have 'Cook-san.' He is the best on Camp Haugen," Barbara Faith chimed in.

"I do want to apologize to Barbara and Sadie for all the 'army talk' earlier. Helen is use to it, but I get riled up when I think how some of our officers are not maintaining standards among the enlisted men. Or for that matter, among themselves," the Major interjected.

"Mac, you 'Woo-Poos' are such tough guys," Don teased.

"Don't give me that. You're the toughest officer I know when it comes to enforcing discipline. When you were with General Ridgeway and the 82nd in Germany, you had quite a reputation. And you know the army here in Japan, not just the 7th Division, is not ready to fight anyone: the Russians, the Chinese—"

"Did you tell General Walker how you feel when you and Helen hosted him and his wife?" Lieutenant Colonel William "Billy" Quinn (USMA 1933) interrupted.

"Okay, boys, I'm starting to hope for another earthquake. So let's talk about more pleasant things, especially since it's Sunday and you'll be back at work soon enough tomorrow. So, Helen, speaking of 'boys,' where are Tom and John?" Barbara inquired.

"Hisashi and Kon, our houseboys, are helping them make parachutes for their toy soldiers and are back in their room. That's why they have been so quiet . . . ."

"Tom, I hear someone knocking on our door."

"Excuse me," Major McDaniel saunters to the front door and opens it to find a private from the 32nd Infantry Battalion he only vaguely recognizes.

The private salutes and hands the Major a message. "Sir, I need you to read this. And if you know, tell me where I can find Colonel Faith."

Moments later, having dismissed the private, Major McDaniel walks back in the room and, without a shred of emotion, addresses his five dining partners: "Well, looks like we are going to find out real soon if our army can fight. The North Koreans have attacked Seoul."[1]

* * *

In only three days, the South Korean capital of Seoul fell to the Reds. The frantic exodus of the Republic of Korea

(ROK) civilians and military soon swelled the town of Suwon a few miles below the capital and on the south side of the Han River. But the burgeoning of Suwon slowed when a retreating ROK general ordered the Han River Bridge to be blown up, heartbreakingly, when it was packed with fleeing South Koreans.

The South Korean government moved to Taejon on 27 June, seeking some distance from the raging battles. It hoped the natural barriers of the Han and Kum Rivers would impede the rapidity of the North Korean People's Army (NKPA) onslaught. The Syngman Rhee government calculated that the Reds could be halted before or at the Kum River, precluding another destabilizing government transplant. (See reference map of entire Korean peninsula on the last page of the book.)

Meanwhile back in Suwon enemy aircraft were strafing the airstrip with impunity while American bombers had begun dropping ordnance all the way from Pyongyang, the capital of the Democratic People's Republic of Korea (DPRK), to military targets in South Korea near the front.

This threat from enemy planes had Brigadier General John H. Church thinking he should reconsider Suwon as the location for the Advanced Command Headquarters (Hq). But when the NKPA was able to ferry their armor across the Han River despite the ongoing monsoon, then the decision was made for Church by the enemy's own audacity and ingenuity. The ADCOM retreat south would not be easy, however, as the dirt roads were clogged with mud several inches deep and with terrified, homeless South Koreans.

So what exactly was the order of battle during these first few crucial days of the war?

The two Korean armies were equal in size—in people, but not in equipment. The commanding general of the NKPA, Marshall Choi Yung Kun, had the initial advantage of strategic surprise; and now on the offensive, he had the tactical initiative and could dictate "the where" and "the when" of his next military move. But most important was the NKPA's advantage in armor. The Soviet T-34 tank was a juggernaut on the battlefield: the Americans and ROKs fighting on the ground, without comparable tanks and potent bazookas, were literally "cannon fodder."

Soviet T-34 Tank Rumbles through Seoul[2]

Moreover, the Union of Soviet Socialist Republic's military "fingerprints" were everywhere. The Russian ambassador to Pyongyang was a Soviet officer, Colonel General Terenti Shtykov. He and other military advisors had spent months planning and readying the NKPA for the invasion. Furthermore, thousands of the NKPA soldiers were not only trained by but had also served in other Red armies. And besides tanks and other assorted vehicles, the NKPA was equipped with sufficient numbers of the reliable Soviet-designed PPsh-41 7.62x25-mm submachine gun or "burp gun"—a devastating weapon if properly employed. In short, every asset—man or machine—in the NKPA arsenal available in Korea could have been stamped "Made in the USSR."[3]

NKPA Small-arms (Front to Rear): Russian 7.62-mm. Submachine (Burp) Gun, Russian 7.62-mm. Carbine M1944, Japanese 7.7-mm. Rifle, Russian 7.62 Tokarev Semiautomatic Rifle with Flash Hider, Russian 14.5-mm. Antitank Rifle PTRD-1941 (Degtyarev)[4]

As for the American Armed Forces being committed to the fray, the 24th Infantry Division (ID), not the 7th ID, was chosen to be the first 8th Army Division to enter combat. This choice was largely driven by the fact that its commander, Major General William F. Dean, was the only one of four division commanders in Japan to have commanded troops in combat and the only one who also knew Korea well. He had been the military governor of South Korea in 1947 and 1948. Otherwise, this selection was problematic, at best, since the 24th ID was the least combat ready.

Its readiness was "optimistically" rated at 65 percent, and on June 27, its total strength was 11,242—roughly equivalent to an NKPA division. Even with levies from the other divisions, the total only reached 15,965 before deployment. In turn, these levies sapped the combat power of the other units in 8th Army programmed to deploy later, especially the 1st Cavalry (Cav) that lost 750 senior noncommissioned officers (noncoms) to the 24th ID.[5]

In addition, the global disposition of US ground forces was strategically precarious. Responding to popular sentiment, the Truman administration had made drastic reductions in defense expenditures. The practical result was an insufficient number of trained combat units available for immediate deployment to Korea. Only twelve combat divisions existed worldwide, two of which were Marine Corps divisions. And every one of the twelve divisions was under strength except the 1st ID stationed in Europe. But with US government officials wondering if Korea might be a Soviet feint, no one was willing to send all or most of the combat divisions to Korea.

Finally, in order to maintain ten combat divisions within fiscal constraints, the army had removed the third battalion from all infantry regiments and made similar reductions in other army organizations. The effect on combat capability of this new regimental configuration was unknown but predictably suspect—at least, in regard to regimental firepower and unit cohesion in combat.[6]

* * *

The afternoon of 1 July saw the first American combat troops arrive at the Pusan airfield via six C-54 transport planes. The 405 infantry soldiers onboard these aircraft with their commander Lieutenant Colonel Charles "Brad" Smith (USMA 1939) represented the first delivery of men that would make up Task Force Smith. This task force was one half of a battalion combat team (BCT) and had been detached from the 21st Inf Regt of the 24th ID. They would be followed by the remainder of the regiment traveling by ship, especially now that the Americans had discovered—with the arrival of Smith's BCT—that the Pusan runways could not handle the weight load of a Douglas C-54 Skymaster aircraft.

The next day, Task Force Smith raced north by rail from Pusan to Pyongtaek and then piled into trucks that then threaded their way through the mass of bewildered and frightened refugees flowing south as the Americans convoyed to their Osan destination. But somewhere, after Chonan and close to Osan, Smith's task force was struck and struck hard by NKPA infantry and tanks. When first hit on the morning of 5 July, the BCT, now the only one left on the road, was motoring north with the soldiers seated in their jeeps and trucks.

Yet despite the inauspicious beginning, from 0800 to 1500 hours after dismounting, this mini-BCT held an entire enemy division at bay, knocking out five tanks with howitzer shells. But when the task force was about to be outflanked, the surviving infantrymen had to abandon all their heavy weapons and withdraw. Even so, two rifle companies, a battery of 105-mm howitzers (eighteen barrels), two 4.2-inch mortar platoons, another platoon with 75-mm recoilless rifles, and six attached teams armed with 2.36-inch bazookas had made a heroic stand. But this baptism by fire dissipated any contempt once held among the Americans for their new enemy. They now knew the Reds were brave, skilled, and well led. And they had far more firepower than the unsuspecting GIs thought possible.

As Task Force Smith fought its way out of their encirclement near Osan, it was eventually able to withdraw through the 1st Bn of the 34th Inf Regt, commanded by Lieutenant Colonel Harold "Red" Ayres. This commanding officer (CO) had won a Distinguished Service Cross (DSC) in Italy and was reputed to be "the best battalion commander in the Far East." His battalion and additional elements from the 21st Inf Regt had established themselves on the road twelve miles south of Osan.

2.36-inch Bazooka Team in Rain Gear near Osan, 5 July[7]

These defensive blocking actions by the 24th ID would mark the start of General Dean's unenviable task, as the temporary ground force commander in Korea, to trade space for time along the railroad line from Osan to Taejon. Simply put, two battles were simultaneously being waged by the South Korean and American Allies: the combat battle was all about holding on to territory and the logistics battle was all about sustaining the Allied force build up. Both had to be won to prevent the Allied ground forces from being pushed into the sea.

It was during these ferocious blocking actions that PFC Ed Slater of 3rd Bn, 21st Inf Regt would become separated from his unit behind enemy lines. Having faced jail time as a teenager, Slater had no intention of becoming a prisoner. He had been with some other soldiers at first, but the group kept getting whittled away as they kept coming in contact with the enemy. Finally, Ed and one other soldier were together being chased up a hill. The other kid, crying, said that he had a grenade and he was ready to end his evasion. Ed told him to wait until he was out of range and then went over the hill to the sound of the exploding grenade. Now alone, it would be almost two weeks before he was finally nabbed by the North Koreans, becoming one the very earliest American POWs of the war.

* * *

Although the situation on the ground was grim, by 10 July, the Allies ruled the air and the sea above and around the whole Korean peninsula. United States and Royal Australian Air Force aircraft could preempt any attack from the sky and, in turn, could strike at will the Reds on the ground. And the US and British naval units had blockaded North Korean ports and now patrolled the length of the DPRK shoreline.[8]

* * *

On the day Lieutenant General Walton H. Walker assumed command of all the ground forces in Korea, the 24th Inf Regt of the 25th ID arrived in the Korean Combat Zone—13 July 1950. This three-battalion Negro regiment would be the last and largest American Negro unit to ever serve in combat. The unit was accompanied by the Negro 159th Field Artillery (FA) battalion and the Negro 77th Engineer (Engr) Combat Company (Co).

Upon arrival in Pusan, the 24th Regt was immediately entrained and given the mission to backstop the ROKs who were blocking the NKPA from seizing the road that ran from Yechon south through Sanjgu to Kumchon. Many Negro soldiers were anxious to prove they could fight. The stereotype of Negroes not being suited for combat was rampant among the white army officer corps. But it was also universally

The Major

acknowledged that the 24th had been saddled with weak white leadership.

On the day the regiment arrived in Kumchon to set up their command post (CP), the commander, Colonel Horton V. White (USMA 1923), had an extraordinary conversation with Captain Charles Bussey, a Negro fighter pilot from WWII and now the CO of the 77th engineers.

The two commanders were standing by themselves in the street, and both were sweating profusely when the forty-nine-year-old colonel offhandedly said, "Would you look at those mountains?" He paused. "I'm not fit to command this regiment. I'm an intelligence specialist and too old for this. I didn't realize it until this morning, but soldiering is for young'uns. Mine is all behind me. I'll do the job as required while I'm here, but I'll have to pack it in soon."[9]

Bussey was flabbergasted, but he hid his astonishment, disappointment, and disgust and simply said, "Sir, I'm just glad I've stayed in shape and stopped drinking like I did sometimes at my old fighter squadron back in Europe."

The 24th Inf Regt spent a week acclimatizing itself to the heat, altitude, and ubiquitous stench—from the rice paddies and kimchi pots—that permeated all of Korea; not to mention the flies, fleas, and lice that thrived everywhere. They spent their days patrolling the road from Kumchon to Yechon. And during this initial period, a key senior white officer on White's staff—who could best be linguistically pigeonholed as a "big, fat, lazy bastard"—faked a heart attack and was evacuated out. But on the more positive side, Colonel White made Lieutenant Colonel Paul V. Roberts his executive officer. This thirty-four-year-old had earned a Silver Star and a couple of Purple Hearts in WWII and was considered "tough as nails and sharp as a tack." Roberts's appointment allowed White to "take it easy" and all the rest of his subordinates to "breathe easier."[10]

53

The ROKs had been fighting hard all over the peninsula, but when the NKPA captured Yechon, Major General William "Bill" Kean (USMA 1919), the 25th ID CO, ordered, on 19 July, the 24th RCT to retake the town. In response, Colonel White gave the mission to a BCT that would be built around the 3rd Battalion, commanded by Samuel Pierce Jr.

Pierce's BCT, reinforced by a battery from the 159th FA and a platoon from the 77th Engr Co, would be the first 25th ID element to go into combat. As the newly constituted unit approached the town on 20 July, the battalion encountered heavy mortar, machine gun, and small-arms fire. Deploying his three rifle companies to the west and south of town, Pierce allowed some skirmishes and then bivouacked for the night, preserving the full assault for the morrow's longer daylight.

The next morning, L Company led the attack. It was commanded by Bradley Biggs, a Negro paratrooper who had been assigned with the Triple Nickles, the "Smoke Jumpers." These WWII paratroopers suppressed balloon-borne incendiary devices launched by the Japanese to ignite forest fires in the North American Northwest. In less than two hours, the BCT retook the town and handed it back to the ROKs with fires still smoldering, but utterly devoid of NKPA.

Tom Lambert, an Associated Press (AP) war correspondent who observed the BCT action from a plateau overlooking the town, penned a vivid account of the fight that was widely published. In it, he declared Yechon was " . . . the first sizeable American ground victory in the Korean War." And as a platoon commander in L Company, Lieutenant JB Smith could stand tall to be associated with this historical event. Unfortunately, this victory would be overshadowed by the Allied debacles that surrounded it temporally.[11]

*   *   *

On 16 July, after devastating losses along the Kum River line, the 34th Inf Regt fell back some twenty miles on the orders of General Dean. New defensive positions were established three miles west of Taejon. At this time, Pappy Wadlington, the 34th Inf exec, was in command. Colonel Jay Loveless had been sacked by Dean and had been replaced by the 24th CO's trusted friend Colonel Robert Martin.

Tragically, Martin's command lasted only fourteen hours as he was blown in half by an 85-mm round as he assaulted a T-34 tank with a bazooka at pointblank range. Colonel Charles E. Beauchamp, who had just flown in from Japan, took command of the regiment next, establishing his command post at the Taejon airstrip northwest of the city.

PFC Allen Gifford (closest), a Medic, Awaits NKPA Attack at Taejon[12]

Colonel Beauchamp (USMA 1930) had been commanding the 32nd Infantry Regiment in Japan. At forty-two years old, he became the youngest regimental commander in Korea and the "greenest"—having never served in a combat unit and only been in command of the 32nd since March 1950. In WWII, he had served as a staff officer in the rear area of the European Theater of Operations (ETO), managing logistics. To assist him, the colonel had brought the 32nd Infantry's plans officer, S-3, Major William T. McDaniel. The Major replaced Major John J. Dunn, who had been captured by NKPA or *In Min Gun* as they were called in the North Korean dialect.[13]

* * *

Early morning on 20 July, Lieutenant Robert Herbert had been ordered by the CO of the 2nd Bn, 34th Inf, Lieutenant Colonel Thomas M. McGrail, to open up the road southwest of Taejon. Reports indicated enemy tanks were seen in the vicinity. But McGrail had no bazookas or grenades to give the lieutenant. Nevertheless, Herbert pulled together his B Company and headed to the designated location, approximately a mile from the center of town.

There, B Co established a roadblock and soon had a tank approaching its position. Herbert was preparing to engage it when someone shouted, "Don't fire! It's ours."

He knew, or at least had been told, that four friendly tanks were in town. But when the T-34 stopped some thirty yards away and the hatch opened, a North Korean "tanker" popped out, saw the Americans, and the tank quickly skedaddled away. Moments later, he saw, through his binoculars, a squad of Americans with bazookas tracking the tank. And General Dean was in the lead.

"Sir," Herbert yelled out indignantly, "what the fuck is going on?"

Dean laughed and said, "Why'd you let that tank get away?"

"We fucked up. We thought it was one of ours."

"I wish it was, Lieutenant. We sure could use some armor right now."

"Sir, my men will stay and fight, but I have to tell them what we're doing."

"We're trying to hold the ground west of town 'til the 1st Cav can get formed up and attack through us."

"When, sir?"

"As soon as they can form."

"When, sir?" the lieutenant was not going to let the general duck this life-and-death question.

"The 1st Cav is just southwest of us, Lieutenant, and in the meantime, I'm trying to kill myself some tanks. Nine of them broke into the city this morning. You just make sure, next time, you kill any you see." And then Dean and his squad departed the area, determined to "bag" themselves a tank.[14]

Herbert thought, "Shit, I guess the general is determined to 'do and die.' The question isn't 'when' the 1st Cav will get here. The real question is 'if' the 1st Cav will ever get here."

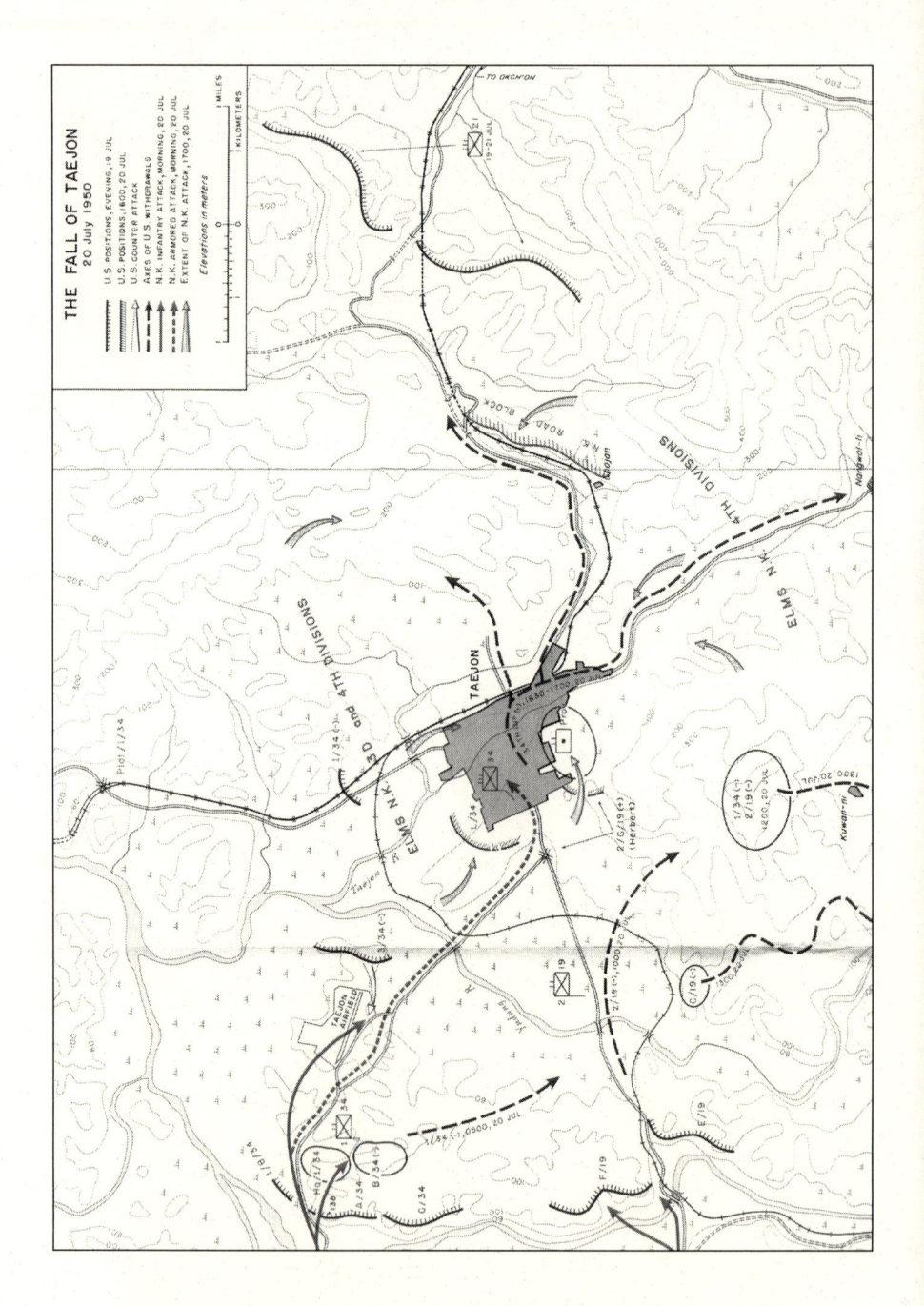

Battle of Taejon, Herbert's Location Southwest of City (See Map Symbols in Appendix 3.)[15]

* * *

After a successful hunting trip where he had finally killed a T-34 tank from a second-story window, Dean returned to 34th CP around noon. There, as he and Beauchamp ate heated C-rations together, the general learned that the colonel may have gotten the first tank kill in Taejon at around 0400 hours that morning with the newly arrived 3.5-inch bazooka; however, their conversation quickly turned to the timing of the withdrawal.

Though the two COs were both ignorant of the enemy's true disposition, their independent excursions around Taejon told them it was time to get the hell out and to do so before dark, which in July in Korea was around 2100 hours. So before leaving the CP, Dean gave the order. Beauchamp relayed it to the S-3, Major McDaniel, who put it in writing and sent it off by messenger to the battalion CPs of Ayres, McGrail, and Captain Jack Smith, the newly appointed 3rd Bn Commander.[16]

3.5-inch Bazooka Team in Action, 20 July[17]

Not being one to stay holed up in a CP, especially one with inadequate comm, the 34th CO jumped in his jeep and hit the road again to ensure the route east was open for a convoy. But as Beauchamp made his way to the Okchon highway, he soon discovered, to his shock, that the soldiers from the 21st Inf Regt were nowhere to be found—their planned exit route out of Taejon was unprotected. So he dismounted and climbed a hill and saw NKPA infantry advancing from the south to the northeast.

Now desperate, he returned to his jeep and went to Brad Smith's 1st Bn CP. Here he discovered the unit knew nothing of orders to move into Taejon and cover the 34th Inf withdrawal. He telephoned the 24th ID CP, only to get Brigadier General Pearson Menoher (USMA 1915) on the phone. The assistant deputy commander was frantic to get any word from Dean and could not seem to absorb the import of Beauchamp's concerns. But the general was, however, decisive in ordering the colonel to report to the 24th ID CP immediately.[18]

* * *

By midafternoon holding onto Taejon any longer was untenable. At 1700 General Dean made an appearance at the 34th Inf CP near the center of the city.

"Where the hell is Colonel Beauchamp?"

The blank stares among the Hq staff only reinforced the general's exasperation. Turning to Wadlington and McDaniel, the general said, "It's time to pack up and get out of here. You two make sure this happens as rapidly as you can. And when you locate your commander, tell him I want to hear from him ASAP."

In executing the withdrawal order, Captain Jack Smith had trucked in the 3rd Bn to the designated initial point at the street corner in front of the regimental headquarters. There he met Major McDaniel.[19]

"Captain, General Dean wants a perimeter defense to protect this initial point. And we may need support to recover a battery of 155s."

"Yes, sir." Smith unloaded L Company and sent the remainder of the battalion to form up with the convoy.

Major McDaniel went back into the building and told Wadlington, "I will lead the recovery. I'll get volunteers from the kitchen, police, and clerks. Just find me some prime movers."

Having collected the "volunteers," the Major addressed the men. "We need to get those artillery pieces back. We've already lost far too many to the enemy. I know some of you are a little rusty, but we will have surprise on our side. They won't expect a counterattack now that they see us forming a convoy to withdraw. We'll move fast and hit 'em hard. And then once we neutralize the position, we'll provide cover for the tractors. We won't stay one second longer than we need to, and what pieces we can't retrieve, we will destroy. Questions?"

155-mm Artillery Piece, Taejon[20]

When the tractors had been positioned for deployment, McDaniel and his motley squad of volunteers clandestinely moved to the south of town. When they had closed within thirty yards of the howitzer battery undetected, they executed a pincer movement. The Reds were actively engaged in firing the howitzers as the movement began and were caught off guard. Before the Korean artillerymen could retrieve their rifles, they were dead or fleeing, all within less than five minutes.

Then, having secured the area, McDaniel radioed for the prime movers to move forward under a *cordon sanitaire* also provided by his squad, and soon, all eighteen pieces were hitched to the tractors and headed back to the center of town to be placed in the forming convoy. (See Silver Star citation in the Appendix 1.)

* * *

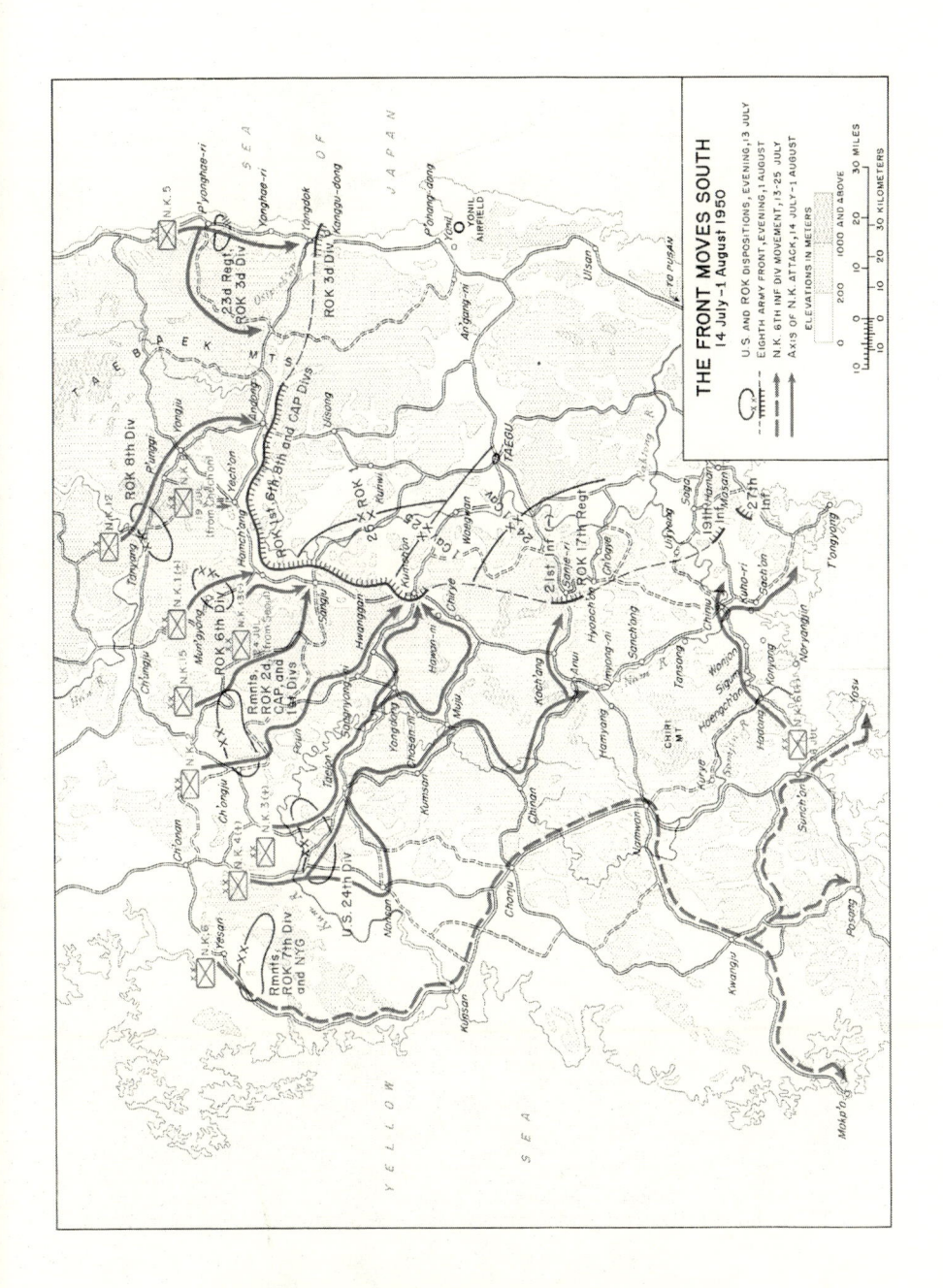

**Disposition of Forces, 14 July–1 August
(See Map Symbols in Appendix 3.)**[21]

* * *

As he sat in his jeep preparing to run the gauntlet of Red snipers, General Dean was already lamenting the fact he had waited a day longer to evacuate his men from the cauldron of death that had become Taejon. When the actual and historical smoke had cleared, there was no disagreement that those precious twenty-four hours would have precluded the annihilation of his forces in and around the city. When the causalities were officially tallied, the numbers were unpardonable.

The losses for the Hq, 34th Inf were 71 of 171 (41.5 percent); the 1st Bn, 34th Inf, 203 of 712 (28.5 percent); 3rd Bn, 34th Inf, 256 of 666 (38.4 percent); 2nd Bn, 19th Inf, 211 of 713 (29.5 percent); C Co, 3rd Engr Bn, 85 of 161 (53 percent); and A Btry, 11th FA Bn, 39 of 123 (31.7 percent), totaling 864 soldiers. As a sad finale for the US Army, the Taejon military defeat would long be celebrated by the North Koreans as their greatest victory of the entire war.[22]

Taejon: Aftermath of Battle, Summer 1950[23]

Chapter Three

Battle, Evasion, and Capture (20 July to August)

You can run, but you can't hide.
—Joe Louis

For the Americans that had become separated from their units during July's and August's combat, the effort to find their way back to friendly lines was particularly daunting. The NKPA were close to pushing the American forces off the Korean peninsula. The friendly line was receding southward rapidly toward the Sea of Japan and the Korea Strait. And the vast majority of evading American soldiers stood out due to their size and the telltale mantle of their skin whether white or colored. Conversely, the North and South Koreans were indistinguishable to the American eye, especially as NKPA infiltrators were often dressed in the traditional white garb of the South Korean civilians.

* * *

Pandemonium reigned in Taejon as remnants of Dean's division tried to extricate itself from the city on the evening of 20 July. Heavy black smoke from ubiquitous fires, driven by hot winds, drifted through the town. Comingled with the dust kicked up from the departing convoy, the visibility was near nil at ground level. Many of the lead vehicles had been hit by enemy fire or were wrecked driving through the smog. With the number of disabled vehicles and wounded soldiers mounting, an "every man for himself attitude" began to prevail, especially as the enemy completed the encirclement of the city. Enemy roadblocks were everywhere, and the whole city was soon engulfed in flame.[1]

As Lieutenant Colonel Wadlington had promised General Dean, Major McDaniel was made responsible for managing the tail of the column. But the Major and his men had been ambushed and were in a horrendous firefight. Soldiers were forced to dismount from their vehicles to find some place safe from the incessant small-arms fire. Soon, small clusters of GIs were making their way on foot to the outskirts of town. In retrospect, the hope of driving out of Taejon and surviving in a vehicular convoy had been doomed from the start. But with ineffective communications, the Americans were blind to their situation and could not appreciate the extent of the North Korean envelopment.[2]

Taejon Retreat, 20 July 1950, Soldiers Crouched to Avoid Sniper Fire[3]

Enemy snipers occupied the high ground. And their abundance was unnerving. Even so, Major McDaniel removed his helmet and told the two soldiers with him to do the same. "The light is reflecting off our helmets. Take them off and follow me." The Major then left the building they were under and began crawling up the mountainside, weaving his way between scrub brush and large rocks, always cognizant to obscure the elevated view of a would-be assassin.

* * *

It was dusk, and Al Gifford was kneeling over the edge of a rice paddy, preparing to take a gulp of water.

"Hold it, Private." Major McDaniel then helped Al to his feet. And as Al and Corporal Leroy Stevens watched, the Major gave them a short lecture. "When you drink, cup your hand like this, then skim the water with your hand, and let it drain some from your hand before taking a sip. These rice paddies are nothing but sewer water."

After imbibing a small amount of water, the three soldiers silently resumed their trek through the mountainous terrain. After a while, Gifford interrupted the self-imposed hush, "Major, do you remember ordering me off the ammo truck?"

"No, but I remember the incident, even though it seems like weeks ago. But no, I did not make the connection until now."

"Yes, sir. You know I was just so intent on helping the wounded man. I wasn't paying attention to where I was."

"No, I realize that. But there was so much incoming fire. I didn't want you blown to smithereens. We needed every medic we had."

"Yes, sir. I just want to thank you."

"Soldier, you were doing your job and doing it well under really bad conditions. I just happened along and noticed the ammo in the truck. That's all. You don't need to thank me."

That first night, as the men continued their journey back to friendly lines, the Major could see and feel the fear and despair in his young companions. He slowed his pace and put his arms around both soldiers while continuing to walk. "Look up in the sky, men. See those stars. Our Creator put them there. You may feel we are lost and all alone and surrounded by our enemies. But we are not alone, the Lord is watching over us. He will help us get home."[4]

* * *

The American lieutenant was plainly all alone, making his way down a brutally steep and slippery path. General Dean was also all alone, hiding behind a large rock with his pistol drawn. When the American came in view, Dean said, "Who are you? What outfit are you from?"

The startled lieutenant, who had no awareness of Dean's presence, jumped but was immediately reassured when he saw the American uniform. "I'm Lieutenant Tabor—Stanley Tabor, 19th Infantry. Who are you?"

"Well, I'm the SOB who's the cause of all this trouble," Dean acknowledged as he struggled to get to his feet.

Tabor had been with Easy Company of the 2nd Battalion. Dean had ordered the battalion to bolster the 34th Regt along the Kum River. Tabor had become cut off during the unit's retreat and started walking south on his own.

General Dean had a more bizarre story of how he ended up solo. As a general officer, he was always surrounded with a couple of aides, a driver, and some bodyguards. And so it was, during his retreat from Taejon. He was in a jeep with a driver and one of his aides, First Lieutenant Arthur M. Clark, an air force pilot. Dean's jeep and the escort jeeps were in tandem—barreling through town, dodging snipers—when Clarke shouted, "We missed the turn!"

But it was too late. There was no going back. At one point, Dean stopped and picked up some soldiers, put them in his jeep, and then caught up with his escort jeeps. But those jeeps were abandoned, and the men who had been in them were taking fire from a roadblock set up on a bridge two hundred yards ahead of them. Dean's jeep swerved at the last second and ended up in a ditch.

There in the shallow gully, Dean realized he had left his M1 carbine on a half-track earlier, and when he looked, his holster was empty. Nonetheless, all the jeepless soldiers began to make their way from the road across a bean field and ending up on the riverbank some distance from the bridge. When Clarke took muster, seventeen soldiers had made it to the river.

"General, I want you to have my pistol," Clarke said as he handed it to Dean with his left hand. "I can't use it anyhow."

Dean hesitated until he saw the wound in his aide's right shoulder. Then placing the gun in his holster, Dean, with Clark, planned their next moves. They decided to wait until after dusk, forge the river, and swing around the mountain to the other side beyond the roadblock.

Later in the dark, the soldiers had little problem crossing the river. The high bank on the other side, however, was more challenging, especially for one soldier shot in both legs. He was in a lot of pain and had to be carried up the mountainside. At one point, the two soldiers carrying the wounded man had fallen too far behind the main group. So Dean, forgetting his age, said, "Hell, I can carry him better on my back."

And so Dean did, but not for very long. But this display of physical prowess and mental dimness was typical of the general: to assume the role of a private and forget he needed to get his thoughts focused above the tactical level—both in terms of the time horizon and the geographic battle space. Within the last forty-eight hours, he had personally assaulted and destroyed a North Korean tank with a newly arrived 3.5-inch bazooka. No doubt, the major general was heroic, but also derelict in exposing himself and not managing his larger divisional responsibilities: delaying the NKPA's push south while preserving the men and equipment of the 24th ID so they could fight again on future days and battlefields.

Around midnight during one of his many rest stops, Dean announced, "I hear some water running, I am going to go down and see if I can find it."

"No, sir, I can't let you do that. I believe there are North Koreans at the base of the hill tracking us," Lieutenant Clarke insisted.

But an hour and half later when Clarke was in the lead of this dawdling seven-man patrol, he realized no one was following him, so he retraced his steps and found five soldiers asleep, but no General Dean. So he waited two hours, hoping Dean would return. Then, with the night slipping away, he roused the men from their slumber and headed off to find the main group ahead of them and, ultimately, friendly lines.

General Dean had let his thirst get the best of him. He had drunk copious amounts of water using his halizone tablets when he was down by the riverbank earlier in the day. Yet climbing up the mountain, carrying the soldier, and letting the wounded man consume all the water had undone his customary soldier's discipline. He told the other men he'd be right back and headed down the steep ridge. The general, helmetless, had not gone far in the dark when his next step met with only air, rather than the ground, and he found himself running down the slope pell-mell.

When General Dean regained consciousness, he was hurting all over. The gash on his head was irritating, but the broken shoulder and some internal injuries to his midsection was almost debilitating. Regardless, he was going to find water and soon did from a small crevice in a rock. He sipped his fill and passed out but came to when he heard North Korean soldiers pass within ten yards of him. It was still in the middle of the night so they never saw him, but he decided to move away from what appeared to be a path and crawled up into some bushes to obscure his presence.

There he lay the whole day, 21 July, half conscious and did not move out again until dark. The going was tough with his injuries, particularly the shoulder. He had to stop, though, on the side of a slippery escarpment when it began raining in torrents. He settled in next to a six-foot flat rock, took out his handkerchief, and laid it on the boulder, letting the cloth absorb the rain. Then he would hold his head, chin high, and wring the handkerchief's sweet nectar into his parched mouth. It was at this rock the next morning that Lieutenant Tabor happened by.

Now that they were together, the general and the lieutenant quickly formed a personal and professional bond. This bond was set the first day as the two made their way south. Dean kept needing multiple rest stops to overcome the pain in his ribs and stomach.

As Tabor pulled the general to his feet in this latest stop, Dean said, "You go on ahead, one person can get through a lot quicker. I'm stove up, and there's no use pooping around here."

"No, two would have a better chance," Tabor would always insist, no matter how many times throughout the day Dean would suggest that the lieutenant leave him and save himself.

Late afternoon, they ran into three refugees—a mother and two teenage sons—from the Taejon area. They were camped out by a stream under a canvass. The Koreans gave the soldiers some rice and told them they needed to stay out of sight until dark. So the two men slept.

But that evening, before they departed, the family informed them that the military situation was far worse than they had expected. The North Korean advance had already extended beyond Yongdong. So the two evaders believed they would have to go east before they could go south to Taegu. Moreover, even before the war, the Yongdong zone had been rife with Communist guerillas. Dean had been told this detail when he was the military governor by South Korean hunters, who coveted the opportunity to hunt there but were afraid of the Reds in the vicinity.

As they wandered the mountainous country side for the next several days, avoiding the low ground and the roads saturated with *In Min Gun*, Dean was in a complete daze. Only with Tabor's encouragement and devotion to his superior was the general able to recover some modicum of mental proficiency. Luckily, it was then that the two Americans stumbled into a village at dusk on 25 July. In seconds, they were surrounded by what seemed like every person in this very small hamlet. Two Koreans in the crowd spoke English—one well and the other, adequately.

The good speaker quickly vanished, but the less adept one took them to a house for food and rest. When they had finished eating and were taking off their boots, they heard a rifle shot just outside the house. The Korean with them scrammed out the front door. And the two men heard the best English to date, "Come out, Americans! Come out! We will not kill you. We are members of the People's Army. Come out, Americans!"

Tabor said, "This is it." He grabbed his carbine, and both men retrieved their boots and flew out a backdoor.

Dean said, "I'll lead," as they hurried up a hill in the dark. "You can cover me better with your carbine. I'll be the point. I'm not going to surrender, Tabor. There won't be any surrender in me."

"That's the way I feel too," Tabor vowed.

Many indiscriminate small-arms bullets soon saturated the hill they were climbing, so Dean and Tabor reversed their flight and ran back into the village where people were crisscrossing everywhere. The human bedlam and darkness got them through the town without any confrontation and to a rice paddy on the outskirts of the community. The paddy was divided into cells ninety feet square with seven-foot-high dikes between them. The water was four inches deep, with rice protruding another four or five inches above the water line.

Dean and Tabor dove into the water and started crabbing on their bellies using their elbows and legs to propel themselves forward. Dean remained in the lead as they went across the first paddy and over a dike. Dean could see two NKPA soldiers silhouetted on the skyline on a parallel dike to his left. The Americans continued undetected over a second dike and then a third. After the fourth dike, Dean turned in the middle of the rice paddy cell to discover Tabor was no longer with him. The lieutenant had vanished, and the general would not see another American for three long years.[5]

* * *

"So this is it," thought Sergeant Tak Kumagai. At the ripe old age of twenty-eight years, he was standing in a row with a handful of other young American prisoners waiting to be executed by firing squad. The NKPA soldiers were having a difficult time getting organized. His Buddhist upbringing gave him the stoic will to stay within himself and manage these final moments of his short life. With little effort, Tak could picture himself as a little boy. He was back on Maui picnicking with his mom and dad. They all sat gazing in wonderment at the gorgeous fully arched rainbow fashioned across the pale blue sky, only recently formed by the confluence of a fleeting squall, jagged hills, and resurgent sun.

He did not contemplate running away, as he knew it would only prolong his few minutes left on earth: no, better to let the squad have a clean shot at his head and torso so the end would be sure and sudden. He opened his eyes. His Red executioners were ready. He closed them again. Tak heard the order to fire but not the bark of the rifles as three bullets slammed into his body.[6]

* * *

By the time the 29th Regiment arrived at the Pusan harbor on 23 July, all the soldiers onboard the *Fentriss* and the *Takasago Maru* were already disabused of the idea that this war was some trivial police action—a mere brawl for the vaunted US Army who had crushed the Oriental in the last war. As they came down their ships' gangplanks, Jim Yeager and John Toney were surprised to be taunted by the sailors from the deck of a docked US Navy destroyer nearby. "We'll be back to pick you guys up in a week after the gooks kick your asses," the unruly and secure sailors shouted.

Every soldier pitched in offloading the ships of all the equipment and supplies, which were taken directly to the railway station and placed on a train. It was miserably hot and humid with no relief from the sun except in the open-covered shed that ran the length of the dock. A glimmer of refreshment, however, was in the offering when a young Korean teenager appeared. He was hawking quart-size bottles of beer, and his market timing could not have been better.

But before the GIs could take their first swig of alcohol, Major Tony J. Raibl, the 3rd Bn exec, grabbed a bottle from a soldier's lips and smashed it on the cement surface where the soldier stood. "The party's over! Did you consider the damn beer could be poisoned? Listen up! You're in hostile country. You cannot tell the good guys from the bad guys. And the last thing I want to do is to write home to your mama that her son died drinking beer. He was too stupid to make it into combat. Now let's get back to work."

That night, with only the aroma of beer in their nostrils, many men attended church services in a large building in Pusan. Then Toney and Yeager later stood guard duty, protecting the train that would take them and their equipment north. At 0100 hours, they witnessed another train come in carrying wounded from the front. They stood and watched as men were loaded into waiting ambulances. Some had wounds so severe, the bleeding could not be staunched and blood was seeping out the backdoor of the ambulances.

Next, much later in the night, the two guards would challenge two lonely figures making their way toward them down the center of the railroad tracks. They had no weapons and were ready to drop. "Where you going? What unit you with?"

"We're from Taejon. From the 24th. We were in terrible fight. We've walked forever. Please tell us where we can go."

Toney and Yeager directed them to the battalion headquarters, but could only shake their heads as the two soldiers limped away, and wonder what the future held for the two of them. So much for these two American privates' first exposure to Korea, the best and the worst thing they could think and agree on was that this inaugural day had definitely been "real."[7]

Bright and early the next morning, the 3rd Bn of the 29th Inf boarded the train. While Toney and Yeager got some shuteye, First Lieutenant Alex Makarounis, the I Company CO, was studying the maps he received in the various company commander meetings that had transpired over the night. The train was headed north to Masan and then on to Chinju where

75

the battalion would disembark. They would then offload all their vehicles and other equipment and convoy east toward Hadong. Their mission there was to find and engage two hundred Red guerillas: to destroy them or degrade them so they were no longer any threat to the area. (See map on page 63, bottom portion.)

The train got to Chinju at 1400 hours. The soldiers got off and marched in formation, route step, in columns of twos to a schoolhouse. Again, the officers met and a decision was made to proceed to Hadong in a "blackout" drive that night. At 2200 hours they began to unpack and uncrate their equipment using the light from their jeeps' headlamps. They got their mortars ready and were all set to go by 0100 hours.

The convoy of jeeps and $2^{1/2}$-ton trucks began to snake their way up the mountainside. The blackout conditions became perilous, especially for the trucks, for the road was more like a trail than a highway with its narrow, ill-defined borders. Lieutenant Makarounis was in the Co Hq jeep with his driver, Private Emerson; his two messengers, Privates Harding and Gardner; and his radio operator, Private Kline. In the moonlight, the soldiers could see the valleys below. But with the darkness and all the dust swirling from the convoy movement, the thirty or more men packed into each truck remained ignorant of the precariousness of their conveyance.

After a couple of hours at the wheel, Makarounis surrendered the driving to Emerson who had awakened and asked to take over. The lieutenant switched seats and was soon asleep. An hour later, Alex woke up with a start when Emerson had dozed off, and the left front tire caught the edge of the embankment and the jeep began careening down the hill.

Emerson and Kline were instantly ejected from the jeep, but Makarounis and Gardner were pinned under the vehicle when it flipped over. All the men started screaming for help and after a dozen or so trucks had passed, some other jeep riders in the long convoy finally heard them. They quickly descended the embankment and lifted the jeep off Makarounis and Gardner. They were lucky. The embankment was fairly gradual and the trailer hitched to their jeep prevented a more violent flip. A medic, soon on the scene, slit Alex's trousers and bandaged his shallow wound and also checked out Gardner's chest pain and deemed him okay.

When Lieutenant Makarounis and his jeep mates had caught up with the rest of I Company, they stayed the night in a small village. The next day at 1200 hours they were told to move forward. And an hour and half later, they had reached L and K Companies who were in defensive positions, awaiting orders. Around 1600 hours, the orders came in and all the companies, again, were directed to move closer to Hadong. This time, most soldiers would march as all the trucks had been ordered back to Chinju.

Six hours and fifteen miles later, the companies stopped, set up a perimeter defense, and dug in on a high plateau above a small village. Though these company commanders did not know it yet, the 3rd Bn CO, Lt. Colonel Harold W. Mott had received orders on the evening of 25 July from Colonel Ned Moore (USMA 1930), the CO of the 19th Inf Regt, back in Chinju. These orders gave the 3rd Bn the mission to seize the road junction at Hadong.

For Alex and his men the night was wet, cold, and quiet, except for the buzzing of huge mosquitoes that sounded like jets. He was still hobbled from the jeep accident, but he was not worried about what the morrow would bring. The battalion had more than nine hundred men, and though only two noncoms in his platoon had combat experience, the enemy, at most, was only three hundred strong and without heavy weapons.

At 0630 hours, 27 July, the battalion started off to Hadong. L Company was in the lead, followed in order by K, M (the heavy weapons company), the battalion staff, and I Company brought up the rear and was in reserve. Five miles out of Hadong at noon, first contact with the enemy was made. The column was immediately halted. From the rear, Makarounis could hear small-arms and then heavy mortar fire. He did not know who was firing, the Americans or the Reds. Many minutes went by with no word from the front.

Then a lieutenant and two enlisted men from M Company came running up and shrieking in voices from another world, "All hell broke loose. There's no protection. We're getting slaughtered."

"Kline, get on the radio to the battalion." The private did and handed the phone to the lieutenant.

"Makarounis, what's my mission?"

"Wait," came the reply. Five minutes went by and Alex tried, again, to get orders. He got the same reply: "Wait."

Ten minutes later, Captain Hacker, the assistant S-3 of the battalion staff, ran up and said, "Get your men forward, now!"

Before Makarounis could ask Hacker "the purpose" and "how far," the captain had disappeared. As I Company advanced, Lieutenant Chamberlain's platoon was in the lead, one hundred yards in front of Makarounis's position. In less than a quarter of a mile, the platoon suddenly came under intense fire, wounding two soldiers right away, and then the lead element became pinned down by machine guns firing from the right side of the road.

"Pull back, pull back!" Makarounis shouted. The fire was withering, and any advance would be suicidal.

Now back to where they first got their orders from Hacker, Makarounis radioed headquarters and, again, was told to wait by Lieutenant Wright, the communications officer. Then a few minutes later, a messenger arrived and told Alex that Captain

Flynn, the S-3, wanted him to take his I Company to the knoll up the road and link up with L Company.

Makarounis got on the horn one more time. "Makarounis, I want to talk to Flynn. Sir, we need to advance through the rice paddy. We can't get up the road."

"Okay, Lieutenant, don't care how you get there. Just link up with Lazy as soon as you can. They're pretty shot up."

Alex gathered his platoon leaders around to explain their new orders when a mortar round hit just yards away. After getting to their feet and dusting themselves off, the I Company officers tried, again, to fully understand the purpose and the task they were about to execute. But then, Captain Hacker showed up and countermanded Flynn's orders, telling Makarounis to set defensive positions right where he was.

Allowing that the battalion staff seemed confused and disoriented, Alex assumed Hacker had the latest information from the front. Therefore, he got his three platoons in positions to repel an assault and/or protect a battalion withdrawal. Then he decided to do a little reconnoitering on his own. But before he could take a step, he was blown off his feet, again, by an incoming mortar shell. When he stood up, he felt a small wound high up on his back, which he instantly dismissed given everything else that was happening around him.

As he stepped back on the road, the first sergeant from the headquarters company came up to him and said, "Sir, the battalion commander wants you to withdraw."

And sure enough, when Alex glanced back down the road behind him, he saw vehicles turning around. So he began to gather his men for the retreat; as he did, the group began to grow in size as remnants from M and L started showing up. When Sergeant First Class (SFC) Applegate appeared, the two men came up with a plan. Applegate had been a Ranger captain in the last war and had great judgment and courage.

Together, they decided to go across the rice paddies in two groups, each group taking turns providing protective fire while the other group moved.

Applegate's group went first, and the covering fire was, frankly, pitiful. Without automatic weapons—machine guns and BARs—the effort was almost superfluous. But it surprised the enemy as most of the soldiers in the first group made it across the paddies. But the enemy was ready when Makarounis and his forty men started across the rice fields. The machine gun fire got so bad that Alex finally halted the ten men with him, and they hunkered down behind a berm, waiting for a miracle.

Alex looked at his watch. He saw it was only 1600 hours: too many hours before dark. He got to thinking how different combat was from how he had pictured it. Like most, he had always wondered how he would perform. And he was pleased that his head was clear and he knew what he was doing. He was not nervous. Scared, yes, but that was different.

"Water!"

Alex snapped out of his musings and handed Frasher his canteen. The squat two-hundred-pound soldier was shot in three places and bleeding badly.

He looked around and saw his messenger, Harding, another Massachusetts boy, who was with him, but no one else from his company was in his rice paddy besides Frasher. Then in the bedlam of machine gun fire, mortar explosions, screaming, and moaning, the killing field went deathly quiet, except for occasional groans scattered across the paddies.

Five minutes went by without a peep, then Alex heard a scared, loud whisper: "Lieutenant?"

Then again, "Lieutenant?"

"Yes." Alex paused to not draw attention to his location. "What do you want?"

"Nothing, sir. I just wanted to know you were here."

The Major

More minutes went by, and then out of the brief respite sprang a deafening rumble that poured out over the entire rice field—not from machines, but from raving brown-uniformed devils, all waving small flags and emitting loud, undecipherable snorts as they advanced. Alex took a quick peek at the countless hordes of enemy soldiers descending upon them and then lowered his head into the fecal water.

Machine gun fire commenced once again, blended with the incessant boarlike grunts, and rained down on the cowering American soldiers from three sides. Alex could feel the sensation of an iron fist pounding him in the back—once, twice, thrice, plus a fourth time. The lieutenant shouted, "Oh god!"

Just like the movies, he thought, "I'm going to start coughing up blood." He spit. He spit harder. No blood? The bullets didn't go through my stomach. Feeling relieved, he prayed, "Please don't let them shoot me in the face. No face shot, please, please." He wanted his mother to be able to open the casket and see her son one last time—not some macabre mask that once was his face.

Even though his body was half submerged in the cooler water, Alex's back was very, very warm. He knew he was leaking a lot of blood before he passed out. But he came to only seconds later to the sound of voices. He finally had the courage to lift his head to see all these GIs with their hands in the air surrounded by the Reds.

"They're taking prisoners, Lieutenant," Private Harding said as he helped Makarounis to his feet. All around, Americans were helping each other get to the standing position. The Reds motioned with their burp guns for all the prisoners to empty their pockets. Some NKPA soldiers did not wait but confiscated the watches off the raised arms of their captives. They even wanted Alex's fatigue jacket now dripping with blood.

Then once all the booty was harvested, the Reds motioned the GIs back to the road via the berms or dikes. With Harding supporting him, Alex made his way out of the rice paddies but was unfortunate enough to see a lone dead American floating in the water, face up, eyes and mouth open, no more than nineteen years old, with a bullet through his left eye. This was Alex's first and most vivid imprint of death, and it would never leave him.

When they got to the road, there was Gardner. He had been shot through the cheek and back. And his left arm had been shredded by machine gun bullets. When the messenger saw Alex, the private pleaded, "Lieutenant! Lieutenant! Help me!"

The guards waved Makarounis and Harding down the road. The lieutenant stopped and looked back. Harding, supporting a lot of Alex's weight, nudged him forward, "Come on, Lieutenant, stay with me."

Makarounis shuddered at deserting his messenger, who had always been at his side ready to deliver any instruction the lieutenant would direct. Only days ago on the ship bound for Pusan, they had all celebrated James's eighteenth birthday. And now Gardner would be executed by the Reds since he was not fit enough to be their prisoner.

In its totality, the ambush at Hadong by the battle-hardened North Korean 6th Division, vice three hundred ragtag guerillas, would become the second worst single-action loss for the Americans in the Korean War with 333 men killed and 100 more captured. In effect, the 3rd Bn ceased to exist and was never reconstituted due to the severe losses.[8]

* * *

McDaniel, Stevens, and Gifford had now wandered through the mountains for six days, foraging on C-rations, and most often finding only discarded crackers. Major McDaniel had employed all his cross country navigation skills honed at West Point to maintain a southerly direction. But they still had no sense of where the American forces were located and they had become famished and unquenchably thirsty. They had sipped as little water as possible in rice paddies. But they were now getting desperate for potable water. Up until this time, they had avoided the roads due to the stream of humanity heading south.

"We need to take a risk, men," Major McDaniel began as the three crouched on the side of a hill in the late afternoon of 26 July. "Even if we had the weapons, we cannot fight and find our way back to our lines without help. But if we are to survive, we need some food and water soon. It's your choice, but I am going down to the road and see if I can get us some food. And with a little luck, I'll run into some South Koreans."

The two young enlisted men looked at each other and nodded, "We're coming with you, sir."

As they made their way off the hill some infiltrators passed below them: they were wearing the customary white clothing, but their pace and loose formation screamed "NKPA." Then, what looked like a family appeared and the three men hurried their descent. They followed the family at some distance to a house where they cautiously entered. The inhabitants, though surprised, were quick to offer the Americans some rice and watermelon.

"Eat slowly and not too much," warned the Major. "If you go overboard, you'll throw up and you'll lose all the benefit." Then the Major, through sign language and simple English words, got a sense from the South Koreans present where they were and the best route south. The three soldiers then bowed and made their exit.

South Korean Refugees in Traditional Dress Flee Taejon[9]

Having barely walked one hundred feet, they were swiftly surrounded by an NKPA platoon. Instinctively, they scattered on the run. Shots filled the void, and Corporal Stevens tumbled to the ground as a bullet pierced his pelvis. McDaniel and Gifford immediately halted their flight, although they were now separated by some yards.

The Major raised his hands and was grabbed instantly while Gifford dropped to his knee and drew a knife from his boot. An NKPA lieutenant, pistol drawn, converged on the kneeling private, pointing his gun at the medic for a head shot. McDaniel calmly but forcefully said, "Drop the knife, soldier."

Al hesitated for an instant, looked into the lieutenant's eyes, and let the knife fall from his hand. The lieutenant hauled off and slapped Gifford across the face. Another soldier kicked him in the back of his right leg. Subdued, Al made no attempt to show any more belligerency, and the blows soon stopped.

The guards then went through Gifford's pockets, relieving him of all his worldly possessions: wallet, bandages, and some stale crackers. At the same time, Major McDaniel was forced to surrender his West Point ring—a prized acquisition that had rarely left his finger since graduation, even during combat in Burma and Korea.

The NKPA soldiers finished frisking the Major, Gifford, and Stevens for weapons and booty. Stevens, in great pain, was then placed on a stretcher. Al was motioned to pick up one end and a South Korean who passed by was commandeered to hoist the other end of the litter. The Americans and their NKPA platoon escort then proceeded on a trek of some distance.

Stevens was unable to urinate due to his wounds, and his moaning gave no comfort to Al. The medic had no remedy for the hurting soldier. Yes, they were all alive. And he and the Major were not seriously injured. But the future looked grim as they found themselves captives of North Korean combat soldiers on the move. At one rest stop, Gifford was finally relieved of stretcher duty when Corporal Stevens was put on an oxcart. But then he and McDaniel lost contact and never saw Stevens again.[10]

* * *

The morning of 28 July, PFC Grady Halcomb was sitting in a chicken coop with less than a dozen other American soldiers in the town of Anui. He had not been cooped up in a stockade since his second AWOL back in Texas during his first enlistment in the army. Now, however, his guards were North Koreans, not his own countrymen. But Grady was content for the moment to be alive since only a couple of handfuls of his buddies from B Company, 1st Bn, 29th Inf Regt were still able to breathe the putrid air of Korea.

When the 3rd Bn of the 29th Inf Regt was sent to Hadong from Chinju, Halcomb's 1st Bn, 29th Inf Regt stayed in the city until 27 July. Colonel Moore, the 19th Inf Regt CO, then ordered Lieutenant Colonel Wesley C. Wilson (USMA 1929) and his battalion north to relieve Lieutenant Colonel Robert L. Rhea's 1st Bn, 19th Inf Regt, so it could return to Chinju. Colonel Rhea's battalion was backing up Colonel Beauchamp's 34th Inf Regt at Kochang. Their units' objective was to block the NKPA 4th Division's drive south to the Naktong River. (See map on page 63: the cities in a line south to north—Chinju, Umyong-ni, Anui, and Kochang.)

When Wilson's battalion arrived in Umyong-ni around noon, Colonel Rhea personally escorted First Lieutenant John C. Hughes's B Company to Anui to replace Rhea's A Company. But upon arrival, A Company was engaged in a small-arms fight and was told by Rhea to follow as soon as they could break from the enemy engagement. Consequently, A Company did not withdraw until 1600 hours. At which point, half of B Company formed a perimeter defense at the base of a hill, and the remainder of the company dug in three hundred yards above them so they could overlook the town.

From his vantage point higher up the hill, Grady was able to observe the comings and goings of white-garbed soldiers in and around the town. B Company had been told that the ROKs were in Anui, and some were even dug in above their positions. They were also assured the 3rd Bn, 29th Inf Regt that had gone to Hadong could come to their assistance should the NKPA begin to pour forces into their sector. After all, the 3rd Bn was supposedly dealing with a small band of guerillas in Hadong and could be shifted eastward if or when needed.

As Grady watched the activity in Anui, unbeknownst to him, to his south the departed A Company had been ambushed and would never make it back to Umyong-ni. Lieutenant

Colonel Rhea waited for five hours, but when a reconnaissance revealed that the NKPA had cut the road, he took the rest of his battalion south to Chinju as ordered. Alerted by this reconnaissance, Lieutenant Colonel Wilson would make two attempts to send help to B Company, but no one was able to break the NKPA roadblocks below and above the city.

By midnight, Halcomb had logged more combat minutes than most soldiers experience in a lifetime. The PFC had gone from a bored observer to the most engaged combatant fathomable. When the NKPA burp guns first began raking the unsuspecting B Company infantrymen, they did so from three sides—their left flank, their right flank, and most devastatingly, from the rear above them.

It was in the dark and after intense street fighting that Lieutenant Hughes, Halcomb, and nine other men made it to the schoolhouse in Anui. There they held out until 0130 hours. But by then they had run out of ammo, and they were tired of dodging all the grenades the North Koreans kept rolling down the hallway of the school. They surrendered.

Now at daybreak, Grady's shoulder wound was bothering him. But it was not life threatening, and he was just waiting in his makeshift jail for the enemy to move him and the other survivors north. A North Korean had stolen his boots, and he was wearing the NKPA procurer's "tennis" shoes. Not happy to be prisoner or looking forward to the nine-day, seventy-mile march to Taejon, Halcomb understood he was lucky to be alive. How lucky he would not learn until after the war. The NKPA butchery at Anui—percentagewise—was the worst single unit fatality rate of the war with less than two dozen survivors out of the 235 American soldiers engaged in the battle.[11]

* * *

After the fall of Taejon, the city promptly became a North Korean logistics hub and holding pen for captured Americans and imprisoned South Koreans. The primary location for detainees within the city was at the central police station, which had collocated jail cells and judicial facilities. The station accommodated around a hundred POWs at a time and many more South Koreans. From the end of July until early September, the Americans were brought here to be housed, fed, and interrogated before moving on to Seoul.

* * *

For most, the stay in Taejon was only a matter of a few days. Unexpectedly, one morning the guards started rousting the current group of POWs and ordered them outside. The guards paced up and down the formation, counting and recounting. By now, the American numbers were approaching the jail's limit.

One guard announced, "We go twenty-two kilometers to train. Train take you to Seoul. Camps in north better. Who cannot walk to train?"

A couple of dozen men raised their hands. They were immediately separated from the group, encircled by the guards, and assaulted. Men were bashed to the ground with rifle butts; some were knocked unconscious.

As the Americans lay there bloodied and groaning, the guard asked again, "Who cannot walk to train?"

Those that could, crawled, stumbled, and made their way back into the formation of unmolested but stunned soldiers. Then after all those who could had returned to the formation, the guard said, "Go pick up your men. They stay, they die."[12]

* * *

The Major

PFC Melvin Rookstool from the 29th Regiment was one of the earliest occupants of the police station jail after being captured on 27 July. And unlike most of those incarcerated with him in Taejon, he was without any wounds. That is until the night a guard tripped over him in the dark.

Melvin was experiencing rapid eye movement sleep, immersed in a vivid dream, nestled between two other GIs on the jail cell floor when someone stepped on him. He sprang to his feet, and the Red intruder smashed him in the face with the barrel of a pistol. In the pitch of near-total darkness, the room suddenly exploded into a universe of stars, and the private sank to his knees. Half-conscious, Rookstool raised his right hand to the area of his pain and was horrified to find his wet eyeball dangling just below its socket.

Melvin spent the remainder of the night trying to reinsert his eye in the now vacuous hole in his head. But no matter how much he fiddled with his eyeball, it refused to stay in its former socket. And the pain was only lessened if he held his eye, so it could not dangle freely when he moved. The optic cord that held the eye to his face had to be uninterruptedly relieved of any tension or the pain was incapacitating. The optic nerve sheaved in the cord was an extension of the brain, and it did not fare well outside the skull. But Melvin found out before dawn, as he tinkered with his eyeball, that if he pinched "the cord" holding the eye to the interior of its socket with his thumb and the fingernail of his index finger, he could numb the pain sufficiently to allow him to withdraw his tired hand and arm—at least, for short periods of time.

His American comrades in the cell with him were mortified when they awoke and saw his fresh wound, especially when he removed his hand from his eye. It was bad enough they had to endure the obnoxious smell of urine and feces that flowed freely from their sequestered cellmates who were unable or unwilling to wait out the undependable guards in charge of managing the latrine schedule.

Now it became more apparent that all their senses had been under assault: from the screams of South Koreans enduring torture and execution, the stench from rotting wounds, the rancid food, and the beveled point of a thrusting NKPA bayonet. But this last visual assault—Rookstool's eyeball dangling—somehow had the effect of accentuating their living hell. The American soldiers, to a man, sought escape in mind and body, even into the arms of "death" if there were no other choice.[13]

* * *

Now incarcerated in Taejon, Al Gifford, the medic, was told by one of his guards that morning to accompany a wounded soldier to the hospital. He was soon joined by a Red escort, a group of wounded POWs and another army medic. The group then took a twenty minute walk from the police station to the nearest hospital. There Al was stupefied as he observed a Korean doctor put a wire all the way through the head of one of the wounded Americans, Auvil Parsons. This soldier's whole face was swollen and he had a bullet hole behind his eyes and in front of his temples on both sides of his head. The doctor was in the process of either putting maggots inside Parson's skull or extracting them from his cranium.

Either way, Gifford was astounded that Parsons was alive and totally lucid as the doctor performed this extraordinary procedure. With his eyes swollen shut, Auvil had to be permanently blind as the optic nerve in both eyes had to have been severed when the bullet carved a tunnel through his head. As he watched, Al could only shudder when he thought about a blind man trying to find his way out of the POW pickle they were in.[14]

* * *

Valdor John and Walt Whitcomb first met in an eight-man jail cell in Taejon. Valdor had been a member of the 34th Regiment and Walt, the 29th Regiment of the 24th ID. They soon found out they shared very similar histories. To begin with, they grew up on Indian reservations with all the attendant problems inherent in Indian communities of their era.

"What tribe are you from?" Walt asked John.

"How ya' know?"

"'Cause I'm a half-breed. My mother is Seneca."

"Oneida, so that makes us Iroquois brothers," John asserted. "I grew up near Green Bay."

"New York, but I had to get away. My dad was hard to live with, even when he wasn't drinking. Mom tried, but she couldn't do anything about him."

"Yeah, pretty much the same for me. I had to move on, but my dad was not happy when I left. He fought in the last war. What do you think about our crazy South Korean collaborator?"

"He's scary," Whitcomb confirmed. "When he put the gun to your head yesterday and I saw him crying and laughing. He's messed up."

"Yeah, he speaks some Japanese, so I could understand him a little bit. He's a true believer. He's as Red as you get. And he doesn't know why we don't want to be Communists like him since we're all from poor families."

"Well, I'm just glad he wants to fool with you, 'cause he is the kind of guy that could be a real killer. The soldiers should never have given him a gun."

"Let's hope we get out of here soon. There's talk we're headed north any day," John concluded.[15]

When it was time for this POW group to depart Taejon, it was none too soon for John, Whitcomb, Slater, Sharpe, and

Rookstool. They had been told by the Reds that the camp in Seoul was better—the food, the medicine, and the living conditions in general. The former capital city was far from the frontlines, and the camp there could more easily be supported by the Reds due to the shorter lines of communication alone. In Taejon the conditions had been deteriorating daily, and the unsanitary conditions were destroying the immune systems of the caged Americans. And the town had become a veritable killing arena for Korean civilians. Kim Il Sung believed all Koreans were his citizens and, therefore, subject to his selective benevolence or his vengeful wrath.

South Korean Political Prisoners at Taejon Mass Grave[16]

Ready or not, the American jail cells in Taejon were emptied one morning, and this time, the guards made no promise of transportation. Every POW understood they were to march or die. The most pitiful soldier in the group was a young man who had several feet of entrails hanging outside his torso. So he could keep up, the GI had tied his intestines to one of his legs to keep them from swinging or trailing on the ground. This undaunted soldier exhibited superhuman tenacity on the march for a day or two before succumbing to this horrendous wound to his abdomen.

At this point in their tenure as a POW, the greatest threat to their survival was the dysentery and associated passing of blood that afflicted almost all the marchers. Yes, the guards would kill stragglers, but dysentery was what made a man straggle. It could very quickly drain all the stamina out of the strongest and most determined to survive.

One day along their slog to Seoul, at a schoolhouse with many small rooms, the American POWs had some visitors. Russian officers were being given a tour. They peeked into Ed's room, and their North Korean guard escort saw a soldier standing against the wall reading from a Christian prayer book. The Red Korean asked him to hand the book over. The kid refused and held his holy book close to his chest. The guard asked again, and the kid shook his head. "No!" The guard raised his rifle, pulled the bolt back, pointed the barrel at the soldier's ribcage, and asked a third time. The soldier started to ball, yet he clutched his holy book tighter as the guard began to count, "One, two . . ."

Ed stood there watching in disbelief and wanting to yell, "Give him the goddamn book!"

Mercifully, one Russian said something, and the Reds all walked away laughing. But the kid had his book and his life—for the time being.

Hours later, the POWs were on the road again. Sharpe and Slater would hang together every moment of their trek north. They would share the near noxious odor of death as each side of the gravel highway was littered with rotting military and civilian corpses. They had thought, back in Taejon in their close confines, the unceasing smell of the urinous and fecal admixture was bad; however, they soon discovered the pungent aroma of death, even in the open, was far worse. But the wear and tear on their feet and legs were atrocious. The blood blisters that caked the soles of their feet and their swollen ankles made them really appreciate the sturdy combat boots they both had once worn.

"Bob, you know what's bothering me the most?" Slater asked.

"No, what?" Sharpe replied.

"It's my bare ass hanging out of my pants. Why did those damn gooks steal my underwear? It's embarrassing."

"Trust me, Ed, no one is taking notice. Everybody we see along the road—man, woman, or child—only has one thing on their minds: how to stay out of harm's way. They have no other goal for themselves or their family."

Before Ed could respond, one soldier about ten yards ahead of them, out of nowhere, started yelling cadence like a drill sergeant, "Hut, one, two, three, four. Hut, one, two, three, four." But he did so in a "Donald Duck" voice that instantly enticed several soldiers around him to get in a tighter formation and in synchronous step, until their momentary fun got the best of them and their guffawing broke up their concentration and syncopation.

Ed and Bob could only chuckle and think: only American GIs would be capable of this brazen act in the throes of an imminent danger to themselves.[17]

* * *

Just having returned to Taegu Air Base that day, 17 August, from a great R&R with his wife Ronda, Bill Locke felt the break from combat had worked some magic. Flying forty missions—thirty-five sorties in an F-80 and five sorties in an F-51—in thirty days can wear down a seasoned fighter pilot. But now Bill felt rejuvenated. And with his first day back coming to a close and having just showered, he was still appreciating the flying lull. Then, at around 1800 hours, an alert came into the ready room for an emergency mission: an NKPA convoy needed to be interdicted near Taejon. The squadron needed a fourth pilot, and Locke volunteered and said, "Hell, I'll go and I'll take lead."

The flight to the target area was uneventful, and the convoy was readily spotted by the four-ship formation even though sunset was forty-five minutes away. Locke peeled off, followed by his three wingmen. He positioned himself and his fellows so their fire would yield the greatest destruction. And they began their first pass. This was followed up with a second pass, and then a third.

On this last pass, the enemy on the ground was ready to respond. As Locke passed over the convoy, he was hit with a 20-mm round. "Shit!" mumbled Locke as he climbed to five thousand feet. He radioed his flight: "I'm hit, and I'm headed to Taegu. Nothing you can do for me. I'm not injured. Get back to base and tell them I was headed for friendly lines. Copy?"

As he pointed his Mustang southeasterly, Bill knew his engine was not responding properly as his air speed and, therefore, his altitude was declining rapidly. He thought if he could just ride his craft into friendly territory, he would feel a hell of a lot better. But it soon became obvious that that outcome was unlikely, given the rate of his descent.

Then, suddenly, time compressed into milliseconds: a fire broke out, he prepared to bail, but the altimeter read: "600 feet." He decided to ditch. The rice paddies were inviting, but trees lined their periphery. He steered for a gap between them, but his propeller clipped some branches as the plane plunged to the ground, shearing off the right wing and breaking in two.

F-51 Mustang Laden with Rockets Rolls through Puddle in Korea[18]

As Bill climbed out of his broken plane, he immediately came under fire. He fumbled for his .45 pistol, took it out of its plastic container, and started crossing the rice paddy. But before he could return fire, he was surrounded by NKPA soldiers armed with burp guns.

A North Korean sergeant stepped forward and took Bill's pistol and began examining it. Then *bang!* the gun discharged, the bullet just missing the huddled group.

"Give me the goddamn gun!" Locke shouted, extending his right hand, palm up, toward the sergeant, who unhesitatingly handed it over.

"Fucking idiot," Bill swore as he emptied the pistol's remaining rounds and handed it back to the still-dazed Korean.

It was only then that Bill realized he was pretty banged up, and blood was flowing from a gash in his scalp. He was ordered to remove his boots, and someone ripped his High

Point college ring from his finger. But, incredulously, Bill watched as the soldiers threw away his gold coins—valued at two thousand dollars. Obviously, the money carried by American pilots to bribe anyone who would help them evade and escape had no effect on these buffoons.[19]

* * *

It was a few hours before marching into Seoul that Rookstool was relieved of his small but loathsome burden. He was pinching the connective cord when his elongated fingernail severed the remaining tissue, and his eyeball plummeted to the road. He almost did not comprehend what had happened since the bouncing eyeball had been his constant companion for weeks. When he did realize his loss, Melvin immediately spun around to make sure no one trampled on his body part. Then he scooped it up off the road, spit on it, wiped it off on his shirt, and put the eye safely in his trouser pocket. For some anthropomorphic reason he was not ready to part with it. In fact, a few more weeks would go by before Rookstool was willing to cast off his optic mate: what he knew to be the "flesh of my flesh."[20]

As the POW column entered Seoul, Ed Slater was astounded at the city's metamorphosis. It was night, but the changes were manifest on every street. He passed a Russian tank whose turret had been blown off. Certainly, Ed expected to see the ravages of recent battle, but he was unprepared for the contrast from when he was last in town. Few structures were left standing in many parts of the city. No street lights were lit. And no shopkeepers or shoppers were roaming the area. It was an urban wasteland. In two months, the Reds had managed to ruin Seoul—the capital city of South Korea and the municipal jewel of the entire Korean peninsula.[21]

Chapter Four

Mr. Kim's School for Propaganda
(August to 20 September)

The darkest places in hell are reserved for those who maintain their neutrality in times of moral crisis.
— **Dante**

Although many POWs had their own unique story of evasion and capture, their lives began to converge in Seoul, for it was in Seoul where some 376 Americans were held for up to seven weeks in a former girls' high school called Muhak. These Americans were not the first group of POWs to be imprisoned at Muhak, but they would be the last staged in Seoul before their movement to camps in North Korea. It is here at this school most prisoners met Mr. Kim for the first time. He would become the face of their enemy and the man most despised when they recounted their entire ordeal as a POW.

The Americans were held in a walled compound that had three large buildings and a courtyard. The yard had two spigots for washing and drinking. The POWs were billeted in seven rooms—designated "A" through "G"—on the second floor of the main building of the school. Each small room was ultimately crammed with about fifty prisoners. One latrine was on the ground level and not attached to the larger building. Another was on the second floor. And one room was designated as the "sickroom" where the most seriously ill would reside. Other rooms in the school were reserved for South Korean prisoners. But virtually no physical contact existed between the Americans and the South Koreans, except for the cries of pain that reverberated through the concrete compound when torture was being administered.[1]

* * *

When Captain Locke got to Seoul and made his way to the latrine for the first time, he met Major McDaniel, the senior American officer in charge.

"God, what a shithole," Locke gasped as he spied the maggots coating the walls and floors.

"Are you in the main building?"

"Yes," Locke said as he started to gag while relieving himself. Then he noticed that the officer talking to him was chained to the wall.

"I am Major McDaniel. We'll talk when I get out of here. Take care of the men for me."

"Yes, sir," he replied as he staggered through the doorway, his eyes and nose burning from the fecal stench.

Captain Locke was glad to discover that Major McDaniel, who arrived in August, had organized the POWs into a functioning network that had a chain of command, assigned work details and a communication system to disseminate orders or to quell rumors. And when McDaniel was released from his punitive stint in the latrine, he and Locke sat down for a one-on-one matriculation brief in an empty classroom.

"Welcome," Major McDaniel said with a smile and a firm handshake. "You're our only airman here. So how would you like to be my second in command so we don't have any interservice rivalry?" The Major had already spoken to some of the other army officers about Locke and gotten their take on him. He also knew his combat history in Korea and Europe and that his date of rank alone would accord him this bestowed authority and responsibility. But more germane, he knew the army officers had quickly solidified their opinion of the fighter pilot: this flyboy had "the presence" to lead a bunch of dogfaces.

The Major continued, "To be frank, I need your leadership now. The men here are young and untested. Only a few noncoms have been in extended combat and none of the officers know much more than how to get mauled by *In Min Gun*. So you and I have to accomplish three things: keep the men alive, maintain discipline, and ensure the men never lose hope."

"Who's running the show here? So far, I can't sort it out."

"There a bunch of major players. Mr. Kim is the front man, our primary interface with the enemy. But that fact is largely due to his command of the English language. I suspect he's trying to carve out as much power as he can, so he can ingratiate himself with the Russians."

"So those Caucasian civilians I've seen are Russians?"

"Most are military men, but I suspect a few are Soviet intelligence agents, and some others are Soviet correspondents. I also believe there may be some Communists from Europe among them. And some of the civilians are definitely Red Chinese. If you noticed, none of these 'civilians' speak in our presence."

"So, Captain, back to your original question. A North Korean major appears to be in charge of the guards and the logistics. But the propaganda effort is orchestrated by this Oriental 'doctor,' Mr. Lee, who is rumored to be Oxford educated. He rarely talks, but his English is excellent."

"I've noticed many of the men are only in fair physical shape. I also understand we have a sickroom, but I haven't been in it. Has the Red Cross visited?"

"No, never. And I believe we never will see them. So you and I have to make some decisions right away. The Russians are pushing the North Koreans hard to get us to broadcast some propaganda for them. I've resisted so far. That's why I was in the latrine when we first met. They thought the experience might get me to cave. And I got to admit, I thought I would die in there."

"But now, Mr. Kim has promised me a carrot—more food for the men, but only if some of the officers will sign some statements and record them for a radio broadcast. I don't know whether I trust him, but I do know the men are wasting away and will start dying soon without some significant intervention. So what do you think?"

"Sir, we can't broadcast for these Red assholes. We are American military officers."

"You're right, and if we do, we will be court-martialed. But if we don't, a lot of men will die. Here's my thinking. We establish some policy and rules. First, I, as the senior officer, am solely responsible for this decision. Second, no American will coerce anyone to make propaganda if they don't want to. But if some officers agree to do so, they will not provide any military information in their statements. And third, we will demand better food and medicine to be given to us immediately—before we sign any statements."

Locke stood up, sighed, shook his head, and said, "Sir, this is a big deal. I got to think hard about it. It goes against everything I believe. You hit me cold. I thought I was just going to get an orientation from you today. I had no idea you were going to make me your exec and then ask me to make the most consequential decision of my entire military career." And then the fighter pilot, sulking, walked out the door.

* * *

Mr. Kim walked into the classroom accompanied by two armed guards. He was about five foot nine inches in stature.

He wore glasses and had a thin moustache on his fat face. Otherwise, he looked like any other Korean with black hair and brown eyes. Mr. Kim was alleged to be a South Korean turncoat who had been a newspaper reporter prior to the North Korean invasion.[2]

Kim went to the front of the room and spoke. "We will begin our instruction today. You will learn how the peace-loving People's Republic of North Korea has come to defend and protect the Korean people from the American imperialists. How America began as a freedom-loving nation and has lost its way. It has embraced capitalism at the expense of its own workers. Not since President Lincoln has America lived up to the ideals of its founding fathers. And now the son of a bitch, Truman, not content to deny his own people the fruits of their labor, wants to enslave the workers in Korea. President Truman is an imperialist, Wall Street capitalist pig who must be taught a lesson by the Great Leader Kim Il Sung."

After droning on for more than twenty minutes, castigating America while employing every Anglo-Saxon expletive within his English repertoire, Kim paused, lifting a container of water to his lips. The room was very hot. And the smell of sweat and the scent from filthy uniforms and raw lice-ridden flesh permeated the air. Even so, Kim resumed his rant, "Truman is a liar and murderer. He—"

"Bullshit!" someone coughed.

Kim grabbed his ever-present twenty-inch wooden baton, left the podium, and waded into the "sea" of seated soldiers, swinging wildly as he came.

Ed Slater started scooting on his rear end to the back of the room. As he and others slid backward, Ed characteristically joked, "I sure hope his arm gets tired before he reaches me."[3]

* * *

The Major

Captain Locke caught the Major descending the stairs alone. "Sir, I've checked out the sickroom and assessed the general condition of the men. You're right. They are in pretty bad shape. Their weight lost is phenomenal. I saw one boy on a cot who couldn't weigh more than eighty pounds. He apparently had evaded thirty days without food before ending up here. So I'm in. I think I can sign a statement and live with myself because I now believe it will save lives."[4]

"Fine, several others have also agreed to perform this onerous, but necessary, task. However, I want you to know I did not give JB Smith the opportunity to volunteer. To make a long story short, one of my West Point classmates, Fowler, was the only Negro in our class. In fact, he was the only Negro at West Point for two years. And we shunned him for his entire four years. No classmate talked to him. He had no roommate all four years. Can you imagine going through the rigors of the academy without any friends? I know, without my classmates, I would have never graduated, yet Fowler did somehow. Well, things have gotten better at West Point, but the army still mistreats Negroes. I don't want Smith to face a court-martial when I know some officers on the court would not give him a fair shake."[5]

"I understand. You know, I'm a southern boy too. And just like you army officers, we air force officers are predominantly from the South."

The Major then refocused and said, "I want you to remember our conversation. When we are repatriated, you must be unequivocal and tell the JAGs that the idea to sanction these speeches was mine and mine alone. If I thought it could help, I would order you to do it, but you and I know it would be an illegal order and you should refuse it. So there really is no way I can inoculate you from prosecution. I can only hope the court will find that in my position as the senior officer, my authority had inordinate influence on your decision."

Locke just nodded his head in assent, and McDaniel concluded, "One last thing. I, myself, won't sign a statement or make a broadcast. As the senior officer, I've established some credibility with the enemy and our men. I cannot and will not undercut my authority. There will come a time when I will need all the 'respect, fear, and love' that I can garner. Of course, it's not about me—it's about my position, my command role. As for your reputation, you already have the respect and love of the enlisted men. They told me about one of your several 'dustups' with Kim. But thank you, Captain, for hearing me out and supporting this morally repugnant initiative. The two of us have a lot of responsibility ahead of us."

"Yes, sir. I can see that. You can depend on me."

* * *

Auvil walked into the sickroom led by the hand of another POW. Halcomb looked up from the patient he was tending to and saw a raccoon-faced soldier with his black eyes swollen shut. "Welcome to the sickroom. My name's Halcomb, Grady Halcomb."

"Auvil Parson's my name. The Reds wouldn't let me take the survey with the rest of our group. Guess they ran out of all their forms in Braille."

"Anybody who walked all the way to Seoul with his eyes closed is much too smart for that survey. It would be an insult to have you take it. Tell me about your wound."

"Not much to tell. I got shot in the head. I have no more pain except around the eyes. And the holes in my head have scarred over."

"You have any other wounds or sickness?"

"No, just the damn squirts."

"Well, here's a seat. I'll set you up a place to sleep and show you how to get to the latrine. Just let me finish up here with this other soldier," Grady said as he guided Parsons to a bench.[6]

* * *

In the early afternoon, while Lieutenant Smith was gazing out the window, two guards entered the room. He started to turn away but noticed that one guard was pointing at him. The other guard put his rifle on his shoulder, walked toward him, stopped an arm's length away, and just stared. Then he licked his thumb, placed the thumb on Smith's forehead, and rubbed the lieutenant's brow hard.

JB stood there, allowing this abuse. He knew this was no racist act but only the curiosity of an ignorant peasant soldier who had never seen a Negro before in person. Strangely, during this awkward episode, Smith did wonder, however, whether his skin color was an asset to his long-term survivability or a hindrance to same. His few private moments with Mr. Kim and Mr. Lee, the Oxford doctor, suggested they knew the history of Negro slavery in America well. So maybe they would think they could exploit his being colored at some point. But then again, they knew he was an officer. And he had given them no indications during their interrogations that he would ever be disloyal to his nation. So in the end, he reasoned once again, his viability would not be influenced by his race but by his own wits and perseverance.

* * *

Major McDaniel got another audience with Mr. Kim. When he knocked on the door to what had become Kim's office, he was accompanied with Captains Locke and Wirt, plus Lieutenant JB Smith. As the Americans entered, Mr. Kim remained seated behind a table and had the senior North

Korean officer, a major, with him and two armed guards who Kim immediately posted at the door outside the room.

"Mr. Kim, we need more food and medicine. One rice ball per day is not enough food for my soldiers. They continue to lose too much weight. And our sickroom has too many patients," McDaniel launched right into his requirements without any preamble.

"Your soldiers eat the same as our soldiers. I will not feed them more unless your officers make and sign favorable statements concerning our 'War of Liberation,'" Mr. Kim declared yet once again.

"We are prepared to do that, but not before we get more food. We need twice the rations we get now—once in the morning and once in the evening. And we need to begin with tonight's evening meal."

Kim turns to the major and speaks to him in their native tongue. The major nods in the affirmative.

"Done! We begin work on the speeches tomorrow. And we will have another parade, and the speeches will be read in the gymnasium with all prisoners present."

"My men are too weak to march through Seoul again."

"They march, or we have no agreement."

"Okay, the sick stay in the compound and the others will march only one mile. You can get all the photos you need for propaganda in that mile. And without the sick in formation, like last time, it will look like you're taking better care of us."

Kim weighed the counterproposal a moment and said simply, "Okay."

"Captain Locke, do you have anything else to add?"

"No, sir."

Thus, the unholy contract was consummated. The Americans departed the room, never witnessing the pure glee on Mr. Kim's face and the slap on the back from the Korean major.

* * *

Although the POWs had heard the disconcerting screams and weeping of South Korean men and women periodically for weeks on end, tonight Al Gifford actually witnessed torture. He was headed to the latrine when he passed the open door of Mr. Kim's office. At that moment, he saw a uniformed man bludgeon a Korean woman with the butt of what looked like a heavy duty flashlight. She screamed as she was clubbed, falling to the floor unconscious or dead.

This battle-proven American soldier had to fight his first impulse to intercede on her behalf. But the room was filled with other uniformed men and other South Korean prisoners. How many, he did not know. He turned and walked back to his room and did not venture out again that night.[7]

* * *

One morning after Kim's indoctrination class, some of the men were in the courtyard soaking up the sun's rays. The sheer "nothingness" of their current existence induced unfathomable boredom and depression, especially with the omnipresent dread of the future underpinning their state of mind.

For a while, Mr. Kim had allowed the Americans to listen to "Rice Bowl Maggie" or "Seoul City Sue." These were the names given by the troops to the spokeswoman who broadcasted for the Communists on their propaganda radio station in the capital. Although the programming had low entertainment value, the GIs enjoyed critiquing Sue's shows. But when Kim found out the POWs had jimmied the radio and "fixed" it so they could listen to Allied radio broadcasts from Japan, he confiscated it, ending their small diversion and access to what was happening in the "real" world.

Yes, the POWs lived in comparative peace, but they only had a scant thread of individual freedom. But time had become their jailer: it stretched minutes into hours, hours into days, and days into weeks. In sum, their minds and bodies craved meaningful activity. This day, however, someone got inspired and suggested a game: "Slice the Lice."

Private Yeager (chin on hands) and Guards in Muhak[8]

Turning to the other four men sitting in a group, one soldier blurted out, "I got a game for us. Let's see how many lice we can kill. The man who kills the most, wins. But you can only kill the lice on your own body."

Grady Halcomb was an eager participant as he removed his trousers and asked, "Who's going to start us?"

"I will," said one onlooker and nonplayer.

The Major

The five players were soon ready—once all their pants were off.

"Go!" the referee shouted as the men started playing "grab ass" on their own person. Their techniques were very similar: extracting an individual louse from their body, pinching it between their thumbnail and forefinger, and then flicking the carcass off before retrieving another pest. It was amazing to watch the body count mount as five piles of the little bloodsucking buggers grew larger and larger with the ever-increasing skill of the participants.

All those sitting around witnessing this "five-guy circus" thoroughly enjoyed the whole spectacle, but had a hard time stifling their laughter so as not to attract any guards who might want to end their entertainment.[9]

* * *

"What's going on?" John Toney asked Jim Yeager as the guards directed the A Group to assemble in the courtyard. No one knew yet, except for the officers, that a propaganda extravaganza was in the works under the direction of Mr. Kim.

"Don't know," Jim replied. But when they got outside, they noticed that the remnants of C Group were in three lines.

"Well, I'll be . . . . They're giving us haircuts," John said in amazement. And sure enough, several Korean civilians were cleaning up the POWs to include all their facial hair acquired in the long weeks of their evasion and detention.

When it was Jim's turn, he was not expecting a shave; his "peach fuzz" face had no discernible beard. But to Yeager's surprise, his barber dipped a brush in a mug and lathered up his whole face, even the forehead and around his ears. Then, for the first time, he noticed the Korean had a straight edge razor without its handle. Seeing the five-inch blade approach his neck gave him the "heebie-jeebies."

Turned out, however, Yeager and Toney both survived their haircuts without losing a single drop of blood. But the "bowl cut" they all received that day, including the American officers, looked like crap. "Moe"—the ringleader of the "Three Stooges"—at least had some sideburns below the top of his ears. The POWs did not.[10]

* * *

As the American officers had planned it, the POWs filed into the Muhak gymnasium and distributed themselves uniformly throughout the large hall. They were surrounded on two walls by civilian observers standing two to three rows deep. They were mainly Korean, but also some Russians and a few Chinese. The third wall was lined with uniformed North Korean soldiers cradling Russian burp guns. The fourth wall encompassed an elevated dais for the American presenters. Motion picture cameras were positioned strategically to capture all the happenings in the room, except for the heavy presence of armed guards. And propaganda signs were hanging everywhere—some with the same jingoist slogans they would be forced to carry on banners in the follow-on parade. This time Mr. Kim, or more likely his Soviet or North Korean masters, had really outdone themselves in orchestrating this contrived "War of Liberation Presidium" purportedly solicited and convened by the American POWs themselves.

When the last enlisted POW was in place, Lieutenant Smith bawled, "Room, a-tent-hut!" And with the most precision they had exercised in weeks, each POW instantly and simultaneously stiffened his torso, jammed his arms to his sides with fists clenched, and caged his eyeballs forward in the direction of the raised dais. The soldiers then held this

The Major

pose while their officers entered the room, ascended to the platform, and placed themselves behind designated chairs and a thirty-foot-long table decorated with indigenous flora.

POWs Assembled in Muhak Gym with Red Onlookers[11]

Major McDaniel looked over the assembly and in his best command voice said, "At ease! Take your seats." The Americans quickly assumed their customary position on the floor: their knees drawn to their chests with both arms hugging their legs. Even in this efficient individual configuration, the floor was filled to its capacity with American GIs, leaving the imported onlookers with standing room only.

As the sham "Chairman" of the sham "Presidium," Major McDaniel began with welcoming remarks, "We have gathered today to express views on the ongoing conflict in Korea. You will hear words from American officers that have been crafted to reach the audiences for whom they are intended. Each officer who speaks before you today is a declared volunteer. His words should therefore be taken as his own without undue coercion or favors."

**Captains Locke and Wirt with
Major McDaniel "Presiding"**[12]

Then, each officer stood and delivered his scripted remarks in the most uninspiring, halting, monotonous manner possible. Captain Wirt was first, followed by Lieutenants Tabor and Boydston and ending with Captain Locke's speech. As the enlisted prisoners sat, they remained mute with no sign of interest or emotion. They most often just stared into the floor knowing the game the Reds were playing and regretting they had a part in the charade. But what could they do.

Then as Captain Locke ended his robotic, insincere diatribe against the war, he, out of the blue, went rogue. In an inadvertent impulse, he departed from his agreed to remarks. With unexpected suddenness Bill assumed his natural persona—the dauntless fighter jock—and angrily uttered this parting shot to all the Communists present, "We are prisoners of war. We cannot fight you now, but very soon American forces will be kicking the shit out of you Reds."

The very few onlookers who understood English were stunned. Mr. Kim was audibly livid. But the American troops who heard or were later told about Locke's prophesy got a huge booster shot to their severely anemic morale on this infamous day of collaboration with the enemy.

Major McDaniel quickly signaled Smith, standing on the gym floor at the bottom of the platform stairs, to call the room to attention. He did so immediately, almost preemptively. The officers filed off the stage. McDaniel grabbed Locke's arm and held him until only the two of them stood atop the dais. The Major roared, "At ease! Dismissed!" Then as their men shuffled out of the gym, he looked Locke straight in the eye and without visible angst said, "I know it felt good. I could see the men that heard it, loved it. But you, Captain, lost sight of 'the objective.' You need to pray the price for your lack of discipline is not borne by the men we serve." And then he let go of the pilot's arm and preceded him down the stairs.

* * *

As stipulated in the oral pact between Major McDaniel and Mr. Kim, the parade marchers were comprised of those POWs fit to make a one mile trek. They would carry eight banners extolling the righteousness of the North Korean cause and soliciting the desired friendship with the peace-loving American people. But instead of a single mile jaunt, Mr. Kim would begin to exact his revenge for Locke's contemptuous indiscretion. The POWs now were forced to walk several hours on a circuitous five mile course from the Muhak School, through the streets of Seoul and not allowed to return to the school until they were demonstratively pooped. Even the vigilant armed guard escorts were glad when the march came to an end, as they had hoisted bayoneted rifles the whole way in case a foolish POW tried to "break ranks."

Parade in Seoul (Halcomb and Yeager Circled)[13]

* * *

On 11 September, in the early morning, Makarounis's group—mainly from the 29th Regiment—entered the Seoul POW compound; scores of soldiers were hanging out the second-floor windows, shouting at the new arrivals.

"Lieutenant, Lieutenant, you made it."

Makarounis immediately recognized some guys from his unit and asked, "What's the food situation?"

"Soup and bread, twice a day," someone yelled.

"Plenty of water," another shouted.

"What about the Red Cross?"

"No Red Cross."

Makarounis could hear some of the newcomers groan. Then someone bellowed, "We got several army medics and a Korean doctor and nurse."

Then the lieutenant and the new prisoners in the courtyard heard a voice scream, "Get the hell away from those windows, you bastards!" And suddenly silence reigned; the windows were abandoned, and Makarounis got his first introduction to Mr. Kim.

Moments later, Kim herded the new men into the building and began administering the standard survey given to every American imprisoned in Muhak. The new guys were astonished to see an American sergeant eagerly handing out the one-page surveys. It was not the fact that he was doing it, but it was his level of enthusiasm and the disdain he displayed to his fellow Americans. The terms "turncoat" and "traitor" fit him like a glove.[14]

* * *

Kim had learned by now, if he waited on the survey, then the newcomers would talk to the "old timers." And the new guys would then provide bogus information about themselves. For example, the stock answer to the question on how their parents made a living became "farming." Every POW soon learned that any person in any way associated with "business" was sure to be part of the Wall Street capitalist class, the oppressors of the working class. And you did not want to be identified as such.

Also, the survey might detect the troublemakers in advance. Walt Whitcomb was one such self-identified recalcitrant. When he filled out the survey, Walt wrote that his dad was "Clark Gable" age "99" and his mom was "Jane Russell" age "21." He also indicated that his family did not have to make a living: "they were too rich to work." And to ensure the Reds had the right first impression, Walt's answer to the question why he came to Korea was pointedly succinct: "To kill gooks."

Naturally, after reviewing Walt's pithy answers on the survey, Mr. Kim "invited" him to his office where two guards adjusted his attitude with their rifle butts by repeatedly slamming him between his shoulder blades. Whitcomb would remain a joker, but he learned to improve his timing and choice of audience.[15]

* * *

As the ranking officer in the newest group, Alex received special treatment from Mr. Kim: he did not have to take the survey. In its place, he would receive a lengthy interrogation in Kim's office.

"What's your name?" Mr. Lee inquired.

"First Lieutenant Alexander G. Makarounis, serial number O58962."

"Are you Greek?"

"I am an American. My father is Greek. My mother is Russian."

"Russian?" Kim interposed.

"Yes," Alex confirmed as he noticed Kim's face soften. The questioning would go on for several hours. But what struck Alex foremost, and other POWs interrogated before him, was the amateurishness of the whole affair. These two Orientals were the "keystone cops" of propaganda. They asked the wrong questions. The intent of every question was obvious. And they did not even try to get any military intelligence from him.

When this initial cross-examination was over, Alex felt almost like they had become cordial acquaintances, if not friends. He would be mistaken, but Makarounis was early in his relationship with these two Communists. Mr. Kim then took the lieutenant to the G Group room and opened the door. Alex stepped in and saw fifty men; almost all were standing. Kim shut the door, and a man in a flight suit approached him.

"I'm Captain Locke. That's Lieutenant Smith. Over there are Lieutenant Boydston and Lieutenant Blaylock." They all walked over and shook his hand.

"I'll put your name on our blackboard, Alex," volunteered Blaylock. "Every room has a blackboard with its inhabitant's names on it. Also, paper records are kept hidden on several different soldiers so we can always account for each other."

Alex could see his room was organized as he gazed at the black board. Not only were the officer's names on the board, but all the last names of every enlisted man in the room were arrayed in three columns under a 1st, 2nd, and 3rd Squad. In G Group, three noncoms—Master Sergeants Sherman, Michaels, and Perry, respectively—were in charge of the three squads. Each sergeant had fourteen or fifteen men under him. Plus, there was a calendar with other info not readily discernible in his quick read.

Locke interjected, "I'll introduce you to the other officers at chow in about an hour from now. But let's walk down to the sickroom and see the medics. Not to get too personal, Lieutenant, but you don't look too good right now. You're awfully yellow."

Halcomb, the chief medic, checked Alex's vital signs and asked him some questions. Grady did not like the answers, but the sickroom was full, so he asked Makarounis to come back in the morning.

At chow, Alex met Major McDaniel and some of the other officers—Thomas, Holt, Tabor, and Wirt, the engineer. But his best introduction that evening was to the food—a bowl of soup with some greens floating in it and a hard-crusted small loaf of bread. He and the other newbies were clearly delighted to partake in devouring this delectable morsel of food.

Soon after, Alex was back in his assigned room for bedtime. Without any working lights in the room, the men had to get settled in before dark. The room was far too small for the throng of sleepers it had to accommodate. So everybody had to find a place on the floor and reduce their body "footprint" to create optimum space for the night's rest. This ritual took time, even for the more practiced.

Lieutenant Smith offered to share his ragged comforter with Alex. And Alex accepted, thus forming a bond between a white officer and colored officer that would only grow with time and their shared suffering.[16]

Sleeping Arrangements in One Muhak Classroom[17]

The Major

* * *

Mr. Kim summoned Major McDaniel to his office. This time the Major was instructed to come alone. When he entered the room, he was told to shut the door.

"That 'airplane guy' is a stupid bastard!" Kim exploded. "You cannot control him. You broke our agreement. Your officers were only to read their speeches. Nothing more! And that crazy son of bitch made me look bad. I am going to cut back on your food."

"Then my officers won't record those speeches," said the Major in his normal, quiet, dispassionate voice.

Kim glowered at the Major for a long spell, but he had found out weeks ago that this American officer was "unbreakable." And he needed those recordings. He had promised his superiors he could get them.

"You record tomorrow. Your food portions will not change." Kim then waved his hand signaling the meeting was over.

The Major was now convinced the improved food situation would end once the recordings were made, so he managed to delay the tapings for two more days. But with Kim's threats to withdraw the scant, but vital, medicine some prisoners were given, McDaniel finally had the officers record their speeches for broadcast. And as he predicted, the daily ration immediately returned to one rice or millet ball per soldier. In the end, the collaboration cost the American officers their unwavering sworn fidelity to the United States of America. But each POW received two loaves of bread and two servings of meat-laden soup every day for one week.[18]

* * *

The air raids starting on 15 September began to intensify in Seoul. It seemed Locke's prophetic utterance during the "presidium" was to be realized sooner than expected. For the POWs the sound of American airpower buzzing all around them was heartening. It even gave Alex Makarounis some hope as he had fallen deathly ill on the second day of his stay in Seoul. He had gone to sick call in the morning as directed by Halcomb and he got to see the Korean doctor who gave him a pill for his jaundice. Then as the day wore on and his diarrhea got worse, he became so weak he checked himself into the sickroom.

Sergeant Rowlette, who Alex had last seen in Hadong and worked in the mess under Lieutenant Tabor, had promised to bring him some food. When he did after the evening chow, the good sergeant also brought a comforter. But by then, Makarounis had lost his appetite and had curled up on the floor to await his fate. There he remained for days fighting for his life. On his third day the young boy on the cot next to him died from extreme malnutrition. This soldier was the first to expire in Seoul and for a while it appeared to Halcomb that Alex would be death number two.

Several days later, however, Makarounis's condition had stabilized when the spectacular miracle occurred. "Grady, I see light. I can see. I can see." Parsons ballyhooed.

The whole sickroom erupted in uncoordinated applause, even among those patients in substantial pain or feebleness. Although it took Auvil a few days to regain the visual acuity to become self-sufficient again, this unanticipated, spontaneous happening soon became common knowledge throughout the POW community and a sign of the Divine to both the religious and irreligious.

* * *

On 18 September, having released Parsons from the sickroom, Grady was taking a rare break in the courtyard when someone said, "Look! Jarheads!" And sure enough, when Halcomb looked up, three marines from the 1st Marine Regiment were being escorted into the compound.

Not missing an opportunity to harass a rival service member, one soldier shouted, "I thought marines never surrendered!"

One marine instantly shot back, "We didn't. We were looking for cunt and got caught with our pants down."

All those Americans in the yard were glad to see this first tangible evidence of the Inchon landing and that these brothers in arms had not lost their humor or grit now that they too were POWs.

* * *

By day eight, Makarounis had made a marvelous physical recovery and was able to leave the sickroom. And by 19 September, the lieutenant really felt good—the best since his captivity began. He thanked Grady for nursing him back to health and made his way back to the Group G classroom.

Little did Alex know that the very next day his wellness would be tested in ways he could never have considered. But not him alone; all the prisoners were about to endure an unprecedented involuntary expedition never before replicated in the annals of American POW history.[19]

Chapter Five

The Longest, Bleakest Trudge
(20 September to 10 October)

Their walk is slow, for they are dead weary, as you can tell even when looking at them from behind. Every line and sag of their bodies speaks of their inhuman exhaustion.

—Ernie Pyle

As they stood there waiting for Mr. Kim and the junior lieutenant to finish their conversation, Major McDaniel gave some final instructions to Wirt, Locke, Tabor, Smith, and Makarounis. "One of us must always be at the head of the column, one in the middle, and one on the end. I plan to traverse the column as often as I can. We have to know what's going on all the time so we can intervene if we need to. Captain Locke, I need you to convince the lieutenant we can march during the day so the air force can 'ID' us."

It was around 2100 hours on 20 September when the march started. The Americans had heard rumors for a couple of days that they might be moved out of Seoul soon, but now the nightmare was actually happening. Mr. Kim had gotten the orders to abandon Muhak. The North Korean junior lieutenant would take the main group, and Kim would follow with those in the sickroom.

The POWs first crossed the city and headed north, colliding with massive NKPA reinforcements that were streaming south on the same road. When the marchers were about five miles out in the countryside, someone rode up on horseback, bumping six prisoners off the road and bringing the POW column to a halt. This horseman shouted something to the guards, and the next thing the Americans knew, the whole column was being turned around. And they were now headed back on the same road they had just come.

Makarounis could not contain himself. He blurted out to anyone who would listen, "We're in luck. By tomorrow this time, the Americans will be in Seoul, and we will be back in the States in a week."

But as the column entered the outskirts of the city, the guards suddenly veered off the road they were on and onto another road that led them north again, but this time the road led into a forest. Makarounis's knees almost buckled; but worse, his spirit and that of the other soldiers dipped to an all-time low.

A half hour later, now under a canopy of trees, Locke came up next to Makarounis and whispered some good news, "Holt and Thomas have escaped. Don't know when. Don't know how. But they are definitely no longer with us."

As they covered some twenty miles that first night, those who knew the lieutenants had gotten away had mixed feelings, especially when the column passed the 38th Parallel. They were, of course, pleased about their daring accomplishment and happy for their newfound liberty, but they were also envious of their presumed freedom and disappointed in themselves for not trying to duplicate the lieutenants' feat.

As the POWs made their way deeper and deeper into the enemy fatherland, Makarounis became more and more disheartened. One simple idea had taken hold in his mind and he could not shake it: suppose the UN forces stop at the 38th Parallel. Sure, it would make military sense to press the attack and destroy the NKPA or, at least, render it unusable for offensive operations. But the politicians may fear a wider war with the Soviets or Red Chinese if Pyongyang's sovereignty is placed in jeopardy.

First Fifteen Hours: Seoul to Pyongyang March, 21 September (Parsons Circled)[1]

So as he walked, he would repeat this argument with himself about what was more likely when the Americans reached the 38th Parallel—a full, permanent stop; a pause; or a continuous push to rout the NKPA. Finally, after several hours he decided to share his fears with Captain Locke.

When Alex was through explaining his unshakable phobia and its implications, Locke only had one thing to say: "I don't care what the higher-ups do. I can't die. I've too much to go home to." And for the moment, this pretentious but elegant assertion was enough to cheer Makarounis.

The march continued through the night and into the dawn. There were very few rest breaks. But shortly after daybreak, the guards' worst dread was realized when two Corsair aircraft came over the horizon. Everyone started to scatter when Locke started shouting, "Stay put! Stay put! Start waving! Take off your shirts! Wave your shirts!"

The guards ran and hid along the road wherever they could—in ditches, behind rocks, in underbrush—and so did a few Americans. But most stayed in place and turned to look at the approaching aircraft. The planes began to descend and line up on the column. They extended their flaps and slowed to about 120 miles per hour. The POWs furiously started waving their white rice bags, their shirts—anything they had. And they hooted and hollered whatever came to mind: "We're here!" "Don't shoot!" "Americans! Americans!"

Corsair Launching from Aircraft Carrier[2]

The propeller-driven single-seat fighters came lower and lower. The roar of their engines got louder and louder. The men on the ground could even make out the faces of the pilots. Locke continued to scream, "Hold your ground!" The soldiers did. And they also held their breath as they waited for possible devastation or deliverance.

The Corsairs passed over the half-mile column, one plane no more than fifty feet off the ground. Then they circled and surveyed the column again, dipping their wings to indicate they had recognized the group as American prisoners. The men could hardly contain their joy, and they cheered as the planes disappeared over the mountains.

It was still morning when the column reached a red-brick schoolhouse where they were told they could get a sustained rest. The overnight march from Seoul had been about thirty-four miles, not counting their early reversal at the start. And the officers quickly ascertained that no one was unaccounted for, except Thomas and Holt who hopefully had, by now, made it back to friendly forces.[3]

* * *

Meanwhile, Mr. Kim and the fifteen sick prisoners had been forced to abandon the Muhak School in Seoul the same morning that McDaniel's group arrived at the North Korean red-brick school. PFC Grady Halcomb, the medic, had shepherded his patients out of their beds and onto the road with great difficulty. The men could hardly stand, much less walk.

The private took command as he had often done before and challenged his patients. "We can only survive if we help each other. The guards will kill anyone who cannot keep up. So we need to stay on our feet. Remember, the guards are really jumpy now that they are being pushed out of here. We can do this if we Americans stick together."

Mr. Kim was clearly shaken by the turn of events in Seoul. The UN advance was evident everywhere on the ground and in the air. The city was engulfed in violence. The POWs could see the fear in his face. Unfortunately, his panic fed his urgency to escape north. And the pace of the march he demanded at first was just short of a run. But after a couple of miles, mercifully, Mr. Kim himself came up hobbled, and he was forced to slow his harried steps.

American Marines Fighting in Seoul[4]

As the POWs settled into a slower slog, all the men began to wither. Yet most of them exhibited extraordinary tenacity and courage, given their medical condition. Corporal Richard Lewis Wilson was assisting one of his comrades in walking when he passed out and was unconscious before hitting the rock-strewn ground. A couple of soldiers kneeled down and tried to revive him by slapping him hard several times. He did not flinch, and the guards motioned the men to move on, raising their rifles to encourage their immediate compliance. As the column moved up the road another fifty yards or so, the captives heard rifle fire. As they turned and looked back, a group of oxcarts came thundering down the road where Wilson had fallen, the ox hoofs trampling anything in their path. Wilson, the soldier, was now history, but a valiant and selfless leader to the very end.[5]

* * *

When Mr. Kim's POW group caught up with McDaniel's group at the schoolhouse, several days had elapsed. And not only were the "sickroom" POWs in terrible shape, so was Kim. The sight of him limping into the school brought a broad grin to Locke's face, and he remarked, "The son of a bitch, I hope he can never walk again." All the men in earshot smiled and nodded in agreement.

At the schoolhouse the now reunited POWs were kept uninformed of what the future held. But, at least, the men ravaged with dysentery had a respite to allow some physiological recovery. They had access to potable water, and Sergeant Robert Morris—one of the section leaders and an army cook—was given a fistful of millet and some rancid fish to dish out to each man daily.

Even so, Sergeant Whited became the second POW to die since leaving Seoul. He had been weak for some time, most likely wasted by intestinal bleeding. He was one of those rare individuals who never complained and always did more than was expected. Despite his deteriorating condition, he had shouldered many responsibilities that others could have or should have. At least, this pause at the red-brick schoolhouse allowed the sergeant a respectable burial.

As men gathered around the freshly dug grave, Major McDaniel began the eulogy. "Sergeant Roy Whited was an American soldier who did his duty. He never once asked for special favors from the enemy or his fellow soldiers. He propped up others when he could barely walk. He always expressed hope and never gave up trying to get home. We will miss him and his courage. But someday, we will tell his

The Major

family what a fine man he was and how, in the toughest of circumstances, he inspired the rest of us to carry on. Now, if you will bow your heads, we will say good-bye to Roy with the Lord's Prayer. Our Father, Who art in Heaven, hallowed be Thy name . . . ."

God's grace having been extended to Whited was also extended to rest of the POWs when a huge stash of potatoes was discovered in a hut on the school grounds. Word spread like wildfire among the prisoners. Everyone who was ambulatory made his way to the hut to secure his share, mysteriously unabated by the guards. It was at this juncture that Locke's Schick razor blade he kept hidden in one of his many flight suit pockets achieved the zenith of its utility. From its former mundane role of cleaning and paring fingernails and toenails, this single blade now became an enabler of culinary delight—potatoes that tasted almost as good as those back home.

On the fourth day the most unnerving event occurred during this particular schoolhouse stay. Allied airplanes had come over the area continuously since their arrival. And from the get-go Captain Locke had told the guards, now that they were north of the 38th Parallel, everyone must evacuate the building when they heard aircraft; plus signs should be constructed that are visible from the air to identify the location of the POWs. Instead, the guards moved all the POWs to the second floor and would not permit evacuations. No signs were allowed. Yet all the guards slept outside.

So on this day, as a lone B-29 bomber was heard approaching at low level, the savvy fighter pilot instinctively, but ineffectually, yelled, "Everybody duck!" They did. They also inhaled and listened to the bombs whine their way toward the school while Al Gifford prayed for the first time in his life. The bombs exploded, jarring the building and showering the POWs with thick dust. The proverbial "could not see your hand in front of your face" was no exaggeration.

Miraculously, all seven bombs missed their primary target, only destroying two adjacent storage sheds. Locke later examined one twenty-foot crater from just one of the five hundred-pound bombs that left no doubt in anyone's mind that they had amazingly dodged a very big bullet. But among both guards and prisoners, the hellish eternity of suspense during the bombs' free fall and follow-on explosive percussions were indelibly imprinted on their psyches.[6]

B-29 Superfortress Dropping Bombs in Korea[7]

* * *

The three Nisei interpreters—Corporal Jack Arakawa, Sergeant Tak Kumagai, and Master Sergeant Robert Shinde—were all sitting together recounting yesterday's near-death experience with the B-29, when Shinde diverted their conversation, "So, Takeshi, what's this I hear about you facing a firing squad?"

The Major

"Well, there's not much to tell. Really, there's not much I remember. I was captured after the *In Min Gun* crossed the Kum River. They were on the march to Taejon, and they had no desire to fool with prisoners. So they lined us up and shot us."

"When I came to, they were gone, and I was surrounded by dead soldiers. I'd been hit in the head, the left arm, and right side. I was drenched in blood—mine and probably the guys' next to me. But all three bullets had grazed or gone through me without hitting any bone or organs. I was weak, but I just got up and walked away. No one else was alive."

"Then, like an idiot, I got captured again. This time the soldiers were support troops, and they turned me over to a group of soldiers escorting POWs headed for Seoul. That's pretty much the whole story."

"So the B-29 was no big deal to you?" Jack joked.

"No, you're wrong. I get nervous whenever I see aircraft overhead, ours or theirs. Remember, I was at Pearl Harbor."[8]

* * *

Later on, still at the red-brick schoolhouse, Major McDaniel huddled with the officers. "We need to get our air force to drop us some C-rations. Captain Wirt and Lieutenant Tabor, I want you to work out a scheme whereby our men can spell out the word *food* when we are on the march. Any time we have friendly aircraft overhead, I want them to be able to form the word without the guards knowing what we're up to. Any questions or concerns?"

Wirt shook his head "no." And Tabor hesitated, then said, "The guards are starting to hide among us when the planes come over. How do we keep them from messing up our letters?"

"Captain Locke, I want you to get word to the guards that from the air, our pilots can pick out which men are North Koreans and which are Americans. And tell them the really good pilots can kill them. Also, we can keep a sizeable group on each end: separated from our four letters. Instinctively, the Reds will find their way into the largest groupings. Anything else, if not, you two get it worked out and be ready to execute before we leave here," the Major ordered.

As instructed, the lieutenants had a plan figured out and had people assigned to specific tasks within a few hours. Essentially, they created four groups—A, B, C and D—with A Group forming the "F," B Group forming the first "O," and so on. In turn, each group had men assigned to a specific spatial position in the formation of each letter. And additional larger groups bracketed "FOOD."

* * *

After six days, the POWs left the red-brick school, having buried another soldier: Master Sergeant Joseph E. Stancel. Again, they headed north for Pyongyang. And it wasn't long before the POWs got the opportunity to signal their vital need for food. Just as planned, when an aircraft was anywhere overhead, the groups unobtrusively formed their letters and the guards hid among the biggest groupings or somewhere off the road depending on their individual perception of the air threat. This spelling exercise was repeated many times, but its effectiveness was not realized until a couple of days later.

For the Major and the rest of the officers, managing the POW "column" was undoable. The length of the column could stretch to three or four miles as it would accordion according to the ongoing natural selection process among the POWs: the weaker ones aggregating and falling to the rear. So as McDaniel tried to be everywhere by crisscrossing the column continuously, in so doing, he not only zapped his energy, the senior American officer also forfeited the opportunity to slow the entire march when he left the head of the column. The other officers, of course, helped in this management task, but only the Major had the gravitas to intimidate or cajole the North Korean lieutenant who had unbounded disdain for his American enemy.

When the POWs left the red-bricked school the number of sick and disabled—in extremis—had almost tripled from fifteen in Seoul to forty-two now. Makarounis was one of those who was unable to keep pace. He had recuperated some, but was still weak. These more feeble POWs would temporarily become detached from the main group and lag some greater distance behind the larger group on their way north. And on some days they would not catch up to the main column and would bed down in a different location. Consequently, it was these sicker men that became the would-be beneficiaries of the airdrop of food.[9]

* * *

On Day 10, a lone C-47 out of the blue appeared approaching Makarounis and Halcomb's sick group. The plane descended and almost seemed to hover over them. Then they all saw the "manna from heaven" falling to earth. Their minds were, instantly if only momentarily, healed as they knew this food would soon nourish their depleted bodies. Moreover, the guards did not impede them as they joyously rushed out into an expansive acreage where the C-rations and water containers had been widely strewn due to the prevailing wind drifts.

The ever-exhausted men labored for hours—gathering the food and water parcels. Under the supervision of the guards, they retrieved, stacked, and eventually hauled their precious air-delivered cargo to a nearby schoolhouse. Hoping to crack open the c-rats for supper and experience what, for them, would be a culinary feast, the POWs, instead, were served their usual rice gruel. But before they could protest, they were assured they would receive their reward in the morning after a North Korean officer had inventoried the entire food and water supplies.

C-47 Airdrop of Supplies[10]

At daybreak, having dreamed of food all night, the POWs awoke to discover every single case of food and water had been surreptitiously transported from the school to parts unknown. The men were enraged and almost insane in the cacophony of their voiced wrath: "The motherfucking gooks stole our food. I want to murder the bastards. How could this happen?" But in the end, their anger eventually subsided into a crushing fatigue and unmitigated desolation that only condemned men can truly feel.[11]

* * *

No one seemed to talk much anymore. Sure, the POWs were dead tired and their mouths were drier than dry. But to talk, you had to think, and nobody wanted to think because there was no telling where it might lead. But Toney was awakened from his walking stupor by a sudden brain "flash" and asked, "What happened to Mr. Kim?"

Yeager was the first to pipe up. "The last time I saw the asshole was when he was punishing Hamilton back at the red-brick school. Remember, when Hamilton found all those cigarettes in the storeroom, and he gave them out. But he got caught handing some to his buddies, and Kim had him beaten out in the courtyard. I remember Kim cussing Hamilton, and Ray had to stand and keep his arms extended in front of him, holding a huge rock in each hand. And if he dropped his arms, the guard would hit him with a rifle butt."

Another soldier added, "Kim never left that schoolhouse. He was too banged up to walk any more. He probably wanted to spend some time alone with that fat nurse. The two Reds make a perfect couple. But he better watch out. She could hurt you, and she loves to shoot that gun of hers."[12]

* * *

The main column had been halted for about five minutes when Bob Sharpe saw the North Korean lieutenant jogging to the area where Bob was sitting. One of the guards had been trying to get a POW to stand, but the soldier refused. He was on all fours when the junior lieutenant got to his guard's location. Even though Bob spoke no Hangeul, he knew that the highly animated and gesturing guard was telling his superior officer that the soldier was not cooperating. And Bob could agree, having witnessed the number of times this soldier had fallen out of formation.

Of course, no one could know what is really going on in another man's head or body. The lieutenant did not care. He had heard enough from his subordinate. He grabbed the

American by the collar, spun him around while he was still on his knees, whipped out his pistol, placed it in the middle of the forehead, and blew a hole in the soldier's skull.

He shoved the pistol back in its holster, put his right hand on the burp gun he carried over his left shoulder, and ordered the POWs to their feet. The march resumed, leaving the POW face up, surprised eyes wide open, on his back with his legs and feet tucked under his buttocks.[13]

That evening when Major McDaniel got wind of the murder, he grabbed Master Sergeant Shinde and approached the lieutenant. He confronted the North Korean—toe to toe—less than arm's length away. "Lieutenant, you shot one of my men. You are an officer. You need to set the example for your soldiers. My men are unarmed. They are no threat to your men. If my soldiers are not following your orders, I, or one of my officers, will get them to obey your guards."

"Your men are animals. They are weak. I will not let them slow the march."

"I am asking you to let my officers control my men. We can do it better than you can. If you start killing them, they will give up and slow you down."

"We will see." The Korean turned on his heel and joined a group of his guards.

"Did he understand me, Sergeant Shinde?"

"Yes, sir. He understood."

* * *

Ed Slater could not stand it anymore. He had long since given much hope to his survival. Only Bob Sharpe's prodding kept his feet moving forward. His throat felt like gravel, and his tongue could no longer feel any moisture along the inside of his cheeks. Then he spied "the melon" some twenty yards from the road in an otherwise barren field. And like a hound dog that just saw a rabbit race past, he bolted—lickety-split—from the column.

When he did, one guard immediately raised his rifle and fired. Ed continued his beeline approach to that melon. Bob started yelling, "Get back here! They are going to kill you!"

Undeterred, Ed swooped the melon up. Held his prize above his head and raced back to the column. The guard lowered his rifle. When Ed reached the road, he threw the melon down, splitting it in several pieces. He knelt down, helped himself to the biggest piece, and began gnawing at its luscious, wet content.

"You fool. You could be dead now," Bob barked as he helped himself to the melon.

"Yeah, right. These gooks can't shoot," as Ed watched other POWs gather up the rind some of the original "eaters" had foolishly discarded.[14]

* * *

Sergeant Leonard Hines was one of only four Negroes among the McDaniel POW group, all from the 24th Inf Regt. Lieutenant Smith, Corporal Milton Morris, and Private William Hodge were the others. But nobody, officer or enlisted, could hold a candle to Hines when it came to his relentless encouragement to persevere. Even the most downtrodden were boosted up whenever he was around. He was from Pennsylvania, and if he held a negative thought in his head, no one would ever know it. Sure, he was a Sergeant and expected to be a leader among the junior men. Yet, by example, Leonard showed every POW how to carry on, in spite of significant and visible wounds he had to his feet and back.

He would come up to another soldier who was struggling and say something like: "Hey, what ya doing? You know, I'm a cousin of Jesse Owens. And I think, right now, I can take you in a ten-yard dash. You want to bet me the next dried fish tail you get? I'm just talk'n the tail now. Nothin' big here."

Or if a more serious tone was needed, Hines would convey some edifying words like: "You're holding up great, soldier. Your high school buddies would be impressed. You know, if I had been as young as you, I'd given up long before now. We didn't prepare you well before we made you fight. I got a lot more training. So I want you to keep doin' what you been doin'—to show the guys that aren't as tough as you how to act."

And then to those POWs who were the most recalcitrant, having lost all civility and were unabashed in their pronouncements: "Who gives a fuck? We're already dead."

Leonard would simply say, "I'm not dead! And someday when I get home or have to stand before my Maker, I don't want to have to make excuses for what I did as a POW."

Sergeant Hines was a gift to every American who had contact with him during their collective journey through hell.[15]

* * *

Having just traversed and surveyed the entire column, Major McDaniel grabbed Kumagai and approached the officer in charge during a brief halt. "Lieutenant, we need to commandeer some oxcarts. Too many of my men can no longer maintain the pace."

"They not walk, they die," the lieutenant turned to walk away.

The Major persisted, "You and I are officers, and the welfare of the prisoners is our responsibility. Some soldiers in your army are also prisoners now. Someday prisoners will be exchanged. You need to help me keep these men alive. Your superiors will not be happy if they die and you could have prevented it. Your commanders will be charged as war criminals under the Geneva Convention."

For whatever reason, the lieutenant listened this time and waited until Kumagai ensured that the Major's words were fully absorbed, then he simply said, "Okay."

As the march resumed, McDaniel soon located Makarounis near the rear of the column. "Lieutenant, I got authority to get us some oxcarts in the next village we pass. But I am going to assign you some tough duty. I want you to consult with Halcomb and decide who rides and who walks. I'll find as many carts as I can, but we will never get enough for all the men. So you'll make the call, and it won't be easy. Any questions?"

"What about the officers?"

"Rank has no privilege. Your decision is based on medical need only. Halcomb knows the condition of the men better than anyone. Use him to decide. But an officer doesn't need to suffer if he is in worse shape than an enlisted man. And if you get sick or lame, I'll give someone else this responsibility to enforce who walks. But I do want you to watch Locke. He's our most valuable man with all his training and experience. He's older and still banged up from his crash. Make him ride if he needs to. Tell him it's an order."

Yes, sir, but what about you? You're policing too much ground, and you are the old man here, sir," smiled Makarounis affectionately.

"I am fine, but thank you for reminding me," the Major responded, mustering up a faux glare directed at his junior officer.

* * *

As dusk approached, the POW column shuffled into yet another village to find shelter for the night. As always, the guards traipsed the column through the main street so the inhabitants could spit and hit on the POWs at will. This day, however, they assembled the Americans into the main square and allowed the villagers to encircle the helpless POWs.

The North Korean civilians were eating and smoking as they enjoyed the unplanned evening's entertainment: taunting and physically abusing the American captives. And this night, for show of loyalty to Kim Il Sung or for genuine hatred toward the Americans, segments of the crowd were more violent than normal. Not content to blow smoke into the GIs' faces and then tease the Americans by stomping the half-smoked cigarette butts out in the dirt, one civilian ground a cigarette out on the forehead of a POW who foolishly stooped to retrieve a discarded butt.

The Americans had learned, by now, that individual North Koreans would sometimes show pity and even offer them food in a village, but they would never demonstrate any coddling of their "enemy" when a Communist government official—military or civilian—was in their presence.[16]

* * *

Around 0730 hours on 8 October, the oxcarts were leading the march for the first time and had separated themselves several miles from the rest of the POW column and Major McDaniel. Several of the officers—Locke, Wirt, and Tabor—were sharing time on the carts with another fifty or so men. Locke's right leg had given out, having never properly healed since his crash-landing. And Lieutenant Tabor had pneumonia, and Captain Wirt's health was failing fast from multiple maladies.

"Captain, I just got nothing left in my tank," Tabor confessed as he and Wirt sat side by side, with their torsos slumped over and their legs dangling from the end of the oxcart.

"Yeah, Stan, I don't like the fact that we are riding and a lot of the men are walking. But you're a combat vet. You fought in New Guinea, and you're twenty-seven years old. And very few old men like us could go through this shitty march. My lungs are better than yours, but this hitch in my giddy-up makes it impossible for me to keep up." Wirt paused and then finished with a tease, "See, we Yankees from Illinois can talk like you Texans."

"I just got to hang on for Kitty. We only had a few days together after the wedding before I shipped out. You know we've been sweethearts forever. God, I want to see her again."

Like every clear day, the American planes could be seen streaking their way to pre-designated targets or searching for targets of opportunity in the enemy homeland. Not unusual, a formation of F-80 aircraft appeared overhead, then the lead plane abruptly fishtailed, turning the formation 270 degrees, aligning the four planes with the road and the strung out oxcarts while rapidly descending. At the same time, they got into a finger formation, three hundred feet apart. Locke instantly recognized the maneuver and screamed, "Hit the ditch! Get off the carts. Now!" He simultaneously jumped to the ground, rolled, and crawled his way into an irrigation ravine.

Within seconds, the sky rained metal projectiles as twenty-four .50-caliber machine guns—six per aircraft from the fast-moving jets, at an altitude of two hundred feet—saturated the hapless cart riders. The flesh of men and beasts were torn apart, comingling with the splintering wood from the wagons and the dirt from the road that sprang into the air from the impact of the metallic shower.

Having delivered their carnage, the air force pilots exited the area. Whether out of bullets, out of recognition of their tragic error, or out of pure luck—they did not execute another pass to complete their annihilation. Even so, the results were devastating to those who remained on the carts.

Locke stood up and surveyed the scene. Most of the oxen were dead or dying, more than half the carts were destroyed, and many men were draped over the wagons, bleeding profusely. He thought he recognized Captain Wirt and limped his way over to a cart. He turned him on his side and saw the gaping, fist-sized hole in his abdomen. He was alive and conscious but had no chance of surviving his wounds. Locke got up in the cart and cradled him in his arms. The captain moaned and violently trembled from the shock of his injuries. Fred hung on for some considerable time, given his wounds; but finally, when life began to ebb from his body, he began to plead for his wife: "Elaine, Elaine, Elaine . . . ." His breathing arrested, his body sagged and he died.

.50-Cal Guns Being Loaded on F-80 Shooting Star[17]

The Major

Still holding the captain, Locke's eyes welled up with tears as he thought of Ronda and how she would handle his death as now Elaine would have to cope with Fred's. The fighter pilot also gritted his teeth as he wept, while cursing his fellow airmen who had committed this reprehensible deed. No doubt existed in his judgment. These pilots were sloppy and derelict in the performance of their duty. In his mind, there was no excuse for this preventable friendly fratricide.[18]

The strafing killed seventeen POWs—many of the most disabled—and one North Korean driver died and a guard was wounded. Among the American wounded was Lieutenant Tabor. He was shot in the nose, side, and leg. His singular hope to be reunited with Kitty was now in grim jeopardy.

Perhaps, having up close and personally shared this disaster, the guards helped bury some of the dead POWs for the first time. Their final resting place was an extended two-foot-deep trench, but in its digging, true compassion was expressed by some of the Koreans, even though this empathy would be fleeting.

By now almost everyone had dysentery, and the pace had already slowed to only twelve miles a day. One North Korean guard, however, showed no sympathy. The lieutenant in charge was enraged. Having felt safe to this point in the daylight, he ordered: "From now on, we move at night!"

"Many more men will die, Lieutenant," Major McDaniel insisted.

"Goddam it, I give orders here. I say we go now." The lieutenant turned and strutted away.

As the march resumed, the Major prayed while he walked, for the safety of his men and the soul of this godless officer, "Lord, give us the strength to endure. Keep me from hating. Remind me that we are all your children and should love each other. And please soften our enemy's heart so my men may live."

This time, the march lasted the remainder of the day and through the bitterly cold night before the group stopped at dawn and occupied another school. After the men settled in, they were given a little millet and some grains of rice. Then they went to sleep, except for some of the officers. Makarounis was so tired, yet he had a bad case of insomnia. Like many others, his mind was a void, but his body would not succumb to sleep. Many POWs just lay there on the hard wooden floor, more dead than alive.

After conferring with Major McDaniel, Captain Locke decided to put his insomnia to good use and spent the day arguing with the junior lieutenant to resume daylight marching. His credibility as an airman or his sheer persistence finally paid off when the lieutenant rescinded his earlier order and told the American officers, "We stay the night."

The twenty-four-hour respite was a godsend for the POWs. Even so, several soldiers were unable to walk at all when the Americans assembled at sunrise for the next day's march. Major McDaniel, with Kumagai at his side, went to the lieutenant and did not mince words.

"Lieutenant, I have six men that cannot walk. We need to leave them behind until they can be picked up by an oxcart. We're so close to Pyongyang. This can be done."

The lieutenant gave Major McDaniel a big grin and spoke in his usual singsong English, "Sure, sure. Leave them here." He paused and fingered his gun. "But if you do, I'll have to shoot them." Then he puffed out his chest and matter-of-factly said, "I already have shot twelve of your men."

Major McDaniel told the men to make some litters. They then had to scramble to construct six pallets from tree branches, rice bags, and rope to accommodate the disabled soldiers. Once finished, the forsaken POWs were on the road again. The litters held together, but four men were needed to carry each litter, and they had to switch off every one hundred yards or so as no one had any stamina left whatsoever.[19]

* * *

Although Lieutenant Tabor had been wounded on the oxcart, his gashes did not appear life threatening—at first. But the day after the strafing he nonetheless grew weaker by the hour as the pneumonia that inflamed his lungs gained the upper hand. Yet, Stan adamantly refused to get on a litter. He knew his ride on one of the makeshift stretchers could cost the lives of those soldiers who carried him, as no POW had the luxury of expending any energy beyond placing one's own foot in front of the other.

Predictably, Tabor soon began falling out of the column, and the guards started assaulting him. Somehow, this abusive stimulus did spur him on for a while. But when Stan became delirious, some soldiers finally coaxed him onto a litter. Mercifully, for both he and his bearers, his supine horizontal ride sped the harm to his lungs and he died before dusk. Compounding his murder, the guards did not allow a burial, and he was left on the side of the road, virtually guaranteeing Kitty would never have the solace of having his remains come home to her.[20]

* * *

Johnny, the friendly guard, sidled up to Makarounis and softly said, "I fight for wrong side." Then he pointed to the skyline and said, "Look, you see Pyongyang."

And sure enough, Makarounis could see a line of structures in the distance. His eyes filled with tears and he muttered a little prayer: "Thank you, God, for letting me live. I won't forget what You've done for me." For this survivor and others, the realization that their circuitous 120-mile, 21-day death trudge was finally coming to an end was both cognitively exhilarating and humbling.

As they entered the peripheries of the city, five soldiers were still on the makeshift litters and another four were being carried piggyback. Sergeant Rowlette suddenly stopped and lowered his man to the ground. Turning to Makarounis, he said, "He's dead, Lieutenant. He just now died."

The contrasts between the countryside just traveled and the city were stark. Where the rural area of North Korea had been a sensory deprivation environment, the city offered sensory overload for what had become POW zombies. To affirm this state of mind and body among the captives, when two pretty young Caucasian women strolled by, Makarounis, the perennial bachelor, impulsively blurted out, "God, look. Americans." To his chagrin, the lieutenant immediately knew they had to be Russians, but more profoundly, he was astounded that none of his soldiers noticed and/or cared about these white women. The ogling and wolf calls that would normally occur among GIs had long since been smothered by starvation, exhaustion, and death.

Even so, the POWs continued to lurch deeper into the city, and the chaotic activity around them increased exponentially. The evidence of a sustained bombing campaign was apparent. The industrial areas were obliterated, but most civilian enterprises seemed unscathed.

Once, Russian officers in uniforms skirted the American column in a jeep, shaking their fists and yelling Slavic profanities as they passed by. Many of the city dwellers came out of the still-standing buildings and silently gawked at the prisoners, as if the POWs were freaks from an American carnival. But everywhere along the bustling streets, the tension was palpable. The North Korean capital was visibly a city under siege—under extreme sociological and physical pressure.[21]

Chapter Six

In the Enemy's Capital (10 to 14 October)

"Duty" then is the sublimest word in the English language. You should do your duty in all things. You can never do more; you should never wish to do less.
—**Robert E. Lee**

"Ain't it a shame," one US soldier remarked as he entered the courtyard of the school and lowered the litter to the ground. "Lieutenant Boydston just died." The second lieutenant was the last engineer alive. And now, with Boydston's death, that left 296 POWs still breathing, though some scarcely, that first night after roll call at yet another school, the Fourth National Grammar School. This one now within the heart of the enemy's capital.

The next day in Pyongyang yielded a small, but significant, morale uplift bestowed upon the prisoners by the same type of aircraft that almost killed their group during their deadly march. Capable of disgorging one million leaflets per sortie, one B-29 dropped its load over Pyongyang. Not surprisingly, some of these leaflets quickly found their way to the cloistered POWs. The Nisei interpreters deciphered the leaflets for the men. These single sheets of $5^{1/2}$ by $8^{1/2}$-inch paper were part of psychological operations being waged against the Communists. They were signed by General Douglas MacArthur (USMA 1903) and called for an immediate cessation of hostilities. But embedded in some

147

of these leaflets was a stern warning not to harm the United Nations' POWs.

These leaflets supported Major McDaniel's repeatedly espoused belief that eventually the UN forces would catch up with them. The Americans just needed the will—and sufficient nourishment—to survive. And the soup and the amount of "Vienna-lite" bread they had started to receive at this new school seemed to have more substance than previous food offerings during their captivity. Plus, a new cohort of guards was treating the prisoners better. They were from the Security Guard Bureau, Home Affairs Ministry. But on the other hand, the daily deaths started to mount from the cumulative effect of the POWs' prolonged medical and dietary neglect.

So even with the marginal improvement in the quality vice quantity of food, the Pyongyang accommodations were ominously worse than Seoul. A hundred and fifty men were packed in one room on the second floor and the remainder in two other rooms. Most of the windows in these rooms were glassless, and despite every attempt to shore them up, the chilly wind howled through them every night.

Two water taps were accessible to the POWs in the courtyard twice a day—for one hour at daybreak and for another hour just before dark. Men would fill what few bottles they had each morning and then nurse their water intake throughout the day. Some soldiers took the opportunity to wash their shredded clothing; however, their garments were so soaked in urine, diarrhea and dirt, any cleansing of them was largely in vain. Some men finally gave up and threw their excrement laden trousers away. These POWS wandered the school wearing nothing below the waist. They had lost any need for personal propriety.

Anarchy among the inmates was already ubiquitous throughout the school compound. The breakdown in military discipline was beyond the tipping point. But now that they were back in quasi-garrison, Major McDaniel sought to reinstitute the routines and structure achieved in Seoul. So he called the remnant of surviving leadership together to direct the way ahead. They met in a corner of the courtyard, out of earshot from the rest of the troops.

"Lieutenant Smith, JB, I want you to handle the burial detail here. We have permission to bury our men in a Christian church nearby. And as always, put the name, rank, and serial number on paper and seal it in a bottle," Major McDaniel instructed—for those new members of the detail.[1]

"Sergeant Morris, Sergeant Rowlette, you all will continue to handle the distribution of food. During the march some of the men serving the chow were accused of hoarding extra food for themselves. So even if these allegations against Eggen are unfounded, I don't want him or any of his buddies on the chow line. Do your best to find some men who will not succumb to the temptation to put themselves ahead of their fellow soldiers. I know it won't be easy."

"Most important, we need better control over the discipline. Fights have broken out already last night when some men disturbed others making their way to the latrine. We can't allow the men to turn on each other. So I want someone in charge in all three rooms. I, Lieutenant Miller, Lieutenant Mulock, Sergeant Shinde, and Sergeant Kumagai will monitor the big room. Captain Locke and Lieutenant Makarounis will be responsible for the classroom nearest the front of the building, and Lieutenant Blaylock and Lieutenant Smith—that's you, Howard, not JB—will maintain order in the other sleep room."

The Major continued, "I've already talked several times to Major Sil, the new officer in charge, to get us some civilian medical assistance from here in the city. I can't read him yet, but my sense is that he is unsympathetic and a man that does not want any involvement from anyone outside his security cohort. So I'm looking to ask Private Halcomb to set up another sick bay."

Then the Major asked, "Captain Locke, anything else?"

"No, sir. I'm just enjoying another day in Red paradise."

"Oh, one more thing, keep your ear to the ground to find out what's happening on the battlefront. Some of the Korean civilians here around the school are willing to give us what assistance they can, even if it is only information."

* * *

Sergeant Kumagai finally found Major McDaniel in one of the classrooms. He was sitting on the floor with his back against the wall. His eyes were closed. He looked totally sapped. No guards were about and only a couple of soldiers were asleep on the floor.

"Major," Kumagai whispered.

Tom's eyes blinked open and he managed a faint smile. "Yes, Sergeant."

"I have been approached by one of the men who work here in the school. He's a Christian and he wants to help us escape."

"Go on."

"He says there is a trapdoor in one of the rooms that goes under the building. There's space for three men to hide out. And he wants you to be one of those men."

The Major closed his eyes, not appearing to breathe for a good minute, and then fastening his eyes on Kumagai's, said, "No, I can't leave the men. But I want you to go and see if Captain Locke and Lieutenant Makarounis would want to go with you. Of course, tell no one else. And you only have to get back with me if one of them chooses not to take this chance. Good luck."

"Thank you, sir, but I wish you would reconsider going yourself."

"You know it's my duty to stay. And if I went missing, there would be an all-out hunt for me. And you might be found. But more important, I might be able to slow or stop some of these killings. Also, I want you to know that I chose Locke and Makarounis for their future value to the military. I know no other way," the Major said as his eyes moistened with his concomitant thoughts of someday, someway, embracing Helen, Tom, and John again.

"I understand. We won't let you down," Kumagai grasped the Major's hand, shook it vigorously, and went off to find Locke.

The Major closed his eyes and silently prayed, "Lord, give me the strength to see this through to the end. I am really tired and need your help. But as always, your will, not mine, be done."

* * *

On 13 October, Locke and Makarounis sat in the school yard basking in the sun, when the captain whispered, "If you had a chance to bug out, would you?"

The lieutenant literally stops breathing, gets a hold of himself and responds, "Captain, I definitely would."

Locke continued, "Sergeant Kumagai has been contacted by a North Korean who is a Christian and works here at the school. This Korean says any day now a bunch of us are going to be moved out to the Manchurian border. And you know not many of us could survive that. He also said he could hide three men. There were no guarantees, but he would do it if some men would take the gamble."

The two American officers then remained silent as Makarounis tried to absorb the full portent of this unexpected opportunity. Then the lieutenant stood up and wandered back in the school building. As he passed a broken window, he spied a red silk piece of cloth inside the sill. He instinctively snatched it and stuffed it inside his tattered fatigue shirt—another layer of warmth for the increasingly colder weather. Was this silk cloth an omen of what was about to come his way?

That night when everyone had settled down to sleep, Makarounis positioned himself close to Locke and whispered one word to him, "When?"

"We'll be told in plenty of time. Don't worry," the airman reassured the soldier. Then both men soon fell into a fitful sleep.

Next morning, with more rumors swirling, Major McDaniel—accompanied by Kumagai, Locke, and Makarounis—approached the lieutenant who had been the principal assassin during the march.

"Lieutenant, we have heard we are going to be moved north," Major McDaniel soberly and succinctly stated.

"Who told you?" he laughed with a maniacal grin.

"We heard talk among your guards. And you know my men are too weak to travel anywhere. Since we got here, twenty-eight soldiers have died," Major McDaniel recounted.

Again, the demented Korean officer snickered and said, "We not move for ten days, maybe never."

McDaniel and his men looked at each other and knew with certainty that their departure was imminent. Even a pathological liar can be read once his behavioral history is familiar.

All afternoon on 14 October, Makarounis ransacked the school building. He began his hunt helping a Korean civilian worker find a blanket for Major McDaniel. Though unsuccessful, he did manage to find some other booty that might aid him in his escape. His plunder of the schoolroom desks yielded thirty-six yen, a bicycle cap, and two plush seat covers—all of which he covertly stowed inside his fatigue shirt.

Just before dusk that day, Locke sidled up alongside Makarounis and quietly said, "After we eat."

At chow, now that it was "pucker time," the lieutenant could not eat but saved his bread for later. As he placed the bread in his shirt, he quirkily thought how crowded his fatigues were becoming, especially with all the bloodsucking lice that lurked everywhere on his person—some of which, he mused, might have been there since Hadong.

When the men were bedded down, Locke and Makarounis went over to Major McDaniel. No one said anything, but they both pumped his arm for a long time. Then the Major whispered, "Godspeed." And they left the room and closed the door.

Sergeant Kumagai was waiting in the hall. He motioned for them to follow, and they quietly made their way down the stairs to one of the empty classrooms. Shutting the door, Tak quickly crossed the room, moved a table and chair, brushed aside some papers on the floor with his feet, and then bent over and lifted a trapdoor.

The sergeant stepped down, and the officers trailed. He then moved some of the papers and placed one leg of the table so it would rest on the trapdoor as he closed it over them. The three were now truly in the dark, as their eyes tried to adjust. All they could see were two tiny windows, maybe one foot high and one foot wide, with bars over them. Their ceiling or floor above them was about three feet high and the "room" fifty feet square in size as they groped to determine the exact dimensions of their new abode.

Their exploration ended, suddenly, when the guards started shouting "*Hanchos! Hanchos!*" for the interpreters. For some reason, this demand from the guards struck the trio as hilarious and they had to fight to contain their laughter, more so as the guards got louder and madder. Then the hubbub above them became very intense, and they immediately sobered up. They went from manic to depressive as all hell broke loose and their defenseless POW brothers began to receive their worst mistreatment to date.

The sounds above them were very disquieting as they heard the screaming guards, some shooting and men running and stumbling down the same stairs they had just used themselves thirty minutes earlier. For more than an hour, the commotion in the building and courtyard remained unabated as the guards counted and recounted the assembled POWs. Then the North Korean lieutenant's unmistakable voice rang out those most hated words, "*Habe! Habe!* And in minutes, all was silent.

Makarounis soon fell asleep as did Locke, but Kumagai kept a watchful eye over his officers. It was a good thing he did because the guards came back throughout the night, searching for them and others who had escaped. And the sergeant had to poke the captain and lieutenant continuously to quell their loud snoring.[2]

* * *

On that same day, Smith's burial detail made several trips to the church to bury seven deceased soldiers and to administer some last rites before placing their bodies underground. Then on their last trip, after prayers, the detail persuaded one North Korean guard to provide a rifle salute. Then they headed back in the dark. When they reached the school, they were surprised to find their fellow POWs in the courtyard. And they soon discovered they were once again being forced to move out even deeper into Red territory.

Lieutenant JB Smith knew this was it. He passed the word to his other four coconspirators: Arakawa, Halcomb, SFC

Morris, and Sergeant William H. Jones. The five had decided days earlier to escape the next time the POWs were moved. They had concocted their plan while conducting their funeral duties. They were not sure how the escape would unfold, but they knew from the start they wanted to keep the group small and ensure all the participants were physically able.

When finally assembled in the courtyard, the POWs were formed into columns and marched into the street. Smith, Arakawa, Halcomb, Morris, and Jones ensured they were in close proximity to each other. It was now dark, and the guards were too few to cover the extended line of prisoners slogging their way through the city. So the guards were aggregated at the head and rear of the column.

As they turned and passed by the rear of their former school prison, Smith suddenly ducked into a side alley closely followed by his collaborators. In the shadows of the adjacent buildings, they waited until the last five guards had passed. Then, as planned, Jack Arakawa assumed the role of a North Korean guard by placing a stick on his shoulder to simulate a rifle and began marching the other four POWs to the outskirts of the city.

The five were making good progress until they came to a guarded roadblock. Jack, however, never broke stride as he headed toward the blockade. Then just yards from the unsuspecting guards, he yelled, "Air raid! Air raid!" in his best North Korean dialect. All the awaiting guards scattered while the POWs raced to the barricade, catapulting themselves over the four-foot fence and running away at their top speed. Shots were fired, but any pursuit in the dark was short-lived. And minutes later, by the grace of God, the group found an abandoned house in which to hide.

When the escapees discovered water and food in the house, they surmised that Providence wanted them to remain. And so they did. With a huge jar of water, about fifteen pounds of flour, some rice, and wheat grain, they concluded they could ration themselves for days without leaving the safety of their hideaway. Moreover, the flour and water were a vast improvement to their recent diet. In short, the food was scrumptious and the accommodations, luxurious to the starving, spent soldiers.[3]

* * *

Meanwhile, back at the school the next day, Locke and Makarounis met their young Korean benefactor when he tapped on their trapdoor and Kumagai handed him their only water bottle. He went and filled the bottle and then hurriedly informed them the train did not depart until midmorning. The guards had been pursuing escaped POWs all night, and they had reportedly shot seven Americans they found around the city. Another four were shot when they were found hiding behind some furniture in a classroom. They had refused to leave the room when given the order and were shot in place, then buried in the courtyard. Then, having delivered this news, the young man scurried off.

During their time in hiding, their "lifeline" showed up every day but one. This brave youth would refill the water bottle, bring some food, and impart some news. Once, he brought a ten-pound rice cake that was laced with sugar. On another occasion, he provided a bag of parched corn, and one day, he gave them some steamed rice that was particularly filling. But the most well received were the comforters he stuffed through the trapdoor one day.

But he also replenished their minds by updating them on the progress of the UN forces. On the third day, he informed them that friendly forces were thirty-eight miles from Pyongyang; on the fourth day, twenty-five miles; and on the fifth day, twelve miles. Then he told them he might have to join them.

The NKPA was grabbing people off the streets and forcing them to fight.

His daily updates correlated well with the sounds that emanated around them; otherwise, his accuracy and optimism could have been discounted by the ever-wary former prisoners. The air strikes had been nonstop day and night, accompanied by the seemingly ineffective North Korean "ack-ack" response. Then artillery fire began to rain down on Pyongyang with ever-increasing intensity. On the fifth day, Locke informed his companions that he could hear liaison-type planes overhead signaling the closeness of UN ground forces. And finally on the sixth day, the sweet, uplifting sound of friendly machine gun and rifle fire filled the air.[4]

US Soldiers in Cold Weather Gear Fight in Pyongyang[5]

* * *

As the time passed, Smith's five-man group's only concern was the old man they saw out a window. He came every day and stayed until dusk, posting himself against a distant building and staring at their clandestine sanctuary. He looked benign, but "what the hell was he doing" preoccupied the thinking of the now-paranoid fugitives.

After five days cooped up in the house, Grady Halcomb and Bob Morris could no longer stand it. They had heard gunfire for a couple of days now, and this morning, bells were ringing in the distance. But the old man was still there and was a conundrum for them. Now short on water and food, they decided to confront him. So the two scruffy soldiers left the confines of the house and approached the Korean at a slow but deliberate pace. And for the first time, they noticed a South Korean flag flying over a warehouse and another pinned to the side of a small building. The old man locked eyes with them, but his body language suggested he perceived no threat from the approaching vagabonds.

"What are you doing here?" Grady asked.

The old man smiled and nodded that he did not understand the question. So Bob tried some sign language while wishing they had brought Arakawa with them. He pointed to the old man and then to the two of them, and then Bob pointed toward what he thought was South Korea. Then the man smiled, thinking they were Russians, and uttered what sounded like "Manchuria."

Grady and Bob shook their heads and said in concert, "Americans, Americans." Then, with obvious understanding, he pointed to the two men and the ground, indicating they should stay here until his return. In only minutes, he came back with several Koreans clad in khaki uniforms.

The Major

Grady and Bob stood their ground as the Koreans neared. Then when the ROKs recognized them as Americans, the uniformed Koreans raced to greet them. Hugs and handshakes were exchanged as they were soon joined by the other three escapees in the house and countless more South Korean soldiers from every flank.

Next, in the midst of their revelry, a jeep drove up with an ROK lieutenant colonel and driver inside. The officer gets out and motions the five Americans to get in the jeep. He talks to the driver and then they sped off, shortly arriving at a facility housing the 1st Cavalry Headquarters. There they are greeted with great fanfare by their fellow countrymen and brothers in arms.[6]

* * *

On the morning of 20 October, what was to become "Liberation Day," the three hideouts greeted their best friend in the whole world. He only stayed a few seconds but talked a mile a minute. When the trapdoor was shut, Tak translated the conversation for Locke and Makarounis.

"The kid just wanted us to know that the North Koreans were running. And I asked, 'How fast?' And he answered, 'Like hell.' That's when we both laughed."

The battle outside was deafening until around noon, and then, dramatically, profound quietness encapsulated their 3-foot, 9 feet by 9 feet, six-day cage. Silent minutes that seemed like hours held back the hands of time. And then, unexpectedly, their aural environment exploded into a profusion of ringing church bells all over the city of Pyongyang.

Almost in the next instant, the trapdoor swung open and their beaming liberator motioned them to come out. As the three exited their temporary dungeon, the Korean told Tak that the South Koreans now were in the city and maybe some Americans. And the NKPA had disappeared. Then the slight Korean lad lifted Makarounis off his feet, put him back down, and slapped everyone on the back. He went crazy with joy as they made their way out of the building, into the courtyard and onto the street.

**Makarounis, Locke, Kumagai with
North Korean Benefactors[8]**

    As their stiff bodies became more ambulatory with each step, Bill, Alex and Tak were soon joined by two other young Koreans besides their savior. As they made their promenade, they encountered South Korean troops coming from all directions. When they had gone about a half mile, they saw the first American jeep. Three men were in it wearing tams. Makarounis shouted, "They're Scotch."

Locke said, "No, they're Australians," and then one rider in the jeep hollered, "Well, I'll be goddamned." The trio knew then instantly they were Americans—in this case, two news photographers, Jim Pringle and Hank Walker, and an AP correspondent, Tom Lambert. They jumped from the jeep still swearing about their damnation and handed a large bottle of "good Communist beer" to the liberated men. Pringle and Walker snapped pictures. But what Lambert saw and really wanted was "the whole story" written all over these ex-POWs standing, unsteadily, before them.

Moments later, however, an American army captain came up and rescued the corralled escapees from the newsmen. He put them and their Korean friend in his jeep and whisked them off to a posh building that had been Premier Kim Il Sung's headquarters. There they let their feet sink into the deep red carpet and drank some champagne the premier had graciously left for them. They toasted their young Korean rescuer over and over and asked what they could do to repay him.

Tak translated his simple, singular desire, "I and my family are from Seoul. I just want to be taken back." And he added, "I'm a gentleman and you are gentleman, and gentlemen help each other."[7]

* * *

After a day of uninterrupted euphoria, the ex-POWs experienced one last joyous occasion that evening when their escorts ushered them into a dining room at 1st Cav Hq. There all eight American escapees were reunited for the first time. Predictably, the bear hugs, laughter and cathartic tears that ensued culminated the happiest day of their lives.

Instead of having a "Last Supper" together as doomed prisoners, these freed men were now eating their "First Supper" together for the balance of their lives. And even later that night when Grady Halcomb and the others were "hanging their asses out the window" due to their overindulgence in food and libation, no one had any regrets whatsoever: "Liberation Day" was like no other day they ever experienced or dreamed of.[9]

Chapter Seven

Train to Manchuria (14 to 20 October)

Helplessness induces hopelessness, and history attests that loss of hope and not loss of lives is what decides the issue . . .
—B. H. Liddell Hart

It was dark, it was raining, and it was cold—which was bad enough. Then they marched into the rail yard and caught sight of their train with its line of cars. To their dismay, the POWs saw only gondola flatbed railcars. They all shuddered at the prospect of riding north in these open gondolas exposed to the frigid elements. Many, if not most, were too weak to survive much longer, even if they had remained sheltered in the temporary unheated prison they just left. Now what little hope remained was, once again, dowsed.

But the North Korean guards were in a frenetic state. They were, yet again, in a panic mode and seemed to be propelled by forces over which they had no control. They began hollering and prodding the stunned and temporarily paralyzed POWs to climb onto the uninviting railcars. And this was no simple task as most men were too weak to pull themselves up on the flatbeds, particularly those gondolas with shallow siding.

Even so, the dazed, frail POWs complied as best they could. They clawed their way up onto the flatbeds—some being pulled, others being pushed up by the more able or determined men. In the turmoil, many men fell onto the gondolas and sustained further injuries to their skeletal frames.

This macabre "lemminglike cavalcade" only lasted minutes, but its psychological effects were more enduring as the men bunched together on the open cars, clinging to each other for solace and warmth.

When the POWs were finally implanted in the gondolas, the train did not budge all night and did not depart the rail yard until late the next day. When it did leave, the train moved north at a relatively slow ground speed; but the airspeed, or wind chill, was numbing to the scantily clad, clustered mass of humanity hunkering down on each car. As the night wore on, several men would succumb to this additional assault to their bodies. Death was, nevertheless, egalitarian—claiming both volunteers and nonvolunteers.

The train did stop the next morning. The track had to be repaired from the previous day's bombing. But no one was allowed to leave their gondola—the living or the dead. Bags of rice crackers were thrown onto each flatcar, but no water was provided that second day. The sun did provide some warmth, but the cramped conditions were unbearable, except for these abandoned souls who, by this time, had been hardened, or softened, to cope with almost any deprivation or abuse.[1]

* * *

On the third day, 17 October, the Americans were finally able to exit the train. And here near a rail yard, they were finally allowed to bury the dead and alleviate their worst thirst to date. The graves were dug by hand and were very shallow, barely covering the remains. But as always, some identification was buried with each man and "words" were said.

Corporal Victor Stevens, still winded, looked at his bleeding, filthy fingers. He sort of wished Locke was here with them, so he could get access to the pilot's "community" razor to clean up his nails. He oddly recalled something in a country and western song about "my hands may be dirty, but my labor is clean."

Having done the lion's share of the digging, Stevens felt personally gratified about burying the young "brown bar" Lieutenant Miller—being the one to perform this small service for another 1st Cavalry soldier. With Miller's death, however, the POW group was now down to three officers: Major McDaniel and two lieutenants, Blaylock and Mulock.

Later in the day, Major McDaniel was sitting on an embankment overlooking the train. His legs were outstretched but bent so he could clasp his hands together and rest each arm comfortably on a knee. But his insides were far from comfortable. His lungs had filled with fluid, and his breathing was greatly impaired. Rounding the final corner of the 440-yard run in college had never required this kind of exertion from him—just to take in oxygen. He was beyond bone weary, and his only consolation was he had convinced himself that many deserving men had successfully escaped—among them Smith, Morris, Arakawa, Halcomb, and of course, Locke, Makarounis, and Kumagai.

As the Major stared out over his pitiful flock of prisoners, Jim Yeager came up the incline and asked, "Sir, can I talk to you?"

"Yes, son."

Then, the private sat down at the Major's feet. Yeager looked up and plaintively posed the central question of their precarious predicament, "Sir, are we going to make it?"

The Major had to go deep to summon a smile and then said, "Everyone is looking for us. And our army won't rest until they find us, now that the enemy is retreating. So we cannot give up hope. I pray all the time and believe we are going to get home. It should just be a matter of days. So when you talk to your buddies, soldier, you tell them it's far too early to give up."

The next day, in broad daylight, some of the Major's prayers were answered when the POW train slammed into another train that occupied the track ahead of it. The accident killed the conductor from the forward train who was crushed between the locomotive and the end car.

Major Sil, still the ranking North Korean officer, ordered everyone off the trailing train and onto the lead train. As the POWS passed the dead conductor, one American prisoner had the audacity to steal the conductor's shoes and make them his own. Other's witnessing the theft could all agree that "payback's a bitch."

This bold individual initiative and sign of good fortune soon extended to the entire prisoner group when they began to board the new train and found it devoid of gondolas and replete with enclosed boxcars and passenger cars—some with wooden bench seats.

It was also at the site of the train wreck that some POWs took advantage of the confusion and made their escape. Among those who escaped here and during the previous stop were Lieutenant Howard C. Smith, Master Sergeant Perry, Sergeant Mounce, and Privates Brady, Hamilton, Jarvis, Morris, and Stamper.[2]

* * *

The passenger cars had only one window at both ends. So in the dim lighting, Slater and Sharpe slumped into the first bench they came to. But when the train got rolling that night, Bob spied Gifford and told Ed, "I am going to talk to Al. He's up front. I'll be back."

Then Bob ducked under the seat forward of him and started crawling to the other end of the car. Not to draw any notice from the guards, he threaded his way methodically through the maze of dangling feet until his head popped up between Gifford's legs.

"Al, it's Bob. I just wanted to say hi."

Gifford laughed, looked around, and then helped pull Bob up to get seated.

They were both anxious to talk since they had so little contact since Seoul. They began, as always, discussing food they had seen in villages along their many forced marches and how these mouthwatering fruits and vegetables were so close, but most often beyond their grasp. Next, they would recall the times back in Japan when they both acknowledged they never had it so good. Then later, they would console themselves when they recounted seeing the American pilots' faces when they flew their aircraft at low level. And the two conveyed to each other, with much conviction, how as much as these pilots would like, they could not save them: only boots on the ground could secure their rescue.[3]

* * *

On the fifth night, the train had momentarily stopped in an open field. Lieutenant Doug Blaylock slid the boxcar door open with the help of Corporals Arlton Craig and Victor Stevens and Privates Auvil Parsons and George Snodgrass. When they did, to their wonderment, the darkness stretched before them into an abyss of impenetrable blackness. And in an instant of simultaneous and shared enlightenment, all five grabbed each other and leaped from the train. Their momentum carried them into some tall weeds where they lay silently and breathlessly until the train started up, leaving them far behind and alone in the grass.[4]

* * *

Major McDaniel had inquired about food several times during the day ever since the train had pulled into a tunnel around 0800, 20 October. Finally, in the early afternoon, Major Sil comes up to Major McDaniel and tells Sergeant Shinde, now the only interpreter: "Tonight we go to our destination. We need some men to go down the track to the village at Myongucham and bring back food for the trip. Also, I want the Major to accompany me on this detail."

Major McDaniel sat shivering on a bench seat. He slowly stood up and handed a blanket back to Sergeant Bomberry. "Sergeant Shinde, I want you, Sergeant Rowlette, and Sergeant Van Dine to come with me and see if you can get a few other volunteers."

Moments later, Shinde returned with more men to the mouth of the tunnel where Major Sil, Major McDaniel, and Sergeants Rowlette and Van Dine waited. Major Sil stepped between the tracks and motioned the group to follow him. The Americans fell in behind the North Korean officer with a half dozen guards bringing up the rear. The group headed south along the rail line, went around a bend, and disappeared from view.[5]

Chapter Eight

Cavalry to the Rescue (20 to 24 October)

Back to the news. No word yet on the Americans being moved north on boxcars by the Reds in Korea. Up and down the line, there is a dramatic order: find those men, quick.
—**Gabriel Heatter, Mutual Radio Broadcast**
(October 1950)

H-Hour was 0800, 20 October. Kimpo Airfield, not far from Seoul, was jammed with transport aircraft. Brigadier General William H. Tunner (USMA 1928), Commander of the Combat Cargo Command, had staged his transport planes into Kimpo. Seventy-one spanking new C-119s and forty old C-47s were ready for departure. The sixty-five paratroopers per C-119 were raring to go. After all, this operation would be the first airborne assault of the war, and it would be deep into enemy territory. Colonel Frank S. Bowen (USMA 1936) and his 187th RCT would be dropped some thirty miles north of Pyongyang at the crossroads of the towns of Sukchon and Sunchon. Their mission was to seal off the major escape routes of fleeing North Korean government officials, trap retreating enemy forces, and effect the rescue of the Communist-held prisoners of war. They would be joined at Sunchon by Task Force Rogers composed of the 1st Bn, 8th Cav Regt and a company of tanks from the 70th Tank Bn.

The Americans were ready, but the god of weather was not. Heavy overcast swept down the length of the Kimpo runway early that morning and would not dissipate.

Combat Cargo Command C-119 Aircraft and Paratroopers at Kimpo, 20 October 1950[1]

"What the hell are you waiting for, Tunner?" demanded General George Stratemeyer (USMA 1915). He was back in Itazuke, Japan, seated next to General MacArthur. Both generals were in MacArthur's personal plane, a Lockheed Constellation. Itazuke was cloudless.

"Sir, we are fogged in. We don't know how far up and out these clouds extend, and we have no intelligence on the conditions at the drop zones."

Bill Tunner put his hand over the "mike" and sarcastically mumbled to the aircrew of his personal C-47 Skytrain, now doubling as an office, "Have any North Koreans forwarded us a weather report?"

This demand for action would repeat itself every hour on the half hour, until in exasperation "Stratty" radioed Tunner around noon, "We are going to cancel the entire operation. It's getting too late."

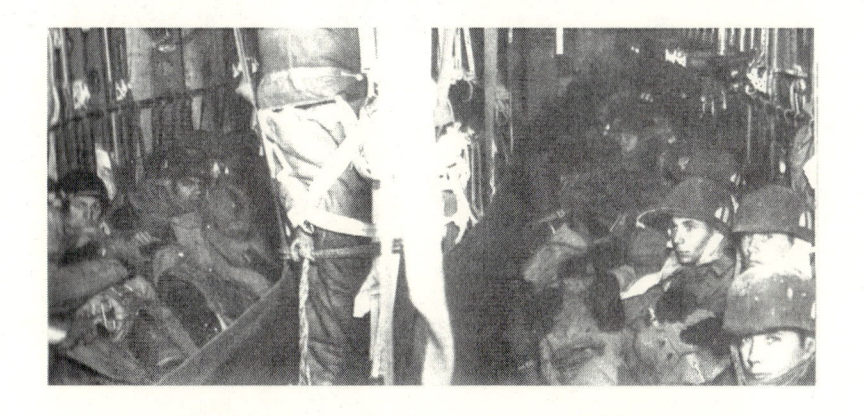

Waiting 187th RCT Paratroopers Inside C-119 Aircraft at Kimpo, 20 October 1950[2]

"Wait a few more minutes, General. I think I can get off the ground myself now. I'll go up and take a look around."

As old Tail Number 5549 lifted off, the aircrew—Tom Collins (pilot), Red Foreman (copilot), Pete Fernandez (radio operator), and Ray Towne—were not sure they could get back down. But even if Korea was socked in, Japan was within reach. And despite all the haranguing from the generals in Itazuke, they now knew Japan enjoyed perfect VFR conditions. No, their real concern as they broke through the clouds at five thousand feet was that their unarmed transport plane was the only friendly aircraft in the air. All of the American fighter escorts were on the ground.

"Follow the planned route, Tom." The highly decorated ex-fighter pilot smiled a "roger wilco" as Tunner began pacing back and forth, constantly glancing out a window. He soon saw that the clouds were scattering, and he went up to the cockpit to gain a more expansive view. In a few minutes, the aircrew could see it was completely clear ahead—unlimited ceiling and visibility. But they had not yet reached the first beacon.

The uncertainty was building and spellbinding at the same time. Their eyes began to ache as they peered into the distance while the aircraft flew the northern leg of the course, and then turned toward the enemy-held coast. Finally, just short of the coastline, they could see Sukchon and Sunchon, both completely bathed in sunlight. Collins lowered a wing and headed back to Kimpo.

Once they were well out to sea, Fernandez broke radio silence and contacted Tunner's command post. "No sweat left! The route is clear all the way to the drop zone," Pete announced, modifying their code word, "no sweat," as he and everyone else aboard the C-47 were ironically drenched in their own stress-induced perspiration.

Tunner then took over the radio, addressing his orders directly to Colonel Edgar Hampton, the commander of the air force task force in charge of the drop. "I want each plane to take off one at a time, climb to five thousand feet, and fly the planned course to Tok-chok-do Island. The planes can rendevous there, form the formation, and proceed as planned. I'll be on the ground in thirty minutes. Make your final preparations, but don't take off. I want to look you in the eye and make double-damn sure you understand these orders."

When old 5549 came through the lingering overcast and had landed, Bill Tunner hurried to Hampton's command post. All the preparations were well under way, being carried out precisely as ordered. The fighters and light bombers out of Taegu were already airborne and enroute to destroy enemy stongpoints in the drop zone. Then the transport planes began launching and heading to the island where they would be joined with Mustangs that would escort them to the drop area.

General Tunner stayed at Kimpo long enough to see everything was under control, then he hopped into his personal plane to go observe the air drop. As 5549 loitered some distance from the path of the extended formation, he proudly watched and exclaimed, "What a beautiful sight, all those white petals falling to earth."

The drop began at 1400 hours over Sukchon and was repeated moments later over Sunchon. The 111 troop carriers had placed the 187th RCT accurately as planned in two drop zones, each only a mile long and a half mile wide. In less than an hour, the Combat Cargo Command had delivered 2,860 men and 301 tons of equipment, including jeeps and artillery. And only one parachutist was killed and thirty-nine injured in the drop. Yes, the six-hour delay was nerve-racking, but as far as the airmen and paratroopers knew, the mission could not be going better.[3]

C-119 Flying Boxcars Delivering the 187th RCT, 20 October 1950[4]

* * *

Bob Sharpe stumbled out of the tunnel, squinting through the sunlight. It was late afternoon on 20 October, and he was happy as he jostled his way into the first group to be fed. He, Al Gifford, Valdor John, and some thirty other men—escorted by ten guards—made their way south along the track. After about fifty yards, the guards veered left and herded the group through some brush into a deep ravine and motioned them to sit. Some cans and bowls were passed out to the seated captives.

Sergeant Hines crossed his legs and stared into his can. As always, his hunger remained unabated. He noticed a beetle weaving its way through the grass and contemplated whether to add the unlucky creature to his meal. Then he heard an unmistakable sound: the bolt of a carbine being driven "home."

Al Gifford stopped wiping his bowl, looked up on the ridge, and saw a guard put a clip of ammo in his gun.

A shot rang out, and a lone POW on the other side of the ravine was hit right between the eyes and slumped over.

Someone yelled, "They're shooting us!"

Sergeant Hines sprang to his feet and started running, as did some other American noncoms. The guards immediately trained their weapons on them and brought them down. Then the rifle and burp gun bullets found their way back to the huddled group.

Al dove into the group on top of Bob who instinctively had flattened out on his back. Then in another instant a second soldier was on top of Bob as everyone was tousled together trying to dodge the incoming fire.

"God help us!"

"Not now!"

"Lord of Mercy—"

The cries of anguish were few and surprisingly muffled. No one begged.

The living and the dead were soon riddled with bullets and became trenched in blood as the burp guns raked the clustered bodies, and the signs of life subsided into an occasional moan or twitch.

Major Sil raised his arm and pointed his pistol skyward. The guards stopped their fire. They then methodically waded into the bodies, thrusting a bayonet or delivering a crushing rifle butt into any cadaver that groaned or appeared to move.

Back in the train, Private John E. Martin was waiting for his turn. He sat in his seat with his head back, alternately opening and closing his eyes. There wasn't much difference. His passenger car was back some distance from the tunnel's entrance, and light had a hard time finding him through the car's only two windows. Even so, in his shadowy world he could hear small-arms fire, and with all the sounds of aircraft earlier, he figured the war was catching up with them. But for the moment, he just hoped he would be in the next group to be fed.

His wait was not long. The second group from the penultimate passenger car that included Martin, Yeager, and Toney was summoned to go outside.[5]

* * *

It finally became apparent to Ed Slater that he was not going to be fed anytime soon. The guards were nowhere to be seen in his seatless boxcar. And given the time lapse and the deathly quietness, he figured night had settled in. So to quell his hunger he sought the solace of sleep and was soon rewarded. Some time passed, but consciousness only returned when he felt the train lurch forward and then Ed could sense some movement although it seemed hesitatingly slow. But he had no desire to contemplate its meaning, so he slipped back into his solitary dreams.

When Ed awoke on 21 October, the gnarling hunger returned. He immediately noted the train had stopped moving and though dim, the light in his car was brighter than it had been yesterday in the tunnel. So he figured the train was in the open, but where God only knew. He gazed at his fellow travelers to see if he could recognize anyone to share his pain. He saw Walt Whitcomb and started to shout out when someone at the aft window screamed, "The guards are running into the cave."

Seconds later, a rocket slammed into the train, and there was a stampede as desperate men tore at the door, finally opening it and leaping from the train. When Ed reached the door, a second rocket exploded, spraying railroad spikes into the fleeing POWs. Body parts and bodies were everywhere. Yet, just as suddenly as their world had erupted into deafening chaos, now the scene for the survivors was abruptly still with only the soft moaning of those sliding into death.

Again, whether through God's grace or pilot recognition, no second pass from their own luckless air force occurred. Ed slumped to the ground, taking it all in. He was numb, but still he tried to understand the "why." Surely, some of these men deserved to live. And why is his body, if not his soul, still intact?

It was not too long before the guards felt safe enough to come out of hiding and start forcing the POWs back on the train. Many had to be helped as they were severely wounded, while others, still drawing breath, were left where they fell. The panicky guards were in a hurry to back the train into the tunnel to preclude another air assault. When the train was finally ensconced under the mountain, Ed, Walt Whitcomb, and Sherman Jones could hear gunfire, but no one spoke of it. They knew with certainty, however, that those that did not make it back on the train were now the victims of a merciless enemy.

As the day wore on in the close confines of their boxcars, Ed, Sherm, and Walt were to remain incarcerated with the dead and dying. Walt sat next to a sergeant, a fresh amputee who could not control his need to express his agony. And his relentless moaning was only abated by others who groaned in a different octave or cadence. Without access to anesthesia, no relief for these poor souls save death was possible. Even when the train headed north again in the night at a faster clip, the resultant rocking had no effect on the din of convulsive pain in every boxcar housing the POWs. So as the helpless Americans had done so often before, they willfully blocked out the reality blanketing them and sought peace in the deepest recesses of their minds.[6]

* * *

At about 1200 hours on October 21, Captain L. D. Van de Voort, F Co Commander of the 187th RCT, set out for the Sunchon Tunnel. He was accompanied by First Lieutenant Maurice A. Johnson Jr. and his 3rd platoon. They had borrowed some jeeps from the ROK, plus a guide and interpreter. The paratroopers were following up on the oral report from two American POWs, Private Lloyd Kreider and Master Sergeant Marion Michael, who had been brought to their command post by some ROK soldiers.

As they drove up to the tunnel entrance, a party of ROK soldiers was already there administering first aid to some wounded Americans. Captain Van de Voort turned to Johnson, "Lieutenant, take your men and comb the area for survivors. Sergeant, radio the command post that we found the POWs, and we will need to evacuate them pronto. Tell them we will give them the numbers and more details as fast as we can."

Once the first aid was organized and the evacuation requirements known to the captain's satisfaction, Van de Voort and Johnson began to investigate the crime scene, trying to reconstruct in their minds what exactly had transpired. As they approached the first stack of bodies in an erosion ditch that ran perpendicular to the track, the captain mused out loud, "Are you thinking what I'm thinking? Could we have prevented this if we had jumped in earlier? Or did our jump yesterday spook the gooks and cause this massacre?"

"We'll never know that unless we capture the bastards who did this. But look at these shell casings along the edge of the ridge. The gooks obviously got our soldiers in the ditch and then fired down on them from up here. I am going down and look at the bodies to confirm that."

"Jesus, Captain, look at these guys. They're skeletons. And they are dressed in rags." Johnson pulled back some fatigue shirts of the dead Americans and could confirm the bullets had entered their bodies higher than the bullets had exited. And most bullets entered from behind, suggesting the POWs had their backs turned toward their murderers when the carnage commenced.

The two officers found two more stacks of bodies in different erosion ditches, again perpendicular to the train track. These stacks revealed the same murderous scenario of the first stack of cadavers: unsuspecting men, corralled in a ditch, executed from above. Then, they examined the fourth and last stack in a nearby cornfield. These POWs had been sitting down at the time they were shot. Most were shot through the head or upper body. And they had been sprayed with .32-caliber bullets.

Then the two commanders ventured into the tunnel. There they found seven more Americans who had not been shot but had died of extreme malnutrition and exposure. They wore native shoes, some were only clad in undergarments, and the rest in shredded fatigues.

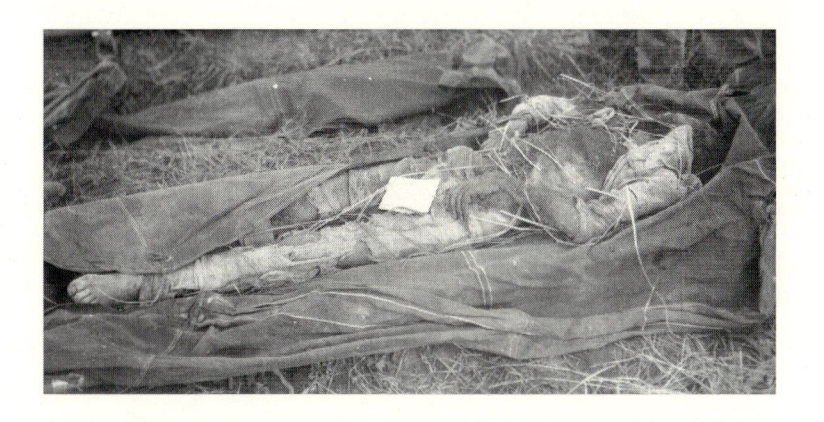

Slain American POW at the Sunchon Tunnel[7]

"We can really never appreciate what these men went through," Van de Voort commented as they departed the tunnel.

"Yes, but what they all went through here at the tunnel is pretty obvious. But to survive this long and to have friendly forces so close and then to be killed like this, that's a shit sandwich no one should have to eat."

When they got back to the jeep, they got in, and Van de Voort told Johnson to take some notes. "We need to write down what we found and turn it in when we get back to the CP. You never know where we will be tomorrow, and this war crime needs to be documented. We were the first Americans here, so start scribbling and make sure we have the same observations so when we're questioned by the JAGs, we'll have our story straight."

When the two officers had finished corroborating and recording their findings, the captain asked Johnson a final question, "Is there anything else we need to document?"

"There is one thing I noticed. The three dead Negro soldiers we found looked in better condition than the other soldiers. I wonder why?"

Captain Van de Voort gave no answer but told the lieutenant to include this observation in the report.[7]

While the two 187th RCT officers were still reconnoitering the massacre site, Brigadier General Frank A. Allen Jr., the assistant division commander of the 1st Cavalry, arrived on the scene at 1500 hours. He was accompanied by his aide, his driver, and two war correspondents: Don Whitehead of the Associated Press and Richard Tucker of the *Baltimore Sun*. The general had first been alerted that morning about a POW train bound for Manchuria by a Lieutenant Blaylock. The former POW and four other American soldiers had been picked up by Task Force Rogers on its way from Pyongyang to link up with the 187th RCT at Sunchon.

General Allen, having ascertained the task force's successful juncture with the paratroopers, went back to Pyongyang, picked up the reporters, and made his way to the command post of the 2nd Bn, 187th RCT. Here he was present when an excited Korean civilian came in and started describing the murder of some two hundred Americans the night before at a tunnel in close proximity to the CP. Allen immediately set out to run down this unimaginable story. On his way, the general stopped at the ROK 6th Division command post in Sunchon and married up with a second jeep that included an ROK colonel, an interpreter, and a driver. The jeeps then proceeded northwest five miles to the railway tunnel, next to the village of Myongucham.

When they had dismounted from their jeeps, the ROK colonel was the first to rediscover the seven bodies in the tunnel. Then the same colonel found five Americans on a ridge top and called to those in the tunnel. Everyone examining the emaciated bodies scrabbled out of the entrance as Valdor John staggered out of some brush.

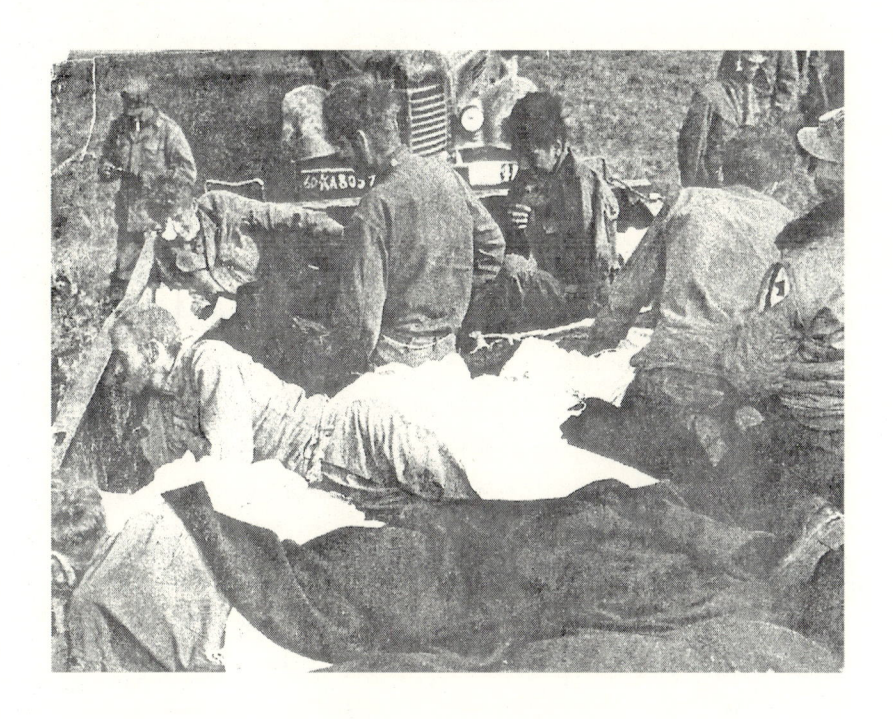

**Survivors Awaiting Departure from Sunchon,
Gifford Kneeling Center**[9]

Upon seeing the shivering, undernourished private, Allen whipped off his coat, wrapped it around John, and said, "I am promoting you to a one-star general."

"Sir, I'm-I'm too dirty. I have lice all over me," protested the stammering, sobbing PFC.

Allen put his arm around the soldier and looked away so as to not betray the heartbreak he felt at this unfolding, unspeakable human ordeal. That morning in Pyongyang, the general had been determined to run down the story, but now this horrific story was running him down. Just getting his mind clear and his emotions in check with regard to what these POWs had endured was excruciatingly painful, even as a mere witness to this final act in their three-month tribulation.

On his own, Don Whitehead, the AP reporter, had surveyed areas of the massacre site, even finding three survivors by himself. He was taking notes all the while and asking questions of those survivors that were physically and mentally able to engage in his gentle interrogations. But it was not long before he found the common theme he sought to encapsulate the ghastly news story he would write: the heroics of the American senior officer in charge.

When Whitehead talked to Yeager, who was sitting at the time on the crest of a hill and had begun describing the massacre, the private suddenly interrupted himself midsentence and burst out, "I hope to God the Major is alive. He may be. But wherever he is, he was a real guy."

"I met him at Seoul. The North Koreans had tried to get him to broadcast for them for propaganda, but he wouldn't. It made them pretty sore, but they couldn't do anything with Major McDaniel. At the time, our ration was a small piece of bread and a bowl of soup made from radish greens and fish. The Major persuaded them to let our own cooks handle the chow. That helped, but when he saw the Reds were shorting us on food, he raised hell with them."

With no prompting from Whitehead, the blond kid from Grand Junction, Colorado, continued a cathartic stream of consciousness monologue about the Major. Addressing the march from Seoul to Pyongyang, Yeager recalled, "Whenever anybody died, the Major held services. He always said a few words and said a prayer. He saw that they were buried. He wrote the man's name on a slip of paper, and he put the paper in a bottle and buried it with the body."

"The Major argued all the way with the Reds. And if anyone got discouraged, he would do all he could to raise their spirits. He never encouraged or discouraged anyone when they wanted to escape. That was always up to the man himself."

"The Reds would give the Major a little more food than the rest of us, but he always shared it. If he was smoking a cigarette and someone asked for the butt, the Major would just hand him the whole cigarette."

"We don't know whether he is alive or not. Friday morning, the Reds took him out of the train, saying they were going on a chow detail. We never saw him again."

Finally, relieved of his moral burden to make sure this correspondent was informed about McDaniel, Yeager lapsed into silence and stared off into the distance. Whitehead put his pencil and pad away, leaned over, squeezed the private's shoulder, and headed back down the hill.

When Whitehead was halfway down the ridge, Yeager called out one last time, "If you write anything about the Major, be sure to say, if it hadn't been for him, none of us would be alive today."

By day's end at the Sunchon tunnel, General Allen and the 187th RCT paratroopers would find seventy-three murdered Americans and evacuate twenty-three attempted-murder victims.[10]

* * *

On the morning of 22 October the POW train had come to stop in the open hills near Kujang-dong, some thirty miles north of the Sunchon tunnel. The North Koreans spent the day performing maintenance on the train, while the POWs languished in their boxcars without food or water. Finally, at dusk the Reds decided they could no longer nurse the train forward. Either from the air assault or sustained poor maintenance, the locomotives were effectively inoperable. Major Sil now had to decide what to do with the POWs on the train.

Sherm was sound asleep when the ruckus began. It was dark and the guards began rousting the POWs from their boxcars.

They yelled, "You no walk, we shoot." Simultaneously, they prodded the men with bayonets and dragged those unable or unwilling to stand to the doors. Many POWs, however, remained frozen where they sat. The guards began to shoot them in place. Flashes from the gunfire lit up the car. Sherm was hit behind his right ear, and the bullet blew out his cheek below his eye. A second bullet destroyed his foot and left him immobilized.

When the shooting and screaming began, Ed skirted the mayhem by staying on the periphery of his seatless boxcar and fumbled his way to the door. Still unscathed, he fell through the door and rolled down a twenty-foot embankment. He was soon joined by other bodies exiting the train. One body landed on top of Ed, and that body was Walt Whitcomb who had taken a bullet to his left arm, which had also ricocheted through his leg. Soon, Walt's blood found its way to Ed's face, giving Slater an aura of death.

As they lay there in a pile of human flesh, the living could witness the execution of other POWs, even some twenty Americans who were all standing next to the train. Then, with most of the killing finished, the guards began dousing the boxcars with some petrol and setting the cars ablaze. Less successfully, they tried to do the same with the piles of cadavers scattered along the embankment. Their intent was unclear, as Major Sil thus far had shown no interest in destroying evidence of his atrocities. Moreover, the major was well aware that one of his junior lieutenants, Hae Do Lee, had deserted his cohort after the Sunchon massacre a couple of days earlier.

Their heinous pyro act now complete, the North Koreans abandoned the burning train in the night. They would continue their journey north on foot with some indeterminate number of POWs in tow to include, at least, two American 1st Cav privates—PFC Ancil A. Roten and PFC Albert Mickelberg—who had shared this death trudge ever since Seoul.

Ed Slater, however, embedded among the dead and dying elected to not move—not a single muscle. He was content to lay under the mass of humanity and soak in the warmth from the flames engulfing the train. He lay in place until daybreak. And when convinced of the guards' absence, Ed began to pry himself loose from the entangled bodies. He did so with great difficulty, as rigor mortis had set into the cadavers and they were unyielding to his squirming attempt to free himself. In his struggle, he awakened Walt who likewise began to unplug himself from the throng of the deceased.

To their surprise, they aroused Sherman Jones. He pleaded, "Don't leave me. Please don't leave me."

But when they saw his bullet ridden body, they knew he could not walk, and they could not carry him. So when they finished covering him with grass and clothing, the two promised, "Sherm, we'll get help and be back as soon as we can."

But Ed and Walt shared a singular thought: to put as much distance as possible between themselves and this holocaust. As they scurried away, they reiterated, "We'll come back. We promise." When the train was out of his sight, Slater and Whitcomb slowed their gait, following the rail tracks south until they reached some sort of dilapidated unoccupied station. They entered and immediately curled up and went to sleep. They came to their senses, though, when they heard noise from some approaching vehicles. Again, they took flight, but not before drinking some water from a green birdbath they discovered as they left the area. They climbed a ridge and then scooted down the other side on their rear ends. When they reached the bottom and looked up, a small boy stood before them.

"Where you go?" the boy inquired as he offered Ed and Walt his hand. Then, leading the way, the Korean child said, "We not go far."

The two Americans followed him like dependent lambs. They really had no choice. They did not know where the bad guys were, and they desperately needed to find the good guys wherever they could be found. And the fact the boy spoke English gave Slater and Whitcomb hope.

As promised, they soon arrived at a small house. An elderly woman was inside, and Ed motioned to her he would like some food. As she prepared them some broth, they crouched against the wall half asleep. Vaguely, Walt heard the boy say, "I go for help."

When the woman finally handed them the watery soup, they sipped quickly as the fear of the guards returning was foremost in their psyches. But before Ed and Walt could leave, loud but unintelligible voices seemed to surround the outside of the house. Ed froze into a prenatal position, expecting the worst. Walt just shook his head. Then this huge master sergeant burst through the door, and with an ear-splitting grin and an extended hand, said, "Let me take you home." Ed cried all the way in the jeep ride to the nearest village.

There, Slater and Whitcomb were quickly paired with General Allen who asked right out of the gate, "Do you think anyone else is alive?"

"When I left this morning, we know at least one soldier was alive," Ed confessed.

"Would you go back with me and help me find him?" the cavalry general implored.

"Yes, yes, sir," Walt answered.

As they came upon the second massacre site, General Allen could only shake his head. His first thought was that they had, at last, caught up with the goddamn "death train." And his second thought was "too little, too late, again," as he surveyed the heaps of charred American bodies.

The Major

Kujang-Dong: Surveying Second Massacre[11]

Ed quickly located Sherm—who was alive, but just barely. General Allen immediately had a helicopter called in to transport Jones to the nearest medical unit. Allen then turned to the two ambulatory privates and said, "Let's get you cleaned up and fed."

Slater turned to Whitcomb and declared, "Walt, buddy, we're going home!"[12]

POW Train Abandoned at Kujang-Dong with Burnt-Out Boxcars[13]

MACARTHUR'S ADVANCE BY OCTOBER 24, 1950

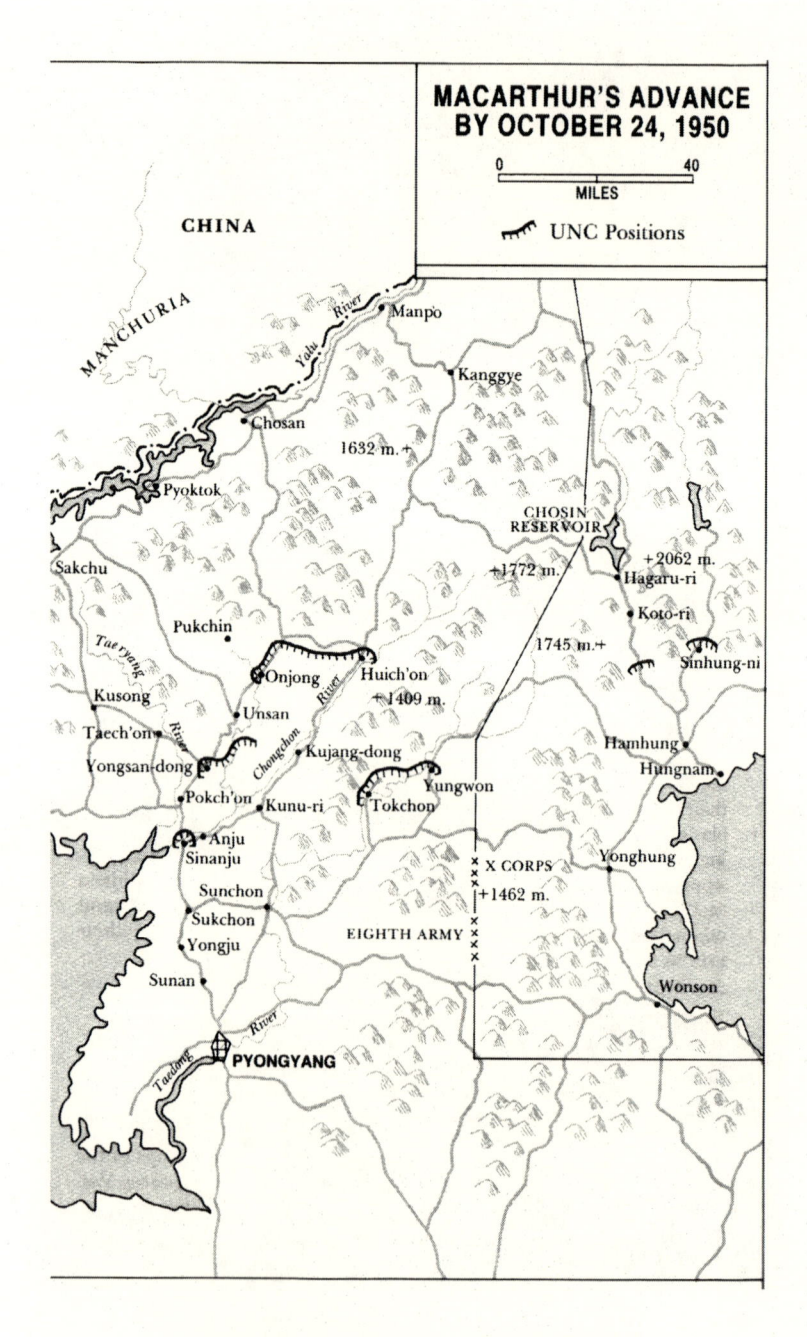

The Disposition of UN Forces after
Sunchon and Kujang-dong Massacres [14]

As the travails of the McDaniel POW group were coming to an end, the war entered a dramatic new phase with the entry of the Chinese People's Liberation Army (PLA). Although the Chinese had crossed the Yalu as early as 13 October, first contact with UN forces was not until 25 October with a full PLA offensive to follow on 2 November. Although the UN military leadership was in denial for some time, the North Koreans were no longer the primary enemy.

The ferocious fighting about to ensue would be almost exclusively a Chinese and UN affair. And the North Koreans would soon hand off the Allied POWs to the Red Chinese. While the bloodletting in combat would get worse, the UN POWs would start to receive better treatment in terms of food and medicine. But now the POWs' indoctrination to Communism would be more probing—psychologically. "Brainwashing" would, henceforth, be done by professionals, as the North Korean amateurs melted away.[15]

Chapter Nine

Home Not-So-Sweet Home
(July 1950 to December 1953)

Earth has no sorrow that Heaven cannot heal.
        —Thomas Moore

For Helen McDaniel the worst part was "not knowing": not knowing why she had not heard from Tom, not knowing where he was, not knowing whether he was alive, not knowing when she would know something—anything.

Tom's last and only letter to her was dated 14 July 1950. In it he had warned her he might not be able to write for a while as he would join the 34th Inf Regt the next day. He gave her logistics instructions on how best to depart Japan and told her his brother, George, would have someone meet her when she got off the ship in San Francisco. Tom even enclosed an automobile insurance card she might need in order to drive back to the east coast. He also listed the names of several officers he had already met there in Korea and who they both knew from previous assignments. And he said he would be seeing Lieutenant Colonel Red Ayres the very next morning.

Then Tom closed the letter with these deeply felt words of his commitment to her and his sons: "Remember I love you with all my heart and love my boys the same . . . Take care of yourself and let me hear from you often . . . forever and forever. Love, Tom."

        *   *   *

The Major

The first news concerning her Major came in the form of a Western Union telegram dated 19 August 1950, 9:50 PM. It was delivered to Frank Harris, the husband of Tom's sister Beryl, in Long Beach. But Helen missed it, having already begun her drive home to North Carolina. The telegram read:

> THE SECRETARY OF THE ARMY HAS ASKED ME TO EXPRESS HIS DEEP REGRET THAT YOUR HUSBAND MJ MCDANIELWILLIAM T HAS BEEN MISSING IN ACTION IN KOREA SINCE 20 JULY 50 UPON RECEIPT OF FURTHER INFORMATION IN THIS OFFICE YOU WILL BE ADVISED IMMEDIATELY PD CONFIRMIN LETTER FOLLOWS=EDWARD F WITSEL MAJOR GENERAL USA THE ADJUTANT GENERAL OF THE ARMY=

Helen had gotten a map from AAA designating which roads to take across country to her destination in Ahoskie. But in a diner on the second day, she was approached by a truck driver while she was finishing up lunch with the boys.

"Lady, I noticed you have Japanese plates. If you don't mind me askin', where you headed?"

"North Carolina."

"I see you got a map, you mind if I take a look?"

"No, go right ahead."

When he saw the planned route, the trucker just shook his head, "This is all wrong. You need to take the southern route. Let me pencil it in for you."

"Okay, because I have never done this before." Then he handed it back and added, "I'll be right behind you all the way."

Helen got back in the Buick Roadmaster, positioned the boys in the backseat, and started off again, this time via a different route and with new confidence. She never saw the truck driver again, but she always believed he was somewhere behind her, and that was comforting. As she often said to herself, "The Lord always looks after you."

Nevertheless, the trip was no cakewalk. With the interminable summer heat, the two-week journey across country by herself with two unhelpful, rambunctious boys was very taxing. But Helen stayed to her routine: up at 6 AM, put sleeping boys in the car, stop for breakfast at 9 AM, stop again around noon for a lunch or snack, and end the driving day at 4 PM for dinner and sleep.

But the challenge of caring for two young boys by herself was about to get a lot tougher. For no sooner had she exited the car in Ahoskie, North Carolina, than some relative among the large group assembled blurted out, "Tom's missing!"[1]

* * *

The second "official" news about her soldier husband came in the same form—via telegram. The 11 September 1950, 8:25 AM telegram read:

> FROM PMGPM MAJOR WILLIAM C MCDANIELS REPORTED AS PRISONER OF WAR BY ENEMY PROPAGANDA BROADCAST MAY OR MAY NOT BE YOUR HUSBAND WILLIAM THOMAS MCDANIEL PRISONER OF WAR STATUS IS NOT OFFCIALLY ESTABLISHED BY THIS REPORT FURTHER INFORMATION WILL BE FORWARDED WHEN RECEIVED=THE PROVOST MARSHAL GEN WASHDC=PMGPM=

Helen had occasionally listened to broadcasts that would list missing soldiers and airmen in Korea on late night radio. But now it would become her daily routine. The boys were always asleep when the broadcasts aired. And she did not sleep well these days anyway. She knew by now that it was pointless to contact the army; they knew nothing about her beloved husband. And if they did, they would be late in informing her. She had better connections through other army wives and Tom's brother George McDaniel.

* * *

Florence Smith, JB's wife, was not a woman to be trifled with. She had gotten notification of JB's missing in action (MIA) status weeks ago. But now, the army was insisting that Lieutenant Smith had been killed, and she and her son would have to return to the States. She, however, knew better. God had "indicated" to her that JB was alive.

After going through proper channels at Camp Gifu and getting nowhere with the local commanders, she decided to go see "The Man"—General Douglas MacArthur, Commander-in-Chief (CINC), United Nations Command and Supreme Commander of the Allied Powers. She found out through her maid when MacArthur was returning to the Itazuke Air Base. The Japanese people always seemed to know the goings and comings of their new emperor.

When he arrived, she was waiting near the airport's VIP lounge as the CINC and his entourage appeared. When he was within earshot, she shouted out, "General MacArthur, I need your help!" Some aides tried to ignore the request and shield the general, but he heard and saw her and was drawn to Florence's piteous voice.

"Yes, madam. How can I help you?" The general inquired with the dignity of an imperial ruler.

"Lieutenant Smith, my husband, is missing in Korea. The army is telling me he is dead, without proof, and is trying to send our family back to the States. I know he is alive. Red propaganda broadcasts have said he is a prisoner. My family needs to stay here until we know his true status."

MacArthur turned to one of his aides, "Get the information you need from this lady. Get to the bottom of it. And report back to me. I'll personally make the final decision."

"Thank you, General," a gracious Florence cried.

"No, I want to thank you for supporting your husband." Then the general left the terminal while the aide remained with Florence, gathering all the facts he would need to pursue the matter. In less than a week, MacArthur ruled that the Smiths could stay in Japan.[2]

* * *

When Ronda Locke left Japan, she was traveling on "blue widow" orders. These travel orders were given to spouses whose husbands had been officially declared KIA (killed in action), MIA, or POW. She was confident, though, that Bill was a POW from a Sue City Sue broadcast she was told about and, more reassuringly, from Bill's flying buddies who had flown over the crash site and could confirm that the Mustang's cockpit was intact.

Ronda knew she needed to get home where she and Karen, the six-month-old, would have family and friends to help her endure what she believed would be a very long wait. Even so, it still took almost a month to sell the car and pack up her household goods. But, this time, thanks to the "blue widow" orders she could fly home.

On the flight, she was accompanied by several other spouses in her same sad situation—their husband's dead, missing, or captured. One very young wife was caring for a newborn. The flight from Japan to Wake Island and on to Honolulu was long, but uneventful. And Karen was a good baby, rarely crying as long as she had her bottle and could get her sleep.

Upon arrival in Hawaii, the blue widows were offered accommodations in a luxury hotel downtown, but most opted to stay on base for an early departure the next day. Aboard this plane, long after takeoff, Ronda had just surrendered Karen to a stewardess. But when she moved over and peered out the window, she noticed one engine was gushing oil. Ronda immediately alerted the stewardess who dashed to the cockpit. Moments later, the captain announced an engine was being feathered, but not to worry, the plane was heading back to the islands. The captain, however, was concerned as they were nearly halfway to San Francisco. But this potentially dangerous snafu would be the last serious hiccup before the Lockes—mother and child—got home, albeit exhausted, three days later.

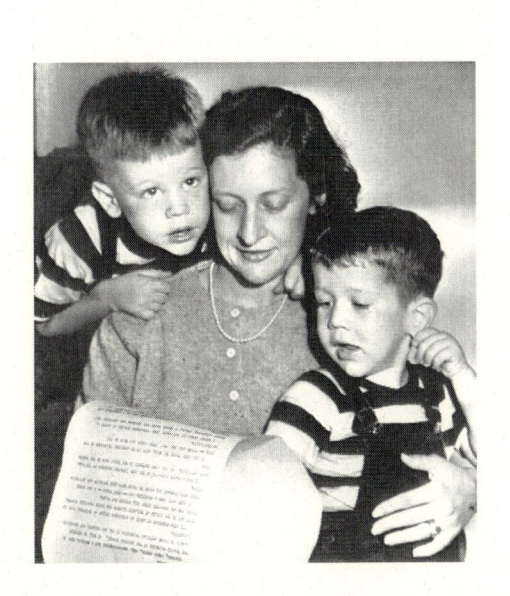

* * *

Helen, Whitehead Transcript, Tom Jr. And John[3]

Early in the morning Helen was alerted by friends and relatives to the streaming mass of front page newspaper articles—with datelines as early as 21 October 1950—of a POW massacre in North Korea. Then, when Don Whitehead tied the atrocity to her husband's POW group, she was deluged with requests for syndicated interviews.

Although overwhelmed with all the attention that followed the publication of her own story, accompanied with the iconic picture of the MIA wife with her two sons, Helen would only be "distracted" for two or three weeks. For now that she knew something concrete about what had happened to Tom, she still had no idea of his fate. And worse, she also knew he had been in the hands of a malicious, coldblooded, godless enemy who had no regard for the sanctity of life.

* * *

It was a gorgeous Indian summer day. Helen wanted some fresh air and decided to drive her two boys and a playmate to the drugstore for some ice cream. As she parked, she saw their playmate's father coming out of an adjacent building. "Look, there's your daddy!"

"Where, where?" Tom and John squealed.

Helen bolted upright in her car seat. Then she slumped and sat stunned, gripping the steering wheel, unable to move and fighting back tears. She never, never mentioned "daddy" to the children unless they asked. Now she had inadvertently, and in a most cruel way, evoked their missing father's title. What was she thinking? Helen vowed to never make that mistake ever again.[4]

* * *

On 21 October, as the C-54 transport plane lifted off from Pyongyang, Grady Halcomb, at last, believed he was really on his way home. And he could see in the relaxed faces of the other seven former POWs that same contentment—that the war was now behind them and the home front lay ahead. For the first time, he felt truly alive, and the thoughts of family and friends were comingled with feelings of great expectation.

It was almost 2300 hours when the eight patients landed in Tokyo and were taken directly to the Itazuke hospital. There they were met by a genial doctor who, without introduction, asked, "What do you want to eat?" Recalling his "First Supper"—this time, instead of bacon and eggs, Halcomb opted for fried chicken. But that night, the result was the same for each special meal ordered: blissful ingestion followed by projectile vomiting and uncontainable diarrhea.

Jones, Smith, Makarounis, Halcomb,
Arakawa, Kumagai, Morris, and Locke

Next morning when the doctor returned and confronted his patients, he irreverently said, "Last night the meal was on me. But from now, on your meals are your responsibility. If you want to heal your insides, you'll stay on a 'soft' diet and work your way gradually to more solid foods." This time, the doctor's ghastly experiment of the night before had a profound behavioral effect on all the doubters. Despite Grady's current

102-pound weight, the desire to put some meat on his bones had lost its sense of urgency.[6]

* * *

At Tokyo's Itazuke Hospital, the Red Cross provided Jim Yeager his first conversation with his family via telephone.

"Dad, it's Jim."

"Son, how are you?"

"I'm safe and getting sound. Better every day"

"Thank God, you're okay. Your mother rode me day in, day out for encouraging you to become a soldier. She would never have forgiven me if you had come back in a coffin."

"Well, I'll be coming home soon, alive and well, and despite all I've been through, I still want to be an officer. You don't have to tell Mom. I'll tell her when the time's right. But I wanted you to know that I have not abandoned our goal."

"Sounds good, we'll keep that between us men."

"By the way, where the hell's Barbara?"

"Salt Lake City. Son, we need to wait and talk about her when you get home."

"No, I heard she was pregnant. I want you to get Tom Hansen to start working on a divorce. I am not—"

"Son, son! Your mom needs to talk. Here she is."

"Jim, I love you, love you so much," gushed Myrtle through her tears of sheer joy.

"I love you, Mom. And I sure do miss you," Jim sniffled back.[7]

* * *

It was interesting when one took a notional survey of the survivors that those privates who had operated under a "buddy system" during captivity seemed more likely to persevere:

Yeager and Toney, Slater and Sharpe, Jarvis and Stamper. This coupling most often occurred before arrival in Korea, but had been reinforced in the ordeal of combat and imprisonment. Their symbiotic relationship sustained the will to live. And now back in Japan under medical care, the buddies would continue to nurture their friendship and assist each other in their hospitalization and recovery. The old adage, "it takes two to tango" was spot-on for these American POWs who were compelled by the Reds to "dance" for three very long months.

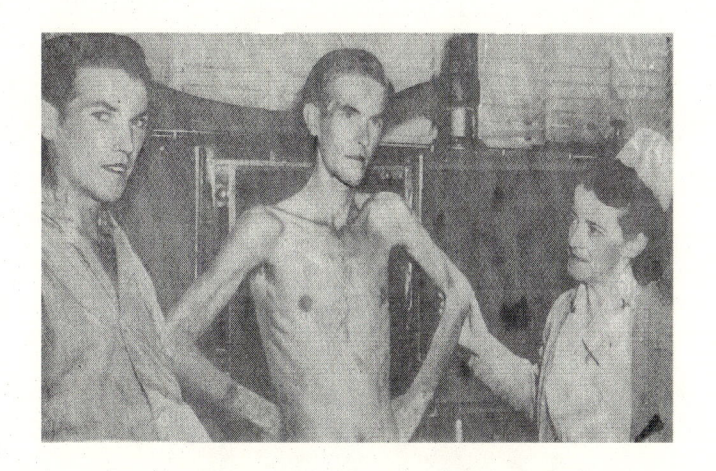

Privates Theodor Stamper and Charles Jarvis in Tokyo's Itazuke Hospital[8]

* * *

Bob Sharpe heard some commotion in the room and opened his eyes. The hospital staff had set up curtains around his bed immediately upon his arrival, but he could peek through a gap between two sections. When he did, he was amazed to see Bob Hope, the comedian, standing there conversing with some doctors. The doctors were gesturing and pointing in the direction of his bed. It looked like the staff was trying to discourage Hope from seeing him. Then the comic broke from the group and smartly strode across the floor toward him and pulled a curtain section aside. He was followed by the comely blond actress Marilyn Maxwell, who walked to the bottom end of Sharpe's bed and clasped the railing.

"How's it going, son?" Hope rhetorically asked. "I'll bet you've visited Korea recently," the mischief maker added.

"Yes, sir, you could say that," Bob responded weakly. He noticed as he spoke that Miss Maxwell was having a hard time containing her emotions as she gazed at him. She did not divert her eyes from his, but was clearly moved by the pitiful piece of flesh in front of her.

"Hi," was the only word from her lips, plus a tepid arching wave from her left hand. She was staying brave, but her heart was being punctured.

Bob Sharpe Boarding Aircraft in Pyongyang for Transport to Japan[9]

The Major

* * *

Beginning the last week of October and ending the first week of November, the survivors from Sunchon and Kujang-dong were interviewed at Camp Zama, twenty-five miles southwest of Tokyo. A JAG unit from the Korean Communications Zone wanted to get signed affidavits from the former POWs related to what would become Korean War Crime (KWC) #76, "The Sunchon Tunnel Massacre."

Valdor John was one of the first to be questioned on 28 October 1950 by a Major Arthur Williams who began by saying, "Please state your full name."

"Valdor (V-A-L-D-O-R) W. John (J-O-H-N)."

"What is your rank and serial number?"

"PFC, RA 16282077."

"How old are you?"

"Nineteen years old."

"Are you married or single?"

"Single."

"What is your Stateside address?

"707 West National Avenue, Milwaukee, Wisconsin."

"Were you one of the victims of the 'tunnel massacre' that occurred near Sunchon?"

"Yes, sir, I was."

"Will you relate what happened?"

Valdor then told how he was in the first group to be shot and recreated what happened. He went on to describe the events once the guards had departed. "I laid there until it got dark. There were eight of us left alive. Then there was four men that got up and moved during the night. There was one more man that died during the night, so that left three of us. Two of them had bad wounds in the leg. There were some civilians that carried them across the tracks. Well, we stayed there all the next day in the bushes, and along about evening again, we heard these voices. They were South Korean voices, hollering, 'GIs come out, you are okay.' I got up and looked around, and I seen a helmet, and I still thought it was a trick. I stayed there and pretty soon, I seen these two news photographers come out, and I seen they were Americans, so I came out."

The major interrogating John next asked a battery of questions about who gave the orders to execute the prisoners, but John had no answers. He only volunteered that he could identify the shooters if he were shown pictures of them. Then the questioning ended with an inquiry on his injuries.

John simply replied, "Well, they just took X-rays today and the doctor said he would look at them."[10]

* * *

On 29 October Earl "Jim" Halcomb flew into Japan to see his younger brother Grady. He had gotten wind of his repatriation and was eager to personally welcome him back. Ironically, he had been a participant in the airborne assault on Sunchon, but had not known that Grady was a POW or the train the 187th RCT attempted to save was his brother's POW group. When he did make the mental connection, he finagled some leave and a flight to Tokyo.

Disappointingly, Grady had departed for the States the same day of Jim's arrival. And the older brother had to postpone their reunion. But now Jim had to find a way get back to his unit. Luckily, he met a colonel who, upon hearing his plight, not only secured a flight to Korea but also a case of whisky. Jim was determined to reward his first sergeant for letting him go despite the fact his unit remained on call for more combat duty.[11]

* * *

Walt Whitcomb would be one of the last to sign an affidavit on 2 November 1950. His interviewer from the War Crimes unit was Warrant Officer Kenneth Washington. After some preliminary questions, the warrant officer started to focus on what happened at Kujang-dong, letting Walt tell his story with little prompting.

"We remained in the tunnel during the day and left that night. We went thirty miles further and remained on the tracks one more day."

"Then what happened?"

"Then we were removed from the tracks that night. About ninety men that could walk were taken further. About thirty-five or forty of us were shot dead."

"Who was in charge of this group of prisoners? Who was the ranking North Korean?"

"Until we reached Pyongyang, a lieutenant was."

"After Pyongyang, along your road of march, who was in charge?

"Johnny."

"He was in charge?"

"Yes, sir."

"A Korean you nicknamed Johnny?"

"Yes."

Then Whitcomb described the shootings and was asked, "Who issued the order?"

"An officer who threw us out from the back cars after the other men moved out."

"Can you describe this officer? How tall was he?"

"Five foot seven."

"How much did he weigh?"

"About 160 pounds."

"About how old did you judge him to be?"

"About twenty or twenty-two."

"Did he have a mustache?"

"He had a small mustache."

"Did he have any scars or moles on him or anything would serve to identify him?

"He had one eye, the right eye, that didn't seem to open all the way."

"Did he speak English."

"No."

"Did he have buck teeth or gold-capped teeth?"

"Yes, sir, he had two on the uppers."

"Do you know what insignia he had?"

"He had two stars on the epaulet."

"Did he carry any sidearms?"

"Yes, sir. A .45 pistol."

"Can you describe any of the North Koreans who were in the firing squad?"

"Outside of him, no."

Walt then went on to describe his wounds and how he, Slater, and Jones were the only survivors within the group that were shot. And he also explained how they were rescued. Then the session was wrapped up with a final question: "After you return to the States and recuperate and get well, would you care to come back to Korea either to work on the war crimes investigation or testify as a witness in war crime trials?"

"Yes, sir, I would. I would like to come back."[12]

* * *

At last released to travel home, Al Gifford was climbing the steps to board his airplane back to the States when he spied his *koibito*, Sachiko, meaning "a child of bliss." And she certainly was. There she stood at the chain-linked fence with both her hands extended slightly above her head with her fingers wrapped over and through the wire mesh. "God, she was beautiful." He paused, gave her one last glance, and ducked into the plane.

He had considered marrying her. He even sent her picture to show his mom, before his deployment to Korea. But marriage was never really in the cards. The army bureaucracy made it excruciatingly difficult for a soldier to bring home a Japanese bride. More to the point, Al always knew he was going home to Rose.[13]

* * *

When Ed Slater got off the train in Quincy, just days before Christmas, he was surprised to see all those gathered to welcome him home. His eyes naturally gravitated to his wife Donna and his two-year-old son Terry whom he had never seen. Of course, he noticed his sister Bernadine and her husband. She was taking care of his son, and Ed always sent her the money for his family. Bernadine was three years older, and he trusted her to do the right thing.

The family, in turn, had not seen him for two and a half years. They were surprised to see him looking so gaunt. But he was slowly getting back to his normal weight of 147 pounds having dropped to 92 pounds during his captivity. And he looked particularly apprehensive, which he was because very few letters had been exchanged over the years. And he did not know much about what had been happening in Quincy.

But in the next three weeks, before he shipped out to Fort Benning, he found out a lot had been going on—most of it had not been good. His wife had her own apartment and rarely saw their son. Donna was cold and distant, and he found some men's clothing hanging in her closets. Ed was not one to jump to conclusions, but nothing felt right in Quincy. He was truly a stranger in an estranged relationship with the people in his hometown."[14]

* * *

Grady Halcomb had found his way back to the States—specifically, to the Letterman Army Hospital at the presidio in San Francisco. It was here that the Red Cross notified his parents by telegram of his whereabouts. And he was soon able to talk to his mom for the first time over the phone. While other patients at Letterman were dispatched home fairly quickly, Grady had some "bug" in his intestines that the hospital wanted to purge before releasing him. So it was not until mid-December that Grady began his journey home to Ohio.

When he landed at the Cincinnati Airport in Kentucky, Grady was not sure how best to get home. He was already surprised that the airport was in Kentucky rather than Ohio. But after some inquiry, he found that the cheapest way was by Greyhound; however, the bus station was in the city. So since he was flush in cash, having recently received his back pay, he found a cab and asked to go to the station.

As they drove, Grady noticed the Negro cabdriver kept glancing at him in the rearview mirror. He was in uniform but could not figure out why all the furtive glances from the "cabby."

Finally, the driver spoke, "I seen your picture in the newspaper. You're from Hamilton."

"You have a good memory," Grady incredulously responded. "Yep, I am finally getting home."

"I'll take you home. It's not forty miles," the knowledgeable cabby suggested.

"No, I got to save my money for my girlfriend," Grady said with a grin.

"No, no, it's no charge. You've done enough," the taxi driver insisted.

"Thank you," Grady spontaneously reacted with wonder at this stranger's generosity.

As they drove on in silence, Grady mused about the impending reunion but also continued to be surprised by all the attention he had received since his escape. He knew he had done his duty the best he knew how. But to be rewarded with such kindness from most everyone he met was a little disarming at times.

"What's your address?" the cabby inquired.

"No, I need to go to the bus station. That's where my parents are expecting me."

"Are you sure?"

"Yes, but thank you again."

When the taxi driver pulled into the Hamilton station, Halcomb handed the taxi driver a twenty-dollar bill and quickly walked away, saying, "It's a Christmas present for your family."[15]

* * *

When Bill Locke came down the stairs of the commercial aircraft that had landed at the Greensboro airport, it seemed every Carolina acquaintance was waiting there for his return. The reporters were shooting pictures, and Bill was hammered with questions. Then the correspondents showed some class and let the family spend some time together inside after being promised that Locke would not leave the airport before granting them a more extensive interview. Even Ronda's parents complained that they had not been able to touch Bill during the arrival commotion.

But this interest in the fighter pilot and his POW journey was only the beginning of the public affairs blitz. Within a couple of days, he was summoned to the Pentagon to brief the military brass. While in Washington, he even briefed Truman's "kitchen cabinet" and got to meet George Marshall, the secretary of defense.

From Washington, he and Ronda were flown to New York where they met Dan Seymour, the host of the television series *We the People*. This weekly evening show wanted to recreate Bill's escape. Bill not only helped the actors and script writers construct the recreation, but he and Ronda were interviewed and taped for the show's ending.

This jet jockey was such a natural speaker and his story so compelling that the general in charge of public affairs at the Pentagon offered him a position on his staff. But Bill was resolute, "Sir, I first have to prove to myself I can get back in the air." And this air force general said he fully understood but candidly told Bill that promotions would come a lot easier at the Pentagon.

* * *

Bob Sharpe's dad, Mike, had spent a lot of his time during his son's captivity cruising the roads of North Carolina. When he found a soldier hitchhiking, he would give him a lift to his desired destination although it could involve hundreds of miles of travel. This was the way a father coped. It allowed him to contribute in some small way to the war effort and to lessen his own feeling of helplessness. It was the only way he knew how to support his son's service.

Now that his son was back in North Carolina and safe, he was on the road again leading a family convoy to Fort Bragg to see his son for the first time since his departure overseas. He knew it would be an emotional reunion with all the women present. So when he saw his son being loaded off the aircraft in a stretcher, he knew he had to set the stage.

As he made his way on the tarmac, the father's and son's eyes met and Bob's lip began to quiver. The father hurried to the stretcher and, leaning down, said, "Son, I got to ask you something before the women can hear."

"Sure, Dad, what is it?"

The women were catching up fast, so Mike got up close to his son's ear and whispered, "Is it true?"

"Is what true?"

"The Oriental women, is 'it' horizontal?"

"Aaah, Dad, come on," Bob smiled as the rest of the family crowded around, all crying and laughing at the same time.[16]

Bob Sharpe Enjoys Family at Home[17]

* * *

Helen's day-by-day existence continued to have its paradoxes, even on Valentine's Day. Instead of hearing from the love of her life on that day, Helen got a letter written on 14 February from Lieutenant General John R. Hodge, commander of 3rd Army. He was offering the opportunity to have a Silver Star presented to her in a ceremony. His closing sentence was most telling: "The award of a Silver Star Medal is a token recognition of the courageous action and devotion to duty performed by Major McDaniel."

Helen thought, enigmatically, to herself the word *token*, when used as an adjective, said it all, when describing this unplanned Valentine gift from Tom.

* * *

In the spring of 1951, Allen Gifford was accorded the honor he so richly deserved for his combat heroism. He was still convalescing at Valley Forge Army Hospital, his award long overdue. Now at a formal retreat parade, the PFC stood at attention as his citation was read for all the soldiers, family, and friends assembled to hear.

Silver Star Pinned on PFC Allen Gifford[18]

"Attention to orders."

"Private First Class Allen J. Gifford, 13282225, United States Army, a member of H Company, 19th Regiment, 24th Infantry Division, displayed gallantry in action on 18 July 1950, near Taejon, Korea. During the withdrawal north of the city when a convoy of trucks was subjected to heavy small-arms fire and suffered many causalities, he went to the aid of wounded soldiers on one of the trucks."

"When it became hopeless to continue in convoy, Private Gifford continued on foot carrying the wounded man. Seeing a group being held up by intense fire, he again went to the aid of the wounded in the face of the withering fire and, with utter disregard for his own safety, administered first aid and endeavored to evacuate them singly to a safer position."

"When last seen, Private Gifford was carrying a wounded soldier to the rear. His gallant example and complete devotion to his comrades reflect the greatest credit on himself and the United States Army Medical Service."

The citation completed, Colonel John M. Welch, the hospital commander, standing at attention by Gifford's side, turns, retrieves the medal from the adjutant, walks up, and pins the Silver Star on the private's chest. The colonel shakes his hand, takes a step back, and salutes Gifford. Al returns the salute, now adorned with the third highest military decoration conferred by the Department of Defense.

* * *

When Al Gifford was allowed to leave the hospital and go home, the nightmares got much worse. The cold sweats were no longer the symptoms of malaria, but were the manifestation of the terrible psychological trauma he underwent in combat, evasion, and detention. Many a night, his mother would race to his bedroom and "pull" her screaming son out of Korea where he was in a firefight or witnessing an execution. Now at home, Al was having a complete breakdown.

But his father, pathetically, had no capacity for empathy and never would or could express any sympathy. Whether his father was self-absorbed or jealous of his son's military record, the dad resented the fact that Al was getting so much attention from the Veterans Administration (VA). Al was receiving some compensation—less than $40 a month—and some scant, inadequate medical follow-up. Nonetheless, the father incessantly groused about the fact that he got "nothin'" from his service in WWI.

So the dutiful son coaxed and prodded his father to visit the local VA office. Al helped him complete all the paperwork to determine if any compensation was in the offering. Although the VA process was long and painful and needed Al to ensure his dad stayed the course, the end result was unexpected and remarkable. The father would receive more than ten times the monthly compensation Al received. It seemed the VA believed that a soldier who never left home, and was only a cook at Fort Dix during wartime, deserved significantly more money than a legitimate combat hero and former POW. The irony was absurd, but the heartbreak for Al was his dad never did say "thank you."[19]

* * *

Unlike the other POW survivors, JB Smith stayed in Japan to recuperate since his family had never left. And he was diligent in writing down his war experiences in a memoir titled *Prisoner of the Red Koreans*. In it, Smith would write about his combat, imprisonment, and the many heroes who shared his plight. But Smith was most effusive about Major McDaniel—"our superior officer" who he believed was "an American of George Washington character."

The Smiths (Florence, JB, and "Peety") Reunited in Tokyo

Moreover, the lieutenant went beyond recording his beliefs in a memoir when he, unselfishly, submitted award recommendations for his fellow POWs. Specifically, while assigned to the Legal Assistance Office at Camp Gifu, he wrote two letters of recommendation, both dated 20 June 1951, to the Far East Command, General Headquarters. One recommended Major McDaniel for the Medal of Honor and the other recommended the Distinguished Service Cross for seven other soldiers. The precise wording of the justifications in the second letter was as follows:

> First Lt. Makarounis, at peril to his life, assisted the wounded, interceded with the North Koreans for humane treatment and the necessities of life for all of the prisoners of war.
>
> Sgt Leonard L. Hines . . . who above and beyond the call of duty, though wounded himself in the feet and back, did physically support many of the wounded and sick men of

the prisoners of war in the forced march to Pyongyang thereby averting their death by shooting as they fell by the wayside. In addition Sgt Hines morally strengthened the men, by his exhortations not to give up, and by the ingenuity he exercised in securing many necessary items of medical assistance and subsistence.

Sgt 1/c Robert L Morris . . . for his constant attendance to the many wounded, physically supporting many, constantly assisting in billeting, feeding, burial, and management of the prisoners of war, at the peril of his life.

Sgt Tack Kumagai (RA10733743); Sgt (first name unknown) Shinde, Cpl. Jack Arakawa; at peril to their life constantly interpreted for Maj. McDaniel, and by constant intercession with the North Koreans enabled the prisoner[s] of war to receive many benefits that prolonged their lives. In the role of interpreters they put in many hours, not required in the line of duty, and saved many lives of men the Koreans wanted to shoot for infractions, or inability to keep pace, with the column; to this end all, at some time or other at the expense of their own strength supported the wounded."

Pfc Edward Halcomb. . . . At the peril to his life voluntarily took the job of administering to the sick and wounded of the prisoners of war. To this end he laboriously put in many long hours tending to the sick, constantly exposed to the many diseases rampant in the group. He received no extra food, yet often shared his food with the sick. He physically supported many of the sick as the group neared Pyongyang, thereby saving many from execution. In addition he assisted in the Christian Burial of many of the prisoner of war dead. He constantly interceded with the North Korean authorities to acquire medical supplies for the group.[20]

* * *

Ed Slater had reenlisted. But he was not sure now that he should have. He hated all authority. And now after several months at Fort Benning, he knew he had no time for officers, especially lieutenants. He blamed his feelings on the officers—Locke, Makarounis and Smith—who he felt had abandoned him and his POW buddies in Pyongyang. But the origin of his anger was far more complex, extending to his life before he entered the army. Ed was drinking too much and not getting along with anybody, particularly himself.

One night when he was out carousing in a Columbus bar, his anger spilled over when he was provoked by a fellow soldier. The guy came over to him and gave Ed this opening verbal salvo, "Where did you get all those doodads on your chest? They can't be yours."

And technically the other soldier was right that Slater did have a chest full of medals for someone so young—the Purple Heart, Army Occupation Medal, National Defense Service Medal, and Korean Service Medal displayed under a combat infantry badge. But Ed held his fire and turned his back on the antagonist.

Later, however, after Ed had a few more drinks under his belt. The soldier returned as Ed was showing someone a picture of his son Terry. This time, the soldier guaranteed the fight he wanted when he told Ed, "The kid's ears are bigger than Mickey Mouse's. And your brat looks nothing like you."

Ed turned and swung, catching the soldier's neck in the crook of his arm and wrestling him to the ground. They were both kicking and throwing punches as others joined in. The fight moved out of the bar into the street, where Ed knocked the guy into the backseat of an open convertible and leaped on top of him. His final blows were arrested by police officers that pulled him out of the car.

Next day, now in the post stockade, he found out he broke the soldier's leg and he would have to stand before a special court-martial. When convened, the trial consisted of a military judge, trial counsel, defense counsel, and three officers sitting on a panel that would determine his innocence or guilt. Ed did not really appreciate the one-day proceedings, but when the commanding officer reviewed the guilty verdict, the major general nullified it. Ed received no punishment whatsoever—that is, from the court-martial. His punishment came a few days later from a different source when he collapsed after the onset of a pronounced chill and fierce fever. After ten months of incubation, the Korean mosquitoes exacted their toll. Ed had contracted malaria.[21]

* * *

It was only days after the 21 June 1951 Medal of Honor ceremony in which General Omar Bradley (USMA 1915) presided in Washington, DC, that Helen and Barbara Faith got to talk on the telephone.

"Barbara, Helen, I've wanted to call you for a long time. But I couldn't wait any longer when I saw you and Barbara Ann in the newspaper. It's been a year. So much has happened since that night at my quarters on Camp Haugen when we all found out that Don and Tom were going to war again."

"I know, Helen, we have both been through some really, really hard times since then. And your letters have helped me a lot. But for me the ceremony has brought some closure. General Bradley was so kind. He told me he '. . . had known

Don since he was a little boy,' and he was 'not at all surprised at his leadership and courage.'"

"Well, you know how much Tom thought of Don. I have never known any man with such confidence. Even officers who knew Don only a short time would follow him to the ends of the earth."

"He was something, wasn't he? I guess that's why I married him."

"Yes, he was."

"You know his father told me we may never get his body back. His flag officer buddies believe the UN will not sacrifice their soldiers like the Chinese are willing to do. So we may never get access to the men who were killed in North Korea."

"I appreciate you telling me this. But, Barbara, no one saw Tom get shot, and his body was not found in the vicinity of the tunnel. And it's been reported there are thousands of prisoners being held by the Reds in China."

"I do not want you to give up hope, Helen. I was the lucky one. Those few men who got out of Chosin could confirm Don's death. But I also learned how badly General Almond fouled things up, refusing to believe the Chinese were in North Korea in large numbers last November. There were actually sixty thousand Chinese encircling Don and his men. Almond helicoptered into Chosin three days before Don was killed, pinned a Silver Star on Don, and told him to attack the 'laundrymen' who were 'fleeing north.' Then, when the general left, Don ripped the medal off his jacket and threw it into the snow."[22]

"Yes, I could certainly see Don doing that." Helen paused, "Well, I need to get off, Barbara, so my telephone bill is not too big. But I just want you know that I love you. Hug Barbara Ann for me, and come see me in Ahoskie if you get a chance. You won't believe how the boys have grown."

"I love you too, Helen, and thank you for your faithful friendship. But don't hug the boys. Pinch them for me 'cause I know they are a handful."

"You're right, they are rowdy. But you know I love boys. Good-bye."

"Good-bye, Helen."

Helen placed the phone back in its cradle, leaned back in her overstuffed chair, closed her eyes, and recounted in her head the emotional calendar of the past year. First, she recalled her shock and then the numbing disbelief that Tom was missing and/or dead. She would deny the reality of her situation to avoid the wrenching pain. This period lasted for weeks.

But when the shock finally dissipated, then the pain became unbearable. Her only escape was tending to her boys. She never drank since her dad was an alcoholic, who had abandoned her after her mother's death from pneumonia when she was only eight years old. But God, she wished she could find a way to drown her feelings of guilt. She would never forget the time Tom told her she was the best mother in the world, but not the best wife. Oh, if God would just give her another chance to be a better wife to Tom.

When some of the pain began to relent, she became angry—very angry. It was the army's fault. They killed Tom. They sent him into battle without the wherewithal to survive. He did not have chance. Ultimately, it was Truman's fault. Why would he care about Korea? It wasn't worth one American life. And then she knew she was beginning to lose all rational thought when she began to blame Tom: he should never have been a soldier. And if that's the kind of life he wanted, he should never have married and had children.

Her emotions often were bursting from the pressure cooker of her mind. She even would lash out at the affable "Buddy

Doug," her mother's brother. He was her favorite relative and primary benefactor in town and kept an eye on her and the boys for the family. But she had several outbursts with him that would be unthinkable in normal times. And also during this phase, she would bargain with God and offer all kinds of promises if she could just have Tom back.

At last the anger did subside and she became much more reflective, but wretchedly so. She was so lonely. She missed Tom so much. Depression set in and she withdrew from family and friends. Her best friend Emily and her husband Jack Barnes became deeply concerned when they visited her, as they often did from across town. She was in the deepest, darkest place she had ever been in her life. All hope had been vacuumed out of her. She was desolate and only able to care for Tom and John. She had finally come to grips with the magnitude of her loss. But utter despair became the order of the day for months.

* * *

On 7 July 1951, in Special Orders No. 135, the Department of the Army promoted William T. McDaniel, 024088 Inf (RA), from major to lieutenant colonel. The promotion would be a significant boost in pay, but all Helen cared about was that this increase in money and benefits would go toward sustaining a family of four instead of a family of three.[23]

* * *

When Valdor John got home to Wisconsin, he found out he was under investigation. Apparently, while he was in Red captivity, his parents were visited by American Communists who had gotten their foot in the door by being the first to inform them of his prisoner status. Conversely, the army had told the family Valdor was missing and later declared him dead.

John had spent more than eighteen months convalescing. He had gone from 227 pounds down to 90 pounds before his weight had an uptick. He had double pneumonia and pernicious dysentery. But what kept him in the hospital longest was the reconstruction of his left arm. His two bullet wounds to the arm had frayed the muscles, and it took a gifted surgeon to repair the arm and a knowledgeable physical therapist to exercise the muscles back to normal.

Once healed and home, the army notified him to appear before a military board. He was given a counsel and advised by his JAG to only answer the questions asked with a simple "yes" or "no" and volunteer nothing more. After a week of grilling, he was excused and never questioned again about his Red associations. Unfortunately, someone leaked this investigation to the newspapers along with his picture. And Valdor John—the Indian—would forever, in a few people's minds, be the subject of innuendo linking him to Communists.[24]

* * *

Surprisingly, Bob Sharpe continued to adjust well to his new life after his many near-death experiences in Korea. He was stationed at Fort Bragg, so home was not far down the road. His family and friends were always close to give him any support he needed. Today, he and his dad were having some Carolina barbecue in a local restaurant, enjoying that great vinegar tartness on their tongues.

"The *Saturday Evening Post* did a great job," Mike recalled.

"Yeah, I never expected they'd include all those pictures of the family. And the people hear in town seem pleased with the coverage. Now the whole country has heard of High Point," Bob asserted.

Then the bubba at the table next to him stood up and casually put his cigarette out in a barely eaten mound of mashed potatoes. When Bob saw this waste, he gritted his teeth, but then could not let it lie. "You know, mister, there are a lot of hungry people who would sure love to eat those potatoes."

"Yeah, who are you—the food sheriff?"

Bob leaped up, and his dad instantly grabbed his arm and pulled him back into his chair. The man glared at Bob, turned, and walked through the open door.

"Sorry, Dad, I just can't stand it when I see people leaving good food on their plates. Don't they know how lucky they are to have it? Nothing sets me off more."

"Bob, they will never know what you know about food. For most people, they can only really appreciate somethin' when they've lost it or can no longer get it. So, son, you need to work on this. People are not going to change, so you must learn to cut them some slack. I know you will."[25]

* * *

By July 1951, Tak Kumagai was back on his beloved islands, assigned to the new army training school at Schofield Barracks in the county of Honolulu. And he had brought home a Japanese bride. But before departing Japan, he had been detailed to the 441st Counter Intelligence Corps (CIC) detachment where he could impart his vast knowledge of the North Korean enemy.

In Hawaii, the army placed Tak in administrative positions, and he became the chief clerk for the provost marshal for more than a year. But even with these considerable work responsibilities and the solace that came from being home, the adjustment to his newfound freedoms and the tranquility far from the Korean war zone was a difficult transition. His marriage dissolved, and he was left alone to deal with the demons that the North Koreans had unleashed on his soul. He knew he would have to emulate the hopefulness of his father, who always believed his son would come home and would be destined to enrich the community with his considerable gifts of hard work and intellectual curiosity.

* * *

Before 1951 came to a close, Bill Locke had reassured himself that he still had the right stuff to fly. He was flying F-84 Thunderjets at Shaw Air Force Base, and these birds carried special weapons—an air force euphemism for nuclear weapons. Consequently, he had to conform to General Curtis LeMay's Strategic Air Command "zero defects" mentality: no mistakes allowed. Under a personnel reliability program, flight surgeons had to certify pilots were psychologically competent to manage nuclear weapons with all their attendant duties. In addition, LeMay personally had Bill flying all over the country, briefing airmen on what to expect as a POW. This all-consuming additional duty made his flying qualifications hard to maintain.

With all this workload on his shoulders, Bill collapsed. But the primary causes were internal, not external. When Ronda got a call, she went to the hospital and found her fighter pilot in a tub filled with ice. Doctors were trying to bring down his 105-degree temperature. His condition warranted a series of tests that revealed he had hepatitis, malaria, and an appendix on the verge of eruption. Although Bill would soon get back on his feet and into the air, it would be several years before he would be free of periodic attacks from these diseases contracted in Korea.

The Major

* * *

In the summer of 1952, Jim Yeager was on the verge of achieving his life's aim. He was at the Sand Hill cantonment, Fort Benning, Georgia, and was halfway through Officer Candidate School. He was in the gym passing a medicine ball around with his classmates when he wrenched his back. This was not the first time, and its genesis went back to Korea. His buddy Toney was used to icing down Jim and giving him a massage to relieve the pain from this recurring injury. This time, however, Toney—although at Benning in a rifle company—was not available to come to Jim's aid. So a classmate tried to replicate Toney's role. And with some success, Jim was able to become mobile enough to sneak off post by donning his enlisted uniform and using an old pass that matched.

Jim needed some medicine to facilitate his recovery. And two six-packs of beer was just what any conscientious doctor would order. Fortunately, he was caught making his purchase by some of his old enlisted buddies from Benning.

"How'd you get off post?" They asked. Then they noticed the stripes on his uniform vice the officer candidate insignia. "Good job!"

"You know, Jim, all the officers in your class are going to Korea after graduation. We cut orders last night. The units aren't specified yet, but all of you are headed to the Far East to break the stalemate."

Jim thanked the guys and, in appreciation, handed them one of his six-packs. When he got back to the barracks, it was near midnight, but he knew what he had to do. He must resign.

Sure, as a former POW, he could get his name removed from these orders. The army would not send a POW back to the same enemy to give them a second chance to kill him.

223

But was he really physically fit to become an infantry platoon leader: to lead men in battle, to charge a machine gun nest and not be a liability to those who followed him? He wrote the one-page letter and slept well.

He was shaving when a soldier told him to see the first sergeant ASAP. In other words, "Now, don't finish shaving."

Jim knocked on the door and entered.

"What the hell is this?" The sergeant waved the resignation letter in the air.

"I've decided to resign. I am not physically qualified to be an infantry officer."

"If you are serious, go back, use official 8 by 10 paper, and get it back to me today. But make damn sure you know what you are doing. After it leaves my hands, if you waffle, it won't go well for you either as an officer or enlisted man."

He did as the sergeant instructed and was standing before the company commander the next day. After knocking, the lieutenant told him to enter. And then the CO kept Jim in a brace for over a half an hour, dressing him down for his decision to quit. Then, when he was satisfied with Jim's answers, he put him at rest.

The first lieutenant then exhibited extraordinary candor with Jim. He had also been in Korea and was shot twice in the back. "What I am about to tell you is for your ears only. One-fifth of your class, around forty cadets, have submitted their resignation. The colonel believes this is due to some organized conspiracy. You convinced me that if such a conspiracy exists, you are not part of it. By the way, I have put in my resignation. I'm never going back to the Far East."[26]

* * *

For Helen, the second half of 1952 was turning out to be a pretty good year. The elementary school staff and some parents had talked her into becoming the president of the PTA. And Tom was thriving in first grade where he was "chosen" to narrate the "Three Little Pigs" play without reading a script. Helen understood the community believed they could best help her and her sons by keeping them heavily involved in "activities," rather than dwelling on the ongoing war and the mysteries about Tom it withheld from her. But then, "the incident" occurred and it changed everything in Ahoskie.

Helen heard a rap at the backdoor. She was in the bedroom in her robe still and the boys were coloring on the living room floor that Saturday morning. She left the bedroom to investigate. She opened the backdoor to see a distant neighbor standing there behind the screen door. And he reeked of alcohol.

He slurred, "Helen, you know I am always close by if you ever need me."

"Well, I appreciate that. Thank you."

"I know you are lonely and I can help you feel less lonely."

Helen, quickly glanced at the latch, and saw the screen door was fastened.

He pulled on the door hard and said, "I want to come in."

"No! Stop it."

"You could use a man like me."

Helen slammed the door, locked it, ran to the front door and locked it. Tom and John looked up. She slowed down, went into the dining room and plopped down in a chair. That way she could watch the boys, but not let them see her uncontrollable, trembling body. The nasty cocktail of rage, fear and shame she had just now been forced to down was having an ugly effect—the short term was deeply disturbing, the long term, incalculable.[27]

* * *

After the interminable military stalemate in Korea, in July 1953, an armistice was officially signed by the warring nations. And a prisoner exchange ensued. First came "Little Switch," and then "Big Switch." In Operation Little Switch, the sick and wounded prisoners were returned in April and May 1953. The UN released 6,670 Chinese and North Korean prisoners, and the Reds returned 684 UN prisoners including 149 Americans. Operation Big Switch commenced in August 1953 and lasted until December. The numbers totaled 70,183 North Koreans; 5,640 Chinese; 7,862 South Koreans; 3,597 Americans; and 946 British. Over 22,600 Communist soldiers, the majority of whom were former Republic of China military, declined repatriation. Much to the chagrin of the UN forces, 23 Americans and 1 Briton, along with 333 South Korean soldiers, also declined repatriation.[28]

With the return of Mickelberg and Roten during the exchange of prisoners, the final tally of survivors from the McDaniel POW group could be ascertained. Of the 376 POWs that were incarcerated together in Seoul, a total of 52 men would ultimately survive and return home to the United States. As captives, members of the McDaniel group trudged from the Korea Strait to the Yalu River—a distance of over 400 miles—over a three-month period, with a survival rate of 14 percent.

In comparison, the Bataan Death March in WWII was a six-day, sixty-one-mile slog with a fatality rate of less than 15 percent, of which 600 to 650 deaths were American POWs. While the Bataan march is the most infamous due to the sheer numbers of Filipino and American POWs involved (approximately 75,000), the duration and degree of suffering are not comparable to that experienced by the 376 American POWs commanded by Major McDaniel.[29]

* * *

Don Whitehead, a Pulitzer Prize winner for his Korean War reporting, composed an article for publication on 10 September 1953. It was printed in newspapers across the country, making the front page in many daily periodicals. In it he wrote:

"Operation Big Switch has ended in Korea, and still there is no word of what happened to 'the Major'—the hero of the Communist-ordered death march from Seoul in the early days of the war."

"For three years, Mrs. McDaniel has been hoping someone will be able to tell her whether the Major still lives—or what happened at the tunnel after he left the train . . . ."

"Major McDaniel reached the front about July 15 . . . fighting a desperate battle for a time around Taejon . . . led a foray to recapture howitzers overrun by the Reds . . . never knew he won the Silver Star and a promotion to the rank of lieutenant colonel."

"Three months later, we heard the story of Major McDaniel from survivors of a Red massacre . . . a wonderful guy . . . gave us part of his food . . . took care of us as best he could . . . never would have made it except for the Major . . . ."

"We never saw the Major again after he left the train . . . don't know what happened to him."

Then Whitehead concluded the article with Helen's own words: "For a long time, I couldn't bear to talk about what happened . . . . But finally, I knew I had to face reality. I still hope there will be someone coming back who can tell me something. Anything is better than this."[30]

* * *

Helen had received dozens of letters over the years—from high-ranking government officials, friends, family, former POWs, and perfect strangers—since Tom became an MIA.

But none were more edifying and poignant than the one dated 12 September 1953, from a Corporal Kreider.

Dear Mrs. McDaniel,

This morning I was reading the Fayetteville Observer and I noticed a write up by Don Whitehead about your husband Major McDaniel. I'll tell you as much as I can about your husband . . . .

At this school, I first met your husband. There is no man in this world from my day of birth that I have more respect for. Major McDaniel thought little of his own welfare . . . and if he was awarded a small morsel, such as an apple or a piece of bread, he would give it to the men . . . .

When we arrived at Sunchon, North Korea . . . toward dusk a Korean guard told me they were taking all the officers to Manchuria. Then the guard told me to tell the other captives that they were taking them away to fix us chow. That was the last I saw of Major McDaniel and the other officer captives. Mrs. McDaniel, I hope and pray that he is safe in Manchuria . . . . I truthfully believe the Commies hold many American captives in Manchuria . . . . I wish you all the luck, for I say again, I'll never forget so honorable a man as Major McDaniel.

Truly Yours

Cpl Lloyd D Kreider
307 Airborne Medical Bn
Fort Bragg, North Carolina.[31]

* * *

Of the 7,190 Allied POWs captured in Korea, approximately 3000 died in captivity. A mortality rate of 43 percent was documented over the first six months of the war, largely from starvation. In comparison, the WWII rates were as follows: 4 percent of US POWs died in Germany (a normal rate reflecting the Geneva Convention) and 34 percent in Japan (condemned as "barbarous"). Among German POWs held by the Soviets, the rate was 45 percent, and 60 percent among Soviet POWs held by the Germans. In their apologias, the Red Chinese claimed that the starvation was caused by US bombing that hampered food delivery; however, the POW camps were right on the border of China whose territory was exempt from bombardment.

In the summer of 1951, the purposeful starvation of US POWs stopped. But when the murder-by-starvation ended, indoctrination in anti-American propaganda ratcheted up with the intensified recruitment of POWs to regurgitate anti-American rhetoric in signed statements and public broadcasts. Stunningly, the Reds were able to coerce or entice thirty-six Allied pilots to sign confessions to having employed germ warfare.

Unquestionably, mass starvation broke the moral fiber of the American POWs in 1950 and 1951. They stopped helping each other, resulting in higher death rates. And any attempts by officers to take command—to get the men to cooperate in their common interest—were broken up by the Reds, unless the officers were willing to become collaborators.

Collaboration was the choice of Lieutenant Colonels Paul V. Liles (USMA 1941) and Harry Fleming. They produced Red propaganda, but in return, they did cut the death rate in their camp near Pyoktong. Later, they were among the thirty-five collaborators who were the most infamous pro-Communist propagandists located at a camp in Pyongyang, which was known by other POWs as "Traitors' Row."

Early on in many camps, things were so bad that men were too apathetic to defend their comrades or themselves against predators like Sergeant James Gallagher and PFC Rothwell Floyd. In one notorious incident (17 February 1951), Gallagher tossed two prisoners who were gravely weakened by dysentery outside the barracks, where they froze to death. Gallagher argued that the stink of unwashed dysentery patients was revolting.

The decisive tipping point in the treatment of POWs, however, came on 27 December 1951, when the Communists finally exchanged the names of POWs with the UN forces. At last, the POWs had some assurance they would not be beaten to death or shot since their Red captors would now have to account for their absence during repatriation at war's end.

This accounting, in turn, emboldened a mass strike by about four hundred noncoms in March 1952 to demand an end to mandatory indoctrination classes. Master Sergeant Ralph Krieger commented later, "It was the first time since we had been captured that we acted like American soldiers." The Reds finally relented, and indoctrination became voluntary.

Subsequently, about 25 percent of the POWs (known as the "progressives") continued to attend, while a smaller number (the "reactionaries") made clear their scorn for Communism and the American collaborators. But for the progressives, the contempt they received from their fellow POWs was outweighed by the better food they received.

Finally, US authorities documented that sixty-six US personnel were kept against their will by the Communists after the end of the war: forty-three air force, twelve civilians, and eleven coast guard or navy personnel. Most were captured outside of Korea, usually in China, and did not come under the terms of the armistice. Tragically, diplomatic efforts never secured their release.[32]

* * *

By the fall of 1953, Helen had become extremely adept at finding who to talk to in the army, depending on the information she sought: personnel, finance, what have you. She finally had found the single point of contact in the army who knew the most about her husband, his history as a POW, and his status as an MIA. That person was Lieutenant Colonel Earnest E. Zeiszler, who was the officer in charge (OIC) of the Determination Branch under the Office of the Adjutant General.

In a telephone conversation with the lieutenant colonel in September 1953, Helen learned that one of Tom's West Point classmates had some information on the Major's captivity. This classmate, Lieutenant Colonel Paul V. Liles, was freed on 1 September and interrogated on the *USNS General Brewster* after being repatriated in Big Switch. In December 1953, a letter sent to her from the adjutant general, General Bergin, quoted the interrogation report:

"In December 1950, Lt. Col. Liles was being interrogated by North Korean Major Kin Dong Suk who made the statement that he looked like Major McDaniel . . . . Lt. Col. Liles stated that he asked the North Korean major if Major McDaniel was still alive. To this, the North Korean major replied that the Major was still alive . . . . This took place in the city of Pyoktong, North Korea."

"In September 1951, Lt. Col. Liles found a Red propaganda pamphlet called 'POW'S CALLING.' On the cover was a picture of Major McDaniel. Inside the pamphlet were the words 'Major presides over POW meeting.' This took place in the city of Pyongyang."

"In the fall of 1951, Lt. Col. Liles saw some propaganda radio speeches. Upon looking through these speeches, he found one that was allegedly written and signed by Maj. McDaniel."

"Again in May 1953, Lt. Col. Liles was with North Korean major Kin Dong Suk in a vehicle en route to Pyongyang from Pyoktong. Lt. Col. Liles again asked the North Korean major if had seen Major McDaniel. The North Korean major did not give definite answers. Lt. Col. Liles stated that the North Korean major was very evasive upon answering and made the statement, 'Maybe he dead.' Lt. Col. Liles was never able to get information from any other POW relative to the status of Major McDaniel. His information is strictly hearsay based on information from an enemy major and a propaganda pamphlet."

Major General Bergin's letter concluded with this paragraph: "Since the foregoing statement does not provide conclusive evidence of the death of your husband, he will continue to be carried on the records as missing in action."[33]

* * *

Helen knew that this day would eventually come. Although she expected the decision, the timing was not good. She had moved to Williamsburg, Virginia, in the summer. And the official letter was properly addressed to her modest Ludwell apartment, close to the College of William and Mary, just across the James River from Smithfield where she grew up. The one-page epistle from the army adjutant general, moreover, was succinct and boiled down to a single paragraph:

"The finding does not establish an actual or probable date of death. However, as required by law, it includes a presumptive date of death for the termination of pay and allowances, settlement of accounts, and payment of death gratuities. In this case, the date has been set as 31 December 1953."

Now that the Korean Conflict was over, the US government was administratively settling unfinished business. They wanted to close the books on this very unpopular war and move on. But moving on would now be harder for Helen; she would no longer be getting her husband's substantial salary. She would have to go to work and find child care for the boys. The only bright spot was she could finally sell the Buick Roadmaster, whose title was in Tom's name and now hers as the beneficiary of his will.

Helen was astounded at the efficiency of the federal government when they wanted to reduce expenditures. By February, the VA had put in place her new income. Every month she would receive $150 for herself, $121 for Tom Junior, and $75 for John. In addition, she would receive a government life insurance settlement of $37.10 every month for life and the commencement date of the insurance would be calculated from the official date of her husband's capture—20 July 1950. This calculation would amount to $1,500. So Helen's cash flow from the government, hereafter, would be $383.10 per month.

This amount could increase, when adjusted for inflation, but would never decrease. Helen's federal income would be decremented when Tom and John turned eighteen years old or sooner if they married or died. Finally, if Helen remarried, she would lose all her monetary allocation and privileges such as using the officer's club, shopping at the commissary, and so on.[34]

Chapter Ten

Judgment Day: Congressional Hearings (December 1953)

> ... *the Major, a West Point officer, was one of the most courageous men you will ever find in the United States Army, one of the most courageous men I have ever met*...
> —testimony before the United States Senate

Judgment day for the dead was legion. But the particulars remain unknown to us mortals on this side of the shroud that separates the finite from the infinite. Yet the numbers available to be judged were staggering by war's end. Both sides managed to kill over 36,500 American; 58,000 South Korean; nearly 3,000 Allied; 215,000 North Korean; and 400,000 Chinese military in addition to another 2,000,000 Korean civilians.[1] On the other hand, judgment day for the quick and the dead, by the living, continues to play out to this day.

* * *

The January 1954 United States Senate summary report read:

> On June 25, 1950, the North Korean People's Army, without warning, attacked the Free Republic of South Korea.

During the ensuing 3 years of warfare, the Communist enemy committed a series of war crimes against American and United Nations personnel which constituted one of the most heinous and barbaric epochs of recorded history. When the American people became aware war atrocities had been committed against American troops, thousands of letters were sent to Members of Congress by parents, wives, and relatives of servicemen, requesting an immediate investigation.

Accordingly, on October 6, 1953, Senator Joseph R. McCarthy, chairman of the Senate Permanent Subcommittee on Investigations, appointed a special subcommittee, chaired by Senator Charles E. Potter, to inquire into the nature and extent of Communist war crimes committed in Korea.

The purpose of the investigation was to bring to the attention of the world in general and to the American people in particular, the type of vicious and barbaric enemy we have been fighting in Korea, to expose their horrible acts committed against our troops, and to foster appropriate legislation.

The report was a summary of hearings begun a month earlier.[2]

* * *

On Wednesday, 2 December 1953, the Subcommittee on Korean War Atrocities met at 1030 hours in the caucus room of the Senate Office Building. Senator Charles E. Potter, chairman of the subcommittee, presided. The senator had enlisted as a private in the US Army in 1942 and saw combat service in the ETO with the 28th ID. He was seriously wounded at Colmar Alsace, France, in 1945, resulting in the loss of both legs. He was awarded the Silver Star twice, the French Croix de Guerre, and the Purple Heart.

Those present for this hearing included Senator Joseph R. McCarthy, Republican, Wisconsin; Senator Henry C. Dworshak, Republican, Idaho; Senator Barry Goldwater, Republican, Arizona; and Robert L. Jones, research assistant to Senator Potter. Also present were the following staff members of the Permanent Subcommittee on Investigations: Francis P. Carr, executive director; Donald P. O'Donnell, assistant counsel; and Ruth Young Watt, chief clerk.

Senator Potter began, "The subcommittee will come to order. The subcommittee is appointed by the chairman, Senator Joseph McCarthy of Wisconsin, chairman of the Senate Permanent Subcommittee on Investigations. With me I have Don O'Donnell, who is a special counsel who has been handling the work for the atrocities investigation. On his left is Frank Carr, executive director of the Permanent Subcommittee on Investigations . . . ."

After setting the context for the hearing, Potter welcomed his first speaker. "We are fortunate in having today as our first witness one of America's most brilliant military leaders, a man who served as commander of the United States and United Nations forces in Korea and who is now chief of staff of the army here in Washington. It is my great honor to have General Matthew Ridgeway present to make the opening statement of this hearing. General Ridgeway, we are pleased to have you with us."

General Matthew Ridgeway (USMA 1917)—"Old Iron Tits" sans his hallmark grenades—was bedecked in full service dress. He had seated himself and pulled close to the microphone, assuming command of this congressional stage,

THE MAJOR

"It is my honor, Senator Potter, to be here. May I first, sir, express my deep appreciation of your very gracious personal remarks, and my high respect for a great combat soldier. Senator Potter, gentlemen. Soon after assuming command of the Eighth United States Army in Korea, I issued a statement to that unified land force setting forth my personal convictions with respect to the issues at stake in the conflict then raging. Specifically, from the text of that declaration, I quote: 'The real issues are whether or not the power of civilization, as God has permitted it to flower in our own beloved lands, shall defy and defeat communism; whether the rule of men who shoot their prisoners, enslave their citizens, and deride the dignity of man, shall displace the rule of those to whom the individual and his individual rights are sacred; whether we are to survive with God's hand to guide and lead us, or to perish in the dead existence of a godless world.'"

"You will note that today, as then, in January 1951 the phrase 'men who shoot their prisoners' has been emphasized. That the Communist armies—North Koreans and Chinese participating in the Korean conflict—are the most brutal and ruthless in the history of modern warfare is established by the overwhelming weight of evidence now on hand within the Department of the Army and in the Far East. Brutality in actual combat can sometimes be expected and, while it cannot be excused or condoned, its stigma can be somewhat lessened by the common knowledge of all military men that violent combat can stir the emotions of participants to the point where, for a time, they cease to control themselves. But a studied and calculated course of criminal misconduct, extending over a period of nearly three years and carried out with such callous disregard of human life and suffering as to indicate a design on the part of the Communist leadership to exterminate prisoners of war in one way or another, should not be expected, cannot be excused or condoned, and not a word can be said in defense or extenuation of it. While loudly protesting United Nations alleged 'mistreatment' of Communist prisoners of war, Red leaders were themselves conducting, or coldly permitting to be conducted, a program of brutality and extermination against military prisoners of war that probably has no parallel in modern times...."

"The premeditated murder of prisoners who had long been in custody, the massacre of 138 officers and men at Sunchon tunnel . . . the execution of wounded, sick, and weakened who could not keep up on the death march from Seoul to Pyongyang . . . the deliberate withholding of food and water. The withholding of medical attention on the flimsiest grounds of alleged noncooperation on the part of victims . . . ."

Ridgeway then provided the latest statistics: "Official casualty figures of the adjutant general, cumulative as of August 12, 1953, provide an interim estimate of the scope of Communist atrocities perpetrated against United States military personnel. A total of 13,239 United States Army, Navy, Marine, and Air Force personnel are known to have been either in a prisoner of war or a missing in action status since initiation of the Korean conflict on June 25, 1950. These figures show that a total of 4,631 have since been repatriated, or otherwise returned to our military control. As may be noted, we now reach a tragic void. I believe most of this discrepancy between the number of men returned and the number of those who are still listed as missing in action, and presumed to be dead, namely 8,608, is directly attributable to Communist mistreatment of their prisoners."

When the army chief finished, the next witness was sworn in and Senator Potter asked, "Colonel Wolfe, will you identify yourself for the record, giving your full name and your present duty assignment?"

"My name is Colonel Claudius O. Wolfe. I have just completed eighteen months' service in Korea and am presently on permanent change of station, from the staff of the judge advocate of the Korean Communication Zone for reassignment in the United States."

Colonel Wolfe proceeded to explain his former organization's role in Korea: "The responsibility was given to the army judge advocate of the Far East Command. On July 27, 1950, field commanders were advised as to the procedure to be employed in the collection and perpetuation of evidence relative to war crimes incidents. This was with the approval of the Department of the Army and the Department of Defense. The judge advocate general of the army was given general staff supervision over this operation. In order to define and clarify the limits of the investigation, war crimes were defined as 'those acts committed by enemy nationals or persons acting for them which constitute violations of the laws and customs of war and general application and acceptance, including acts in contravention of treaties and conventions dealing with the conduct of war as well as outrageous acts against persons or property committed in connection with military operations, whether with or without orders or the sanctions of commanders.' The investigations thus made would perpetuate all available evidence so as to document criminal acts and retain for posterity the evidence thereof and thereby fix responsibility at levels above that of the immediate perpetrators."

"In early October 1950, a letter order from the Far East Command transferred immediate responsibility for war crimes investigation to the commanding general, Eighth Army, and directed the establishment of a war crimes division within the judge advocate section. An organization consisting of a maximum of twenty-six officers, one warrant officer, and thirty-five enlisted men was provided for the investigating agency. This organization was initially divided into three branches: administrative, investigative, and apprehension. This group began operations at Seoul, Korea."

* * *

Private Martin would be the first POW from McDaniel's group to testify. As he settled into his seat, Senator Potter said, "Would you identify yourself for the record? Give your full name and your present military assignment?"

"PFC John E. Martin, 359th Engineer Aviation Supply Port Company, Bordeaux, France."

"What is your home address?"

"590 East Lewiston, Ferndale, Michigan."

"Tell the committee about the time you went to Korea and in what unit you were assigned to at that time?"

"I landed in Korea the twenty-first of July with the 29th Regimental Combat Team."

"Can you give the committee information concerning how you were captured?"

"It was during the withdrawal to the Pusan perimeter. The squad I was attached to became separated from the rest of the unit during the withdrawal. The next day we reported to the battalion headquarters and were put on a hill outside of the city of Chinju. We were told to stay on this hill as more or less of a check point and not fire on any troops or the road because they were our own battalion retreating.

Somewhere along the line someone forgot to set up a check point on the road. During the night our battalion had gone by and the North Korean Army had been going by for quite a few hours."

"I think if you could speak just a little louder. If you moved your chair a little closer or moved the microphones a little closer to you it would be better. You may continue."

"During the night and early morning the North Korean forces had been going by our position and when the sun came up the next morning we spotted them down there in the road. A firefight started. It lasted until about 12:30 that afternoon.

Just toward the end, we were surrounded and they had three tanks on the hill. I asked a friend of mine to toss me a grenade, and I could not see the man. A grenade landed in the foxhole and I picked it up, and it turned out to be one without a pin or handle."

"Without a pin or handle?"

"Yes, it was from the enemy. I threw it away from me, but the concussion knocked me kind of silly and I was captured then."

"You were captured by North Korean troops?"

"Yes."

"Was this in the Pusan perimeter area?"

"The perimeter had not quite been formed yet, sir. They were in the process of withdrawing to the perimeter."

"What was your location?"

"Chinju, Korea, just about ten miles from the city of Masan there." (See map on the last page of the book, both cities in most southern part of Korean peninsula.)

"Would you point out Chinju on the map? What happened after that. Did they take any clothing away from you?"

Indicating the location on the map near his table, Martin continued, "I went down to the bottom of the hill, sir, and there was a North Korean lieutenant there. The first thing he did was knock me down and he picked me back up."

"Did he knock you down with his fist, or rifle?"

"Pistol, sir. He picked me back up and asked me why I was fighting the People's North Korean Army. And two other soldiers came down from the hill and they told us to call for the rest to come down. We told them that there weren't any more people up there because to our knowledge there weren't. But he called again and a few of the men did try and come down walking and crawling, but they shot them as they came down."

"They shot them as they came down to give themselves up?"

"Yes, sir. Some of them were wounded and could not walk, so they just shot them there."

"What did they do to you after that?"

"They took us to what appeared to be their company aid station. We stayed there for about four or five hours. They asked us questions, not a very thorough interrogation, wanted to know our outfit. We all gave them different answers."

"You what?"

"We all gave them different answers. They marched us into Chinju about three miles away, and we met seven more prisoners there. We were met by a man wearing a Red Cross band that claimed to be a member of the International Red Cross, and he said that we would receive shelter and medical care and food."

"He said that you would receive it?"

"Yes. We were taken in front of one of the larger buildings in the city, and we were kept there until about five or five thirty that evening."

"How many prisoners did they have at that time?"

"We had ten men then. They brought in two wounded men a little while later. One was walking. The other one we had to bring in on the litter. About five o'clock that evening, the Red Cross—so-called Red Cross—man came back again and gave us all four or five little rice cookies about that big around." Martin showed the committee, making a circle with his forefinger and thumb.

"About the size of a half-dollar?"

"Yes. And some water. We were told we could rest there for the night, and we slept out in front of the building. The next morning, they came around and told us we were going north to a big prison camp with a lot of Americans. So we started out. They let us take the man on the litter at first, but in the middle of the afternoon of the first day, we had to put the man on the litter down. They would not let us take him any further. They said that he would receive medical care. We left him at a little village. I do not know what happened to him yet."

"You have never heard what happened to him?"

"No, sir. The other man was wounded through the hand, not seriously. He managed to keep up pretty well. It took us, I think, about five days to walk to Taejon."

"You started out from Chinju?"

"Yes."

"And marched to Taejon?"

"Yes."

Senator Potter directed his next question to Major Fenn, seated at the table with Martin. He was the army's technical witness. "Major, how far is that in mileage?"

"As the crow flies, it would be roughly eighty miles, but the road is quite windy."

"Had they relieved you of any of your clothing for that march?"

"No, sir. At the time, the only thing they had taken was my watch, a ring I had, and my wallet. We would have made it a little sooner, but we had to go across country the last two days. Their troops were coming from the north down the same highways that we used, and when we passed at night, they started moving us around and slapping us around in the road there. I don't think they moved us across country so much for our benefit, but just to keep their troops moving."

"When you would meet their troops, would they molest you?"

"They all stopped and took turns slapping us, yes. We went across country and got to Taejon. I think it took about five days. There was a large group of American prisoners there, about sixty men."

"How long were you in Taejon?"

"I spent my eighteenth birthday there, so we were there about six days."

"Did they confine you in Taejon?"

"We were, I believe, in the ... police station.... We were in the upstairs part of the compound, and the CP or whatever it was downstairs."

"Were you interrogated there?"

"They didn't bother me too much with interrogation that time as far as military stuff goes because, I suppose, I was so low ranking. But they wanted to know all about your family, what your parents did for a living, whether you had a car, whether you were reactionary or not. I told them my father was an electrician."

"Did that please them?"

"Yes. They were happy."

"I assume that they thought if he was an electrician then he was not a capitalist?"

"Maybe they thought he was part of the party or something, I guess. They kept us there, I think, about six days. During that time, there was a man in there who was later killed and had a badly infected leg. It had been infected with maggots and everything, so they found that they either had to cut it off or let the man die, so they did take him to some kind of hospital or something to cut it off, and one of our medics went with him, and when he came back he said they didn't use any anesthesia whatsoever."

"They amputated his leg without anesthesia?"

"Yes. They brought him back, left in a couple of old rags, and left him there."

"Were you beaten by the guards while you were there?"

"Only once, sir, when one of the guards wanted my shoes."

"The guards took your shoes at the prison?"

"Yes. He threatened me with a bayonet and poked me around a little bit with it, and one of the men that spoke Japanese said it would be a good idea if I gave them to him because he would probably use the bayonet on me. He took my shoes off and gave me his."

"Did his shoes fit?"

"No, sir. I wore a 9, and he wore about a 5."

"Could you wear his shoes?"

"I cut the toes completely out. I had about half my foot hanging out the open end. It was better to go barefooted."

"What were the circumstances under which they moved you?"

"I don't know exactly what the marching order was or anything, but they came through early in the morning. I don't know. *Bali, bali*—that's the only word I ever learned: 'hurry, hurry.' And took us outside when we started off on the march. They told us when we were going to Seoul we would be able to keep a more or less slow pace so our wounded could keep up and we could help them along, but it only took us, I believe, five or six days to go from there to Seoul."

"From there to where?"

"To Seoul. We did go about fifteen miles on a truck at one time, but the air traffic was so heavy we had to get off."

"The rest of it was by walking?"

"Yes."

"Were all of the men too weak to keep up with the march?"

"There were quite a few that were too weak. There were some of the men that were in Taejon when I got there and had been there for two or three weeks and some of them shot up pretty badly and they didn't get any medical attention to speak of. Maybe a doctor would come around and give them a bandage or something like that, no drugs or disinfectant."

"What would happen to the stragglers in the march?"

"The largest part of them, sir, if there was a village close, they would take five or six men and say, 'Well, we'll keep them here, and they will join you later in Seoul as soon as we get transportation,' but none of them have ever showed up. Some of them, if we were traveling pretty fast, some men fell out. I don't remember seeing them shoot anyone there, but I remember they hit one guy on the back of the head with a rifle pretty hard. He never got up."

"He stayed on the ground?"

"Yes."

"And the march continued?"

"Yes."

"What happened when you reached Seoul?"

After some generalities, Martin chose to focus on Mr. Kim's indoctrination classes and the fact that the Reds tried to compel the Americans to lead some class discussions. "At first, they tried to force the officers to do it. Then I think they more or less had the NCOs . . . . I think they kind of ran a roster on them, kind of a turn like. When it didn't take—the guys weren't paying much attention to it and arguing about it—they separated the officers from the enlisted men, thinking that the officers were instigators. They told us we needn't have any fear anymore, they would remove the officers. They took the officers in a room for about six days and beat them and didn't feed them so well. That made us worse, and they let us have them back."

Potter changed the topic, "Did the wounded receive medical treatment while they were in the prison in Seoul?"

"For a while when we first got there, sir, there was some kind of medical aid. There was a doctor that I actually believe was trying, but he wasn't given anything to work with and he didn't last very long. He was there just a week and a half or two weeks, and they moved him out."

"Were the prisoners beaten by the guards?"

"Yes, especially during classes."

"What other types of propaganda did they use at this camp?"

"Well, at first they had a few of us puzzled. Myself, I was only eighteen and puzzled. I didn't have my mind on world affairs very much at that time, didn't know much of the history of the last World War, and they used to throw one argument at us: about the Russians had invaded Korea as soon as the war had ended, whereas the Americans stayed offshore for a day or two, and that way they let the Japs loot everything where the Russians hadn't been afraid and we had, and actually I didn't know what to make of that."

"They didn't tell you that the war was over at that time, or practically over?"

"Well, we understood that it was the closing days of the war, but one of the officers of the group—I don't remember which one now—stood up and explained to all of us in the class that the reason we waited was because after two days we could make a peaceful landing and otherwise we would have had to make an armed invasion. And they were very angry and called him a liar, said that wasn't a fact at all, that the Americans were afraid of the Japanese. The officer said if we were afraid of them, how did we whip them all the way across the Pacific? And they told him to shut up and sit down. They didn't get very far with their classes."

Once the questions on the captivity in Seoul were complete, Martin would testify about the march to Pyongyang, beginning with the first significant halt.

"We went into some small village. I am not quite sure of the name. It was something like Kaesong. It may even have been Kaesong. I don't know. They put us in a factory building there, an old factory building. They claimed it was a school building, but it was built along the lines for a factory. I think we were there about four or five days. I lost track of time. During the time we were in there, the Koreans wouldn't even come inside the building to sleep. They slept outside, dug holes around the outside of the building." (See map on the last page of the book: along 38th Parallel.)

"Did they do that because they were fearful of Allied air attack?"

"Yes."

Then the questioner wanted to get some sense of the distances Martin walked as a POW.

"What happened from there? You were captured near the lower part of the Pusan perimeter."

"Yes; just above the ocean."

"And you marched by foot past the 38th parallel so far?"

Martin nodded in the affirmative.

"What would happen to the stragglers, to the POWs that were so weak they could not keep up with the march?"

"They were shot, sir."

"Shot?"

"Yes. Some of them were bayoneted."

"Who was in charge of the march?"

"North Korean officers."

"Were the men shot on orders of the officers?"

"Yes, definitely. There was a march order, a set pattern laid down from the beginning to the end of those marches."

"Were any of the prisoners beaten by the guards with their rifles?"

"Every once in a while. The officer at front always tried to hold the pace down."

"You are speaking of the American officer?"

"Yes, not others. They always walked behind where the shooting wasn't—"

"You walked about two-thirds of the length of Korea; did you not?"

"Yes."

"What happened at Pyongyang?"

"They put us in another school building, and our diet changed there from rice to bread. We had some kind of bread, not exactly like ours. It was so hard you couldn't bite it off. You had to break it off and then try and chew it. We got one loaf a day, about the size of two hotdog buns. I would say two good-sized hotdog buns. We stayed there. We had a lot of people die there from yellow jaundice, malnutrition, bad infections in their legs, and so on. And sometimes they wouldn't let us bury them for a day or two. They would be right in the same room."

"They would be in the same room as the ones who were living?"

"Yes. In fact, the men who were actually sick, almost dead, were right beside the dead ones sometimes for hours on end in the same room."

"How long were you there?"

"We were there—I'd say five days, sir. The night that they got ready to move us out we had quite a number of men in the sickroom, and the rest of us I think everybody was thinking about a break then. We thought we would try to get in the sickroom, too, and perhaps they would leave a little litter guard on there and we could get away. We went up, and the guards came in. They started really working the guys over. They left some of them right there on the floor. They beat them up so bad they never could get up."

"With their rifles?"

"Yes. I got my nose broken there myself."

"By a rifle butt used by a guard?"

Then Martin went on to describe the journey north on the train from Pyongyang to the Sunchon tunnel and how erratic it was due to Allied airpower.

"We thought at the time because of the air force."

"Our air force?" Potter asked.

"Yes. They did a very good job on trains. I thought they were afraid that the train could get tore up. Later on, it turned out that the air force was looking for us, that they found out in Pyongyang that we were on that train and were trying to throw us air drops. We were on the train two days, and while there, we had several of the men die there from malnutrition and different things. We didn't get fed. We got a little something the first night we got there, if I remember right, but we didn't get fed from that time on. When they finally did get ready to feed us, it was about three o'clock in the afternoon on October 21. They had us all get off the train. We were all in the tunnel there. The highest-ranking officer, two sergeants, and another corporal had already left earlier. There was some money collected by the prisoners supposedly to buy food. They haven't come back yet. They told us we were going to a small house to eat, and the reason we were going in groups was because it was so small."

"How many groups, did they say?"

"They were different sizes. I would say on the average of forty men to a group. The first group went out, and the guards were gone about twenty minutes to a half hour. When they left, we heard a lot of small-arms fire, but I never thought anything about it, and I don't think too many other people did either because we had been hearing quite a bit of fire on and off there. They came back for my group, and we started out and we went down the track about four hundred yards, and I had fallen back to the rear. My feet were pretty bad, and I had to keep falling back. I couldn't keep up with them. We went around the corner into this ditch. They said, 'Get down, the planes. Get down, the planes.' So when we all ducked down, some more of them come up on us over a little rice paddy and they just opened up."

"They fired on you?"

"Yes."

Martin then related what happened after the exterminations. "I stayed there until it got quite dark. Just after they left, until say an hour, we had heard small-arms fire after that time. We heard the train whistle blow and we all thought that they pulled out. So all the ones that were alive began to look around for others, and there was a man in the same ditch with me that was alive and wasn't hurt and a few others that weren't wounded bad, and there was a lot of guys that were all shot up, and everybody that we could move, we moved away from there."

"How many out of your group were alive?"

"Out of my forty—four, sir. There were more than four alive, but there were only four that lived until the troops got there."

"Only four that survived?"

"Yes. We crawled off in a field not far from there and hid in a hole—a hollow space. After they harvest their sugarcane, they stack the stocks together. We hid in there until the next afternoon, and people were coming around yelling for us to come out. We weren't quite sure whether it was friendly or enemy, but we took the chance and came out and the air force was there, and General Allen, and some of the 1st Cavalry Division, I think it was, and then we were all right."

"Then you were brought back to the States?"

"Yes."

"Were you hospitalized after you got back?"

"Yes, nine months."

"Nine months?"

"Yes."

Mr. O'Donnell intervened. "Mr. Chairman, I would like to have the record show that the Department of Defense, primarily JAG (Judge Advocate General's Office) in the army has the photographs of the actual marches. However, because the faces of many who are in the march were victims who did not survive, we have refrained from using those photographs, but they are a matter of evidence if ever needed in a court of law...."

Senator Potter then addressed the soldier, "Private Martin, you have experienced communism in its rawest form. Would you have any comment to make on communism as a way of life?"

"I don't think I have anything defendable to say, sir."

"I think that answers itself."

And then Senator Potter wrapped up the session, "I would like to say on behalf of the committee, and I think I can say on behalf of the American people, that we look to you with a great deal of pride. You certainly have been a great credit to your country and to your friends and your family. I know they are as proud of you as I am. You are a great American. Thank you."

* * *

Next to testify would be the soldier who wrote the most touching, but most haunting, letter to Helen as he suggested Major McDaniel was taken to Manchuria and not executed at Sunchon.

"Corporal, will you identify yourself for the record," Senator Potter asked. "Give your name, and your present unit assignment."

"Mr. Chairman, I am Corporal Lloyd D. Kreider, A13266788, 307th Airborne Medical Battalion, 82nd Airborne Division, Fort Bragg, North Carolina. My home address is West Willow, Pennsylvania."

"Corporal, when did you go to Korea and what was your unit assignment at that time?"

"I believe my unit was the first unit to reach Korea at the beginning of hostilities of the United Nations forces. We arrived the third of July 1950 a few miles south of Seoul."

"And you were a medical aid man?"

"Yes; I was a medical aid man with the 24th Division, 34th Regiment."

"Will you briefly describe to the committee, the circumstances under which you were captured?"

"The 34th . . . had been pushed back to the Pusan perimeter, and on about the fourth of August 1950, I believe the 34th was practically annihilated, overrun. Early in the morning of the fourth, the North Korean forces cut all through our lines, and I was taking care of a wounded man. I was trying to get him back to our rear from the Allied front."

"In the meantime this man died, so then I laid down during that day. I couldn't be seen during the day. On the night of the fourth, I traveled south trying to find my way back toward Pusan where I knew the Allied forces were. Then early on the sixth of August 1950, it was getting daylight when I was traveling, and I came into a ditch. There was a high bank on each side. I saw this communication wire laid across through this ditch."

"On the lengthwise of the ditch. So I followed the communication wire, thinking that this communication wire was an Allied communication wire, not knowing that the North Koreans answered the same. I followed this for quite a few miles, and I saw up on the bank some soldiers. I could not recognize them. They looked like American soldiers. So I came out of the ditch and walked up toward the hill and I was almost certain they were American soldiers, and about that time about four or five North Koreans walked down in front of me and raised their rifles, so I yelled to them in Japanese, as I can speak fluent Japanese."

"You speak Japanese?"

"Yes. I yelled to them to wait a minute in Japanese. At that time they hesitated, drew back their rifles, so I fell and started rolling down the hill and they started shooting at me. So then I went in the opposite direction, and I traveled most of that day, and toward the afternoon it was real hot and I was so tired. I could hardly walk anymore, and I heard the Koreans yelling at me, so I kept going. I didn't want to turn around and face them. Then they began to shoot, and one bullet ricocheted off a rock and just cut across my face right here, and I passed out."

"All this while you were still wearing your Red Cross armband?"

"Yes, I was."

"And was your helmet marked with your Red Cross?"

"My helmet was not marked at that time. I had a fatigue cap at that time, but I had a Red Cross band, and I had my medical aid pack with me."

"Was your band noticeable enough so they could tell?"

"I am sure they noticed it. They did not believe in the Red Cross because they told me later in the prison camp they did not recognize the Red Cross. It was a reactionary People's Red Cross. The only Red Cross was the People's Red Army Red Cross."

"The International, so far as they were concerned, was a reactionary organization?"

"It was supported by capitalists and things like that. That's what they told me. When I came to, the Koreans were standing right in front of me and I thought they were going to shoot me. They had their bayonets fixed, and I was thirsty and I asked them if I could have a drink, and they shook their heads, 'yes,' and I took a drink. Then they wanted all my clothes, everything but my pants, including my shoes. They took those too. The only thing they gave me was a Russian boot, but it wouldn't fit me."

"Just one boot?"

"Yes. I think that's about all they had. The only shoes that they had were a type of gymnasium shoe for their army. A lot of them didn't have very good footwear, and they were after American equipment. Then they kept me on the frontline for approximately a week, and they would make me carry water for them as they were afraid to show themselves in the open because of the Allied force. So I would carry water for them and carry them around to the trenches. At nighttime, they had a guard standing watch to see that I couldn't escape. They kept me there for about a week, and then they moved me on toward Seoul."

"They kept you near the place where you were captured?"

"Yes. I believe near Masan, right along the Naktong River, on the Pusan side." (See map on the last page of the book: in most southern area of Korean peninsula.)

"In other words, they kept you in a frontline unit?"

"Yes."

"Were you questioned at all while you were there in that frontline position?"

"I was questioned a few times. They wanted to know how many planes we had, how many tanks we had. I was only a private first class, but I guess they thought I knew everything we had and everything else, but we gave them any guess—one, two, five. They knew we were lying, so they'd keep asking us, and one day they took me and put a pistol to my head and said they would shoot me if I didn't tell how many planes we had, and so I figured they'd shoot me anyhow so I told them we all had a plane. They said, 'Where's yours?' and I told them I wrecked it. Then after that, they let me go. They didn't ask me about that anymore. Then they said, 'Why you come to Korea?' They asked me in Korean, 'Why you come?' I passed out at that time. I guess mostly from fatigue."

"It takes more than a Communist mind to understand a GI."

"When they questioned me, they get off the military angle. They begin mostly with the political angle. They wanted to know if I had a dad, what kind of a job he had. I told them he was a carpenter, and so they said, 'That's good. That's people's work, not the capitalist's work.' They asked what I was. I said I was a carpenter before. Then they moved me and about a week after they moved me, along the Naktong River they had a few more prisoners, American prisoners—believe approximately twenty-one or fifteen—and a good majority of these were pretty well wounded. One was shot right along the heart, came through the lung and came out the back."

"'You are a doctor. Cure him.'" They pushed me around. "'Why don't you heal him?'"

"Why cannot you what?"

"Why cannot I cure him. Cure his ills. So when we went out on the road march, we would travel all night. They took the wounded men and beat them up because they couldn't travel, and let them stay along the road. I guess they were killed, but I didn't see them being killed. They beat them with rifles and every sort of way."

"They beat the wounded men with rifles?"

"Yes, with the stock of the rifles. Every night we traveled. They would keep us at schoolhouses and churches, but they hated religion, one thing especially, Christianity. They didn't believe in Christians or any religion. That's one thing they really hated, and I noticed they still had churches. They said it was all right to have churches, but had to be under Stalin. They had Stalin's picture in every church and all over the place. In every building was pictures of Stalin and Kim Il Sung, the North Korean premier."

"It was all right for them to worship, but they had to worship according to Communist doctrine."

"They had no freedom of religion. They had to go by the laws of the Communist state. It seemed to me that way. I believe there was a lot of Koreans that had religious faith and they didn't want to suppress it too much, so they told them they could have their religion, but then they gradually shifted away into a dictatorship under Communist doctrine."

"How long did it take you to reach Seoul?"

"I would say approximately two weeks to get to Seoul."

"How long were you in Seoul?"

"Approximately three weeks or more, sir. I'm not sure. I have lost count of time and days, but I'd say approximately three weeks."

"What happened after you left Seoul?"

Kreider recounted the death march, the stay in Pyongyang and the train ride north. "So in the daytime we went right through Sunchon City. When we got on the other side of the city they took us off the train and took us to the other side of the field, and I figured they were going to shoot us. When the planes came over, they put us back in the train. We were so weak we could not hardly run or stand up. It was impossible to stand up, and we couldn't escape. Some of the men were so sick in soul and heart they didn't care if they lived anyway. They would as soon be dead as to go through any more torture."

"We got into a tunnel near Sunchon and they put the train in the tunnel. It was the morning of the twentieth of October. We were hungry. We made an SOS with our bodies lined up on the ground a few times. Our planes a few times dropped supplies to some of the men, C-rations. I believe the Red Cross dropped too, but I am not sure. But the North Koreans took the supplies and kept them. We saw a lot of planes going over that day, and we figured they were planes going to send food, but it was one of the 187th Airborne drops at Sunchon."

"About how many were in your group, Sergeant?" Potter asked, erroneously promoting the corporal, but remembering the Sunchon massacre involved multiple groups.

"I believe there were approximately forty in our group. They took us out in groups of forty."

"And out of the forty, were you the only two that survived?"

"That I know of there were only two, I and another survivor, a master sergeant. And I helped to take him back to Sunchon, helped to carry him back, because he was too weak to walk. We stayed in a corn shock that night."

"How long were you hospitalized?"

"I was hospitalized for two weeks."

"You are in the regular army now?"

"Yes, sir."

"Are there any questions?"

"Just one question, Mr. Chairman," Mr. O'Donnell intoned. "How much weight did you lose all told, Corporal?"

"I lost approximately 45 pounds. I was around 145 when I went there and came back with 100 pounds."

Mr. Carr, the committee's executive director, went next. "There was a lack of food along these marches, and in the camps. How about water? Did they give you water during the march?"

"That is something they would never hardly give us is water. I wouldn't understand. They said it would make us sick because the Americans poisoned the wells. They were telling us that, but we drank everything we got hold of. We didn't believe them, because many times we stole the water wherever we found it. They said it had to be boiled. So every once in a while they would give us a pot, very little for all of us, and they said it was boiled. It was cold, but they said it was boiled and it would be good for us! It was propaganda and it didn't make sense."

Mr. Carr continued. "When you were taken out of the train for this final shooting, was there any doubt in your mind but what this was a decision of somebody in authority?"

"I am sure it was a decision of authority because they took us out to shoot us that morning, and all the guards were in conference together. They took us out in the field that morning and put us back on the train and shot us the same evening. I am quite certain it was authority from higher up."

Then the chairman began his wrap up with the witness. "Corporal, I wish to thank you for relating this terrible experience that you have gone through to the committee. I know that it is an experience you would just as soon forget. I know that you feel, as does the committee, that if the American people know the true character of communism and the Communist leaders, that communism will hold little brief as far as they are concerned. After the experience you have had, do you care to make any comment concerning communism as a way of life?"

"Sir, I believe many people are of the opinion that because of this war that they commit these atrocities just to these soldiers. But I think it is the Communist theory all through to kill every subversive, to their theory of thinking everyone is subversive, and they want to destroy them. I believe communism in every country is the same thing."

"In fact, I believe the Communist in this country is even worse than over there, because these people know better at least have a little intelligence and know what a great country this is. In Korea a lot of those peasants had very little education and didn't know what they were doing, but did what they were told. But Americans, I think, know better than that."

Senator Potter expanded. "It seems inconceivable, doesn't it, Corporal, to understand how an American who has enjoyed the fruits of a good education, many of them have enjoyed material wealth in their own right, can accept and adopt the Communist doctrine as a way of life?"

"Right."

"We are very proud of you. I wish to thank you kindly, Corporal."

* * *

To break up the testimony of atrocity victims, Senator Potter called a high-ranking expert witness to the aftermath of both massacres of the McDaniel POW group—the cavalry officer.

"General Allen, we are pleased to have you here, and to have you supply some of the evidence which we have collected for this hearing. Would you identify yourself for the record, please?"

"Yes, sir. I am Frank A. Allen Jr., major general, United States Army, serial no. 07415, stationed at the Joint Chiefs of Staff in Washington, DC."

"General, you were in command of what unit while in Korea?"

"I was the assistant division commander of the 1st Cavalry Division. I went to Korea with the division about the fifteenth of July 1950 and remained with the division until February or March of 1951."

"You were in command of the troops that moved into the area near Sunchon tunnel, is that correct?"

"Well, may I explain it this way, sir, that the 1st Cavalry Division organized a task force, consisting mostly of armor that was sent in to the vicinity of Sunchon to make contact with and be of assistance to the airborne drop of the 187th Airborne Regiment. That force was commanded by a Colonel Rogers, the tank commander of the battalion of tanks which was organically a part of the division. It was one of my functions as the assistant division commander to see that those operations proceeded as well as could be expected. At the time the junction was to be made, I flew over and watched the armor column join with the 187th in the vicinity of Sunchon. I came back to Pyongyang, which was our command post at that time, where my jeep awaited me, and with an aide and a driver and two newspapermen, Don Whitehead of the Associated Press and Tucker of the *Baltimore Sun*, who happened to be at the airport. They said, 'Where are you going?' and I said, 'To Sunchon, to join up with the task force.' They said, 'We have lost our transportation, can we go with you?' I said, 'Yes,' and I proceeded then with them and my aide and the driver of the group and made contact with the battalion, Task Force Rogers, and then went in and made contact with the 187th Airborne Division, who told me that a ROK regiment was then coming into the town. The town was about a mile and a half or two miles from the road junction where the drop was made. I went in and joined up, I think, with the 7th Regiment of the 6th South Korean Division, ROK Army. It was there I learned of the shooting of the American prisoners."

"You went to the scene where it happened, is that correct? What did you or your troops find?"

"That is correct, sir. I was told through an interpreter that this trainload of American soldiers had been taken out, and they had witnessed the shooting of these people, this North Korean civilian. I was of the opinion that if they were that anxious to get rid of our people that they must have been in a very great hurry and unquestionably some of them must have remained alive. So with an interpreter and with one or two officers of our army stationed there with the ROK as advisers, we proceeded in ten to twelve miles farther and deeper into the North Korean country, to the vicinity of this tunnel. Our first visit to the tunnel brought out these seven cadaverous corpses. They apparently had starved to death. There wasn't a speck of flesh on their carcasses."

"Were they right in the tunnel?"

"They were right in the tunnel, near the north end of the tunnel. No train or anything in the tunnel save these seven bodies, naked. One of the local civilians in that area said that he thought there were some Americans loose. We shouted and made considerable noise, and finally, a response from the top of a hill about two hundred or three hundred yards away indicated there were Americans up there. I recall that my aide and I went up the top of that hill and met a group of five, four of whom were quite badly wounded. I think that my driver and Mr. Whitehead had proceeded the other way looking for some evidence of American troops in that vicinity. Then I heard a cry, from another source, of an American, so we came down the hill, and there we came across the most gruesome sight I have ever witnessed. That was in sort of a sunken road, a pile of Americans dead. I should estimate that in that pile there were sixty men. In the pile were men who were not dead, who were wounded. With the aid of one or two of the North Koreans in that area, we removed the dead from above the bodies of the wounded and brought them out. We, incidentally, found a very shallow grave, it must have contained at least sixty bodies, the other side of the road down maybe fifty yards from that place. We unearthed some of the bodies, but apparently, there were no live soldiers in that group."

"This first group that you met, that you ran into in the sunken road, had they been buried?"

"No, sir, they had not. There was no attempt to cover them with dirt whatsoever. They were just there, and one or two of them very badly wounded sitting on the side of the bank, unable to move farther. Others were called out of the hills. As has been testified to the committee, some of them came very reluctantly, not believing that we were Americans. After we discovered that we had, I think about thirty Americans alive out of that group, I sent my aide-de-camp, a Lieutenant Jack Hodes, with the jeep and a driver into Sunchon to contact the 187th Airborne and advise them that I would try to get the wounded in to them. They had no transportation, so we got the ROK Army to provide us with trucks, with straw in the trucks, and taking advantage of the number of people in the nearby village, we made them carry the wounded to the trucks, placed them in the trucks, and brought them into Sunchon, some ten to twelve miles, where the doctor from the 187th Airborne took care of them that night. Two died that night, I am sorry to say. I think we got out twenty-eight alive."

"General, you have had considerable military experience?"

"A lot of it, sir."

"And we know by your reputation and the awards you wear, that you have seen considerable combat."

"Correct, sir."

"Have you ever in your vast military experience witnessed the evidence of such beastlike treatment of prisoners as you ran across this time?"

"It was beyond my comprehension that any human beings could treat other human beings as badly as our men were treated by the North Koreans. I could hardly believe that a human being could be so bestial as these people were."

"Thank you very much, General."

* * *

When Senator Potter chose to call JB Smith to testify, the fact that he was a Negro army officer had implications beyond the Korean war crimes hearings: the evolving politics in the army and the nation with regard to Americans of African descent.

"Lieutenant Smith?"

"Will you raise your hand and be sworn. Do you solemnly swear that the testimony you shall give this committee will be the truth, the whole truth, and nothing but the truth, so help you God?"

"I do."

"Lieutenant Smith, will you identify yourself for the record, and give your full name and present duty and assignment?"

"My name is 1st Lieutenant James B. Smith. I am at present a student at the Infantry School, Fort Benning, Georgia."

"And where is your home? At present my home is in Franklin, Indiana, I was born in Columbus, Ohio."

"Will you tell the committee, Lieutenant, when you went to Korea and your unit?"

"Yes, sir. My regiment went to Korea on the 9th of July 1950, with the 24th Regiment of the 25th Division."

"I am sorry, I did not hear you."

"The 24th Regiment of the 25th Division."

"Would you tell the committee under what circumstances you were captured?"

"Yes, sir. Our regiment was fighting around Sangju, Korea. We were entrenched on a hill position north of the town of Sangju. The North Koreans struck the company I was in, the L Company of the 24th, about six o'clock in the evening, about dusk. I at the time had gone back by order of the CO to get chow for our unit." (See map on the last page of the book: southeastern portion of Korean peninsula.)

"Were you a platoon leader at the time?"

"Yes, sir. I was, and also the exec. I had brought the chow up to the base of the hill and it was about a three hour climb to our positions. That is when one of the other lieutenants came down and told me that the company commander wanted the battalion commander to know that we were under attack by a superior force, and he wanted further instructions. I immediately went back to the battalion commander's CP and told him the situation as had been told me, and asked what his instructions were. His instructions were for us to hold at all costs what we had, to tell the company commander that he was going to send in another company to reinforce and help us. As I went back up toward our positions, some of the men—the position had been overrun—some of them were filtering down. We held those who were not badly wounded there, and reorganized them. I say we, another lieutenant and myself."

"At the same time, we had to lay down a base of fire so that some of the other men that were coming down could make our positions there at the foot of the hill. About forty-five minutes later, the company that was to reinforce us came up the hill and we joined forces with them, the men that were able. I took a BAR and with the first squad of this reinforcing company I was directed to go up a saddle which would flank the access road which led to our positions. I went up this saddle with the first squad, reinforcing squad, and as we neared the top of the hill instinctively I noticed that it would be bad to walk up and expose ourselves, so we went around to the right flank on the inner side of the valley."

"We had gone maybe about three hundred yards when they opened fire over on the adjoining ridge, the ridge which ran parallel to the saddle. At that time they opened fire all around us and we found out that we had walked into an ambush, also. It appeared that bullets were coming from every direction, and we had to use grenades to kind of get ourselves out of the situation, because most of the men had tracers in their rifles and those tracers were giving away our positions."

"After a firefight of maybe, I would say or estimate, an hour. I was conscious that, well, I wasn't conscious of any other men being around with me. I was also conscious that there was a machine gun chattering up on the top of the ridge.

It wasn't too far away. I was about fifty feet down from the top of the ridge. So I worked my way up to the top, and I could see this machine gun firing with a group of figures around it."

"I used the BAR on the position and, after a while, ran out of ammunition. I started working my way back down the flank. Immediately hereafter, I noticed that our men didn't appear to be firing to the front anymore. They were firing to the rear and over to my right. That is where the main part of the fire seemed to be coming from. We started getting artillery on the hill, this ridge where I was, and one burst landed behind me and showered the ground with fragments. I started working my way down the hill and I could hear Korean or foreign voices. I assumed they were Korean. So I decided to try and figure out just what was going on. Well, I waited there maybe about fifteen minutes, working my way down a little further toward my lines, and then I heard a loud explosion in the valley."

"At that time I didn't know what it was, but I assumed that the North Koreans had come down the main road and had hit our battalion CP. I later learned that our battalion commander had to blow his ammunition, and they had orders to withdraw.

Later I also learned that they had sent up word for us to withdraw, but it never got to us. I stayed on the inside of the ridge for most of that night. I could hear North Koreans moving up on the top of the ridge and down in the valley all during the night. I figured that rather than run into them, I better wait until a little light came along so I could see where I was going and make my way out of there."

"The next morning in the valley the side that I was on, I could see North Korean troops coming down out in the open, and making no attempt to conceal themselves, going toward my rear, toward our lines. I then decided to work my way up to the top of the ridge close enough so that during the night I could work over the nose of the ridge and get on the other side and find out what was going on over there.

I had my field glasses to see if I could find out where my lines were. So that night I did that. I went over the nose of the ridge and worked my way down about a third of the way down this same ridge, on the opposite side. The next day I searched the surrounding country with my glasses and all I could see were North Koreans, down the main road, at our CP, and all over the area. Our artillery fire was landing around the CP, and around the road there, and the liaison airplane was flying over."

"Well, I decided that night, then, to work my way across the valley. I figured if I could work down to the road and across the road, I would get on the far side, which would be the east side of the road, and maybe outflank the enemy positions and work my way around to our lines."

"That night I went down the side of the ridge, which was a steeper side than the inside, the valley side, and it was quite difficult, but I was able to get down into the valley and work my way down there and across to a group of hills, say, approximately at the base, at the nose base of the hill. I stayed over there for the next day in some bushes and trees and things, a clump of small trees. North Koreans were still passing by on either side and making no attempt to conceal themselves, which I thought was rather odd."

"I finally figured that maybe our forces weren't very close. The liaison airplane was still coming over, so I concluded that our forces were still somewhere in the area. But firing had died down quite a bit, and artillery was no longer hitting us. The next night, I worked up over the group of hills and closer toward the road. That same night I struck . . . ."

"Incidentally, I didn't have any sleep. I stayed awake day and night because I didn't want to be captured. We had been shown pictures in the *Stars and Stripes*, about two or three days before, of our men with their hands tied behind their backs, and our battalion commanders told us to instruct all of our men that this is what they could expect if captured, to be shot in the back of the head with their hands tied behind their back. I made this blind, and during the night I also searched for food. I didn't have any food. I wasn't very fortunate. I knew there were potatoes in the area, but every time I would dig up a bush or something there would be no potatoes there."

"I was getting rather hungry. I got some water about the third day. Anyway, after constructing this blind I stayed awake the rest of that night, and mosquitoes helped keep me awake. They are very plentiful in Korea, and it is hard to sleep at night with them biting you all the time, anyway."

"The next day I fell asleep out of fatigue, sheer fatigue. I do remember as I wakened that I had one foot outside the blind, and I don't remember whether I snored or what, but I was conscious of a loud shouting. When I finally realized that the noise was real, and it was not an American, I sat up and when I sat up I looked right into the muzzles of four guns. There were four North Koreans facing me, all of them were facing me, and they had their guns leveled at me."

"Their rifles pointed at you."

"Yes, sir."

"What did they do to you then?"

"They were motioning for me to get up, and put my hands up. But I didn't catch on right away. I thought that they would shoot me. I mean I expected that. They kept gesticulating and waving their bayonets for me to get up. Finally I caught on so I stood up. Immediately they all rushed toward me, the four of them rushed toward me. One of them stood back a little bit and three of them started going through my pockets. I was pretty well loaded with—I guess you would call it booty, to them. I had a match, I had field glasses, I had my compass, and an extra pair of socks, a canteen, a mess kit."

"You were a lucky find for them."

"Yes, sir. I had practically all of my gear with me, and they were having a field day dividing the stuff up. Then they found I had one grenade left. I had carried it with me down the hill. I had a habit of hooking the handle in my pocket. I had saved that one grenade in case. I planned if necessary I would have to use it on myself rather than be captured."

"I had put it in my pocket, after losing it a couple of times coming down the hill and retracing my way up the hill to find it. I put it in my pocket and buttoned the flap. They found the grenade and started to get irritated. They started making signs as though they were going to throw it at me. It didn't faze me because I really expected they would do something like that."

"Then they gesticulated for me to go to the road. I started out ahead of them. I kept looking back. I thought they might jab me with a bayonet, and I wondered if I could catch it if they did. Anyway, they took me down to a group of officers in our CP. They said something to them, and they took me down farther to a road juncture, I would say maybe about a half mile toward our lines or toward the direction I thought our lines were. I didn't know at the time, but our men had been shifted fifty miles from the position where they were. There were no American troops in the area. They evidently didn't know that either because they were all holed up, rather entrenched, on the reverse slope of a ridge that paralleled what would be our front. They got me in there and they turned me over to some more of their troops, and a junior officer and the guards that had originally captured me went away. While I was there, no one spoke English very well. They did speak Pidgin English."

"They were coming up and asking me what I was doing there, and why I came to Korea, and 'Pretty soon you die,' and then they would point a pistol at your head and sometimes they would click the trigger. They would point a rifle at you. They would just take turns. One group would come up with the pistols and rifles, and then they would go away and another group would come up."

"Did they remove any of your clothing?"

"Not at this time. No, sir. Just my belt and all my gear. A little bit later on another officer came up—apparently a lieutenant, if I remember the ranks—and they took me down to the road and started walking back toward the CP, what had been our battalion CP."

"As they got up there, they got into a Russian-type jeep. No, let's see. We stayed on this hill until it started getting late in the afternoon. About dusk a Russian-made jeep came down with some officers in there, and they put me in there and turned around and took me north to what I believe was the area commanding unit, his CP."

"The reason I believe that is because it was well guarded all around by troops, and it was high up in a ridge. We had to walk up this ridge and it took us about two or three or about four hours, I guess, to get to the top of the ridge. He had a very good hideout up there where he could look at our lines. That is the place where I was given interrogation."

"What was the nature of the interrogation?"

"This one was strictly military."

"Strictly a military interrogation?"

"Yes, sir. They wanted to know how many men we had."

"Did they treat you pretty rough or not?"

"They started out treating me very kindly, and then when they found out that in answers to a lot of things I told them I didn't know, and a lot of things they suspicioned or knew were incorrect, finally one of their colonels, he had the shoulder epaulettes that I remembered belonged to a colonel, grabbed an American carbine up, and took the bolt back and made as if he was going to shoot me. This high ranking officer who took no part in the actual asking of the questions, he smiled when he did that, and the interpreter told me, he said, 'You have made the colonel very angry. He said you are lying, and he is going to shoot you if you do not tell the truth.'"

"I told him. I said, 'I have only told the truth. I don't know any more than what I have told.' They stopped right after this happened. The fellow who was interrogating me claimed he was a civilian, just going with the People's Army to write the glorious history of this particular campaign, and that he didn't understand English too well, he told me, but to speak and use simple words so that he could interpret for me. He told me that. They got another person in civilian clothes, carrying a burp gun, who came up and he spoke English very well, very fluently. He asked the same questions over, and I gave the same answers."

"So evidently that satisfied them. Then they took me from there and said they were going to send me up to Seoul where I would get chicken and rice, pork and rice, beef and rice every day, play cards, and everything would be real nice up there. It would be very good."

"They took me up there later on that evening. It happened that evening that the officer that was supposed to take me back, that they had assigned to take me back, evidently, either got separated from me or else in the confusion of the troops moving around we got separated, and I wound up going with the unit when they moved out. They moved the CP that same night, later on in the evening, or early morning. They moved the CP and I had to march with them."

"You marched with their troops?"

"I marched with their troops. I was still wounded and I was rather fatigued. I had had one meal by this time. After marching all that night I found it was pretty hard to keep up. But anyway, I kept up and they marched about three or four days until they got down near Waegwan." (See map on page

61: city just west of Taegu in southeastern portion of Korean peninsula.)

"You were marching south?"

"South—yes, sir. We got to Waegwan and we went through a tunnel. It was late in the afternoon. As we came to the mouth of this tunnel, the south end of the tunnel, they received rifle fire. So immediately they withdrew and I felt real happy. I said, 'Well, at least I know where our lines are, and maybe I can make a break and get away.' The unit took me then, the guard that had me, the unit that I was with, they waded across the Naktong River that night and evidently tried to flank our positions. But they weren't successful. We laid up on a hill across the Naktong River, the south line ridge, for about two or three days more. All this time, the airplanes were working us over, the artillery were working us over, and you could hear machine gun fire chattering to the front."

"Were you pretty well guarded?"

"Yes, sir. I was pretty well guarded, but my guards were beginning to get a little bit lax. Later on, about the third day, I attempted to make an escape, which was unsuccessful, and the next day I got hit by one of our rounds that landed about five feet from us—got hit in the hand. I had blood all over me, and this North Korean lieutenant sent me to the rear of their lines and back toward Seoul. I think his aim was just to send me to the rear of their lines. But anyway, I got back there, and I got picked up by another group, and the next thing I knew, we were walking again. I was the only GI in the group. It was a group of their wounded they were taking north toward Seoul. At least, I think they were going to Seoul. We started out in the group and got up to Yongdong. All this time, I had been with the army military personnel. At Yongdong, I was turned over to the civilian police." (See map on page 61, center of map.)

"Turned over to the civilian police?"

"It is some sort of a . . . well, they are in uniform and they had a green band around their hat. The red bands were usually the ones that the army had. And then there was also a group of civilians there. They put me in a jail there. I there met my first other Americans. There were about a dozen Americans in this particular jail, and they were about two or three to a cell, and the rest of them were South Koreans."

"How long did you stay there?"

"We stayed there about eight days."

"Did they interrogate you there again?"

"No, sir. No interrogation. They just took away my shoes there, and my underwear."

"Shoes apparently were quite a prized possession for them."

"Yes, sir. They were very valuable. I don't know why they took away my underwear, but they did. And it was rather cold there, and I tried to keep it. But it was a choice of getting a rifle butt or giving up my underwear, so I let them have it. It was at Yongdong that I saw one of our men clubbed with a rifle butt. He kept asking for water, and you got water twice a day, and in between that time you got a cup of water, a small cup. And in between that time, you just had to suffer. This man, evidently someone else might have taken his water and he kept begging for water. They came and struck him through the bars on his kneecap. It kind of lamed him. He never was able to walk very good after that."

"Also, they had another American there that they beat out in the center. The jail was circular. The cells were in a circle, and the big room was in the center of the circle of cells. We gathered from a few Koreans who could understand a little English, and some of them that could understand a little Japanese. I could understand a very little Japanese—we gathered they were trying to get this American to confess that he killed some civilian Korean. Eventually, they took him out.

I don't know what they did to him, I never saw him anymore. They made you sit on your haunches in a very uncomfortable position. You couldn't lay down until ten o'clock at night, and they would then give a signal, and everybody would stretch out in the cramped quarters they had. The food was very poor and very insufficient. It was kind of like millet."

"Did they treat your wounds there?"

"No, sir; they did not. Finally, on the eighth day, they took the Americans out and a few of the South Koreans, and they wired us all together with regular communication wire around our wrists. We saw the truck there, so we figured they were going to put us in a truck, which they did. The truck was so crowded that we had to stand up, and it was very uncomfortable."

"The airplanes were still out patrolling at night, B-26s, and every now and then they would have to stop the truck and jump off. The guards would jump off and leave us on the truck, while they would run and hide from the airplanes. Quite often the planes dropped flares but never strafed our particular truck. We went on up to about, I would say, twenty-five or thirty miles from Seoul. I think it is Chungju, or something like that, and there we were put in another jail, a red-brick jail, where we met some more Americans that they had collected there. (See map on the last page of the book: city southeast of Seoul.) Here the food was about the same . . . and the treatment was about the same, except that they had one guard who delighted in blowing cigarette smoke through the peephole and asking if you wanted a cigarette. If you said yes, he would blow smoke through. That was about the only diversion."

"We started out from Chungju, and they had two vehicles. They were just taking Americans. They had a three-quarter ton and a jeep. Practically all the men tried to get into the three-quarter ton because it provided a little more cover from the chilling winds. It was nighttime."

"What time of the year was this?"

"This was the middle part of August. No, it was late in August. I am sorry. It gets especially cold in Korea at night. We started out. I and another GI were left to go in the jeep. The jeep had a radiator that leaked, and the mechanical condition wasn't very good, and it kept stopping. Pretty soon the three-quarter-ton left it."

"In this jeep, also, there was a high-ranking civilian, a North Korean, a judge of some type who was carrying some valuable papers, I later learned. We begged them for something to throw around us, a sack or something, because it was so cold. They denied it."

"We were huddled together for warmth. We got up to the Han River bridge at Seoul, and for some reason the driver tried to go across the bridge, which had been bombed out in the early days of the war. He was supposed to take a ferry across there. Why he didn't know that, I don't know. But we heard a cry of alarm from one of the guards, and he jumped off the jeep. At the same time I happened to look out in front, and I knew that there wasn't any road there. About that time, and it all happened so quick, the jeep started dropping down toward the Han River. It seemed to be about a hundred feet or more drop."

"When we hit the water, it flung me out up over the other GI; we just crossed over in the air and into the water. As I went out, some cans hit me, and a spare tire that he had in the back. We got in the water and splashed around. It seemed for a period as if my back was broken. I was trying to make a girder. Part of the bridge was down there in the water, and I was trying to get over to one of the railings that was not too far away from me."

"I finally made it over there, and one of the other guards had climbed up on this same railing, and the guard that jumped off at first was up on the top shouting in Korean. I don't know what he was shouting. The fellow who was with me was clinging on the opposite side to the roadway railing. Pretty soon a ferry came out, and they put us on this ferry, the bottom of it. We had trouble getting in. They had to haul us in. They tried to find this civilian North Korean, but they couldn't."

"Well, they took us in to the shore, and we were able to crawl out on the bank. They asked us if we could walk, and the other fellow had the same difficulty I had. For some reason or other, we just didn't seem to be able to get up. They threw rice mats over the top of us, and we got as close to each other as we could to try to get warm."

"That night, several times, guards would come down and lift up the rice mat and kick us or something like that, and then go away. The next morning, one guard came down and told us to get up. We made an attempt to get up but were going too slow for him."

"He let us know if we didn't get up, he was going to shoot us. So we got up, and we supported ourselves. Each of us supported the other. With that assistance, we got up into the village. They took us to a police station there, a checkpoint, and then later on they brought up the body of this North Korean civilian. He had slit his skull open when the jeep went down, and it killed him. Evidently he was of such high rank and of such importance that they were very much disturbed that this had happened, because a lot of high-ranking officers came out during the daytime and rode a jeep, which is something. They weren't traveling too much in the daytime, and they rode out there to view this man's body and to get the briefcase. Also, they got this driver, and they were giving him a hard time for how this accident happened."

"The driver, you could tell by his motions and so forth, was trying to make out as if the other GI had tried to grab the wheel. He kept mentioning, *hongo, hongo*, like airplane came over. There never had been any airplanes over."

"This other GI, he made a movement that caused him to go off the bridge, is what he said. They didn't appear to be believing it. We were hoping, both of us, that they would take time out and shoot him. What happened, I don't know. The officers came out, and the one who received the briefcase took us into Seoul proper in a jeep. We thought we were going to get medical attention. They took us into what I thought was formerly a hotel there, one of the large buildings in Seoul, and took us in the basement of it. It had blackout curtains around all the windows. When we got in there it was a big, plush office and they asked us why we came to Korea—there was a civilian there—and a few questions along that line, with nothing military."

"We kept asking for medical attention. They said, 'You will get medical attention later,' which we never did. They were going through this briefcase. They were very much interested in the contents of the briefcase. It was very important. Anyway, they took us the next morning from this hotel to a compound in the city of Seoul."

"To a compound in Seoul, did you say?"

"It is a compound, but it wasn't the prison compound. It was an area that had a large, very decorative oriental gateway, and it had a fence around it, a very decorative fence. It reminded me of a palace, an oriental palace. It might have been.

Anyway, they took us in there, and we were interrogated separately by a—"

"Mr. Kim?" interrupts Mr. Jones, the staff researcher for Potter.

"No, sir, not Mr. Kim. A person in what appeared to be civilian clothes. I had never seen before that time a Chinese army uniform. I didn't realize that it was a Chinese army uniform until after I was back in Japan and the Chinese got into the war."

"But this was a man in a Chinese military uniform. He asked the usual questions about why we came to Korea, and were any Japanese troops there, and what did my father do, what kind of work. I told him my father was a carpenter, which was true. That made him feel pretty good. He asked me what I did, and why I was fighting against the North Koreans. I told him I was a truck driver. He said, 'That seems funny, but all the Americans that we have captured are all truck drivers.' He said, 'None of them are combat soldiers.'"

"He went on from there, and he said, 'You don't seem to have done very much hard labor. Your hands are soft.' That is one thing they did all along the line, they would look at your hands. I guess they were trying to find out whether you were a machine gunner, a worker, a laborer, a capitalist, or something of that type. He wanted to know who my relatives were, and if I knew Paul Robeson, if I ever went to see him, and if I ever heard him. And if I had ever been a member of the party. He always got negative answers and seemed to be very disturbed. The thing that disturbed me most was when he asked me if I was a Christian, and I said 'Yes.' He shook his head on that. He couldn't understand that."

"Did he try to raise the racial issue?"

"Yes. He tried to raise it. He asked me if I had ever seen any lynchings or things like that. First he asked me if I had ever been lynched, and I wondered how he expected me to be there. So he said the next day that I would go to the rest of the American prisoners in Seoul, get good food and everything else, play cards all day, and have a good time."

"Well, we went the next day to this compound. We got there late in the evening. That is where I met Mr. Kim, and he always wanted to be called Mr. Kim. You had to be very polite to him. The fellow that was with me made a little error as he came in, and he called him *boisun*. Kim just blew his top when he said that. He tried to get the fellow, but it was dark and he couldn't locate him again. They had a radio going when I came in, and it just seemed by coincidence that Sioux City Sue, we called her Rice Ball Kate, was broadcasting that I had been captured, and with me two other lieutenants of my company, the same company that I was in. That disturbed me greatly, and I wondered if that were true. I had reasons to doubt it, but I didn't know if she was telling the truth or not."

"Anyway, Kim had told me when I came in, he gave me the interrogation when I came in, and told me where I was to be quartered, and what I was not supposed to do. I wasn't supposed to go downstairs in the hall. If we had to go to the latrines, you had to go around the end, and use the upstairs hall, things like that. He said, "You are to listen to radio. Rice Ball Kate comes on in the evening, and it is very good for you to listen."

"The next evening the radio was taken out, or I guess it was the third night it was taken out. The reason for it being taken out was this: Kim went in on that particular day, the third day, and he caught one of the GI's tampering with the radio. He asked the fellow, 'What are you doing.' They had one station they kept it on and they had all the knobs off it so you couldn't change the station and the fellow didn't think and he said, 'I am trying to get Tokyo!' That did it. Kim started cursing, and he took the radio out."

"The reason he wanted to get Tokyo is the fellows told me they had been getting Tokyo every evening when Kim wasn't around, and they could get the true picture at that time, when they heard the newscast from Tokyo."

"How long were you in the prison at Seoul?"

"I was in Seoul I think for about two or three weeks. Anyway, I was up in Seoul until about the twentieth of

September. Most of this time, I was lying flat on my back, allowing my back to heal."

"Evidently, there were no bones broken, but if there had been any broken, I wouldn't have received any care for it. About the last week, I was walking around pretty good. I still was shuffling, and the other fellow with me was doing the same. He was able to shuffle around."

Having heard about Smith's capacity to walk before departing Seoul, Senator Potter turned to the lieutenant's observations on the Seoul to Pyongyang death march. "Did they treat the stragglers pretty rough?"

"Yes, sir. The little lieutenant that was in charge of the group, you could tell he hated Americans worse than any of the Koreans, apparently, that he has ever come across. He shot two that I saw, personally, and one of the guards—"

Senator Potter stopped Smith. "This lieutenant shot two of the wounded? Were they wounded?"

"Practically everyone in the group was wounded someplace. They each had straggled blindly, and he had shot them. One of the guards shot another man who had not even straggled. He had fallen out of line. He had dysentery. If you had to relieve yourself, you had to run up to the head of the column or get someplace where the column's end would come past you. If the column's end got to you and you were not finished, you had to get up and run further. This man had made the attempt and was getting up to run forward and this guard came up and he shot him right through the head. I saw that because the Major in charge of the group, the senior officer."

"The American?"

"Yes, sir. He had various officers get to the end of the column every now and then to try to keep down that type of thing by trying to ask the men to keep up in line, and also to give him reports on what went on there. He had officers at the end of the line and the front of the line, and in each group.

Also, the men were so hungry that they would try and dart out of the column to pick squash and cucumbers and things like that, and corn, out of the field. Every time they did that, the guards would shoot at them or throw rocks at them or run up with a stick, to get them back in line. They said all of that food belonged to the people of North Korea, and we weren't to touch it."

Then Smith recalled the stint in the North Korean capital. "When we got to Pyongyang . . . the Major had me in charge of the sick up there in Pyongyang, the sickroom. Each officer was assigned a room, one of the schoolrooms, with a group of men. The men were dying pretty fast there, and he asked me to go along with them and see that they were decently buried as much as possible, under the supervision of the North Korean guards, and also to make a record of where they were buried and to see that they always prepared a bottle with the man's name, rank, and serial number and other data that we could gather placed in this bottle in the graves."

"How many men did you bury?"

"I buried about twenty men at Pyongyang."

"Did they have other burying details too?"

"Not in Pyongyang. No, sir. They did along the road, though. After we buried about three men, some of the North Korean civilians seemed to be in sympathy with us, we noticed. They would come up and give us apples and a kind of a cake, a grape sugar-flavored cake, and chestnuts and corn. We would carry this back and divide it mostly with the sick men or someone that was in need, and then we would eat some of it ourselves. We had almost a permanent burial detail and used the strongest men."

"How were the men buried? Did they have a deep grave?"

"Yes, the grave was pretty deep. We would dig down about four or five feet. We were only able to do that because, quite often, the civilian North Koreans would jump up and help us dig the graves. This was done only because they were friendly to us."

"In other words, you had some North Koreans that, while they were still under Communist control, were still sympathetic toward the Americans and some South Koreans, is that correct?"

"Yes, sir. That is correct."

"From there, well, that is where I made my escape, I and four other men. Before I tell you about the escape part, I would like to bring in another thing. While we were working during the day, every now and then we would get a pamphlet from one of the civilians, pamphlets that had been dropped from airplanes."

"From our planes?"

"From our planes, yes. It said, 'Do not harm the prisoners of war. The war is lost. Surrender and treat our prisoners well, or you will be brought to task for it.' It was signed by General MacArthur."

"We would carry these back and show them to the Major. We would try to figure out what was going on. We figured maybe our forces were coming north, or maybe going to plan another end sweep. We found out they had landed at Inchon because three marines were added to our group as we traveled north, and they told us about the landing at Inchon."

"About this time the men started making plans and trying to escape. They all concluded they would not travel north, that they couldn't make it. The Major said that was fine, that they had his blessing but that he would stick with the main group so that he could try and see them through."

"Were you hospitalized as a result of your experiences?"

"Yes, sir. I was. I went down to 114 pounds."

"114?"

"Yes, sir, from 165."

"Any questions?"

Mr. Donnell spoke up, "Mr. Chairman, I would like to get a quick recap, if I may. Actually, how many American POWs during the march did you see killed?"

"That I personally saw, was three, sir."

"How many do you know of that were actually killed?"

"I got reports from the men in the group that I was with, in the back, that would total twenty men."

"From the time you were captured and started your march until you escaped, how many American POWs did you assist in their burials?"

"From the time that they started the march? From the time we started the march, I have accurate notation on that."

"What I would like to get is a summation, if I could."

"Yes, sir. I made notes of everything that went on a piece of paper I had which was turned in when I got back to American hands."

"Take your time, now, in looking at your notes."

"Eighteen, sir."

"Eighteen?"

"Yes, sir."

"Thank you very much."

Senator Potter asked if anyone else had questions and when there were no takers, he said, "Lieutenant, I wish to thank you for giving us the benefit of your experiences. I would like to say this, as I said before today, that it makes you proud to be an American when you hear the valor of the men who have testified here today.

I think probably the history of Korea when it is written will go down as having some of the most courageous action of any military experience that American troops have participated in. I think that you who have been fighting the war in Korea, whether you are Irish, Jewish, Negro, or whatever race you might be, are a great credit to us as Americans. We are all a mixed race. I know that the Communists put on a great effort, made a great effort, to incite race hatred, to pit one group against another. I am proud of the record of American soldiers of all races, and the Negro race. The Negro soldiers that are fighting in Korea can hold their head very high. You are a credit not only to your race but you are a credit to our country. To you, Lieutenant Smith, who testified here today, I am saying this to you, but I mean it for all Negro troops."

"Thank you, sir."

"I would like to ask you one question before you are released, a question that I have asked others. Did the Communists endeavor to indoctrinate you when you went through their propaganda mill?"

"Yes, sir."

"What do you think of communism as a way of life?"

"Sir, personally, I hate communism and anything communistic. As a way of life, I believe that they are totally wrong. I personally would relish fighting against it any place at any time."

"Thank you. The committee will recess for today. We will begin tomorrow at 10:30."

* * *

On the second day of the hearings, only Bob Sharpe from the McDaniel POW group testified. He was now a noncom, and his army career was already taking off.

When Sharpe was seated, Senator Potter began, "Sergeant, will you identify yourself for the record giving your full name and your present unit assignment?"

"I am Sergeant First Class Robert Sharpe. I am presently assigned to the 14th Antiaircraft Artillery Battalion, Fort Myer, Virginia. My home address is Pledge Street in Burlington, North Carolina."

"Sergeant, when did you go to Korea and what unit were you assigned to at the time?"

"I landed in Korea the Fourth of July, 1950. I was a medical aide attached to the 19th Infantry Regiment of the 24th Infantry Division."

"Can you give the committee the circumstances under which you were captured and your assignment at that time?"

"I was a member of George Company, attached as a medical aide man, and along the Kum River we were having a battle. My company was just north of Taejon. My company was assigned to run a blockade and get the 1st Battalion free.

We went on foot and they were in vehicles. We broke the blockade and the vehicles got through, but we were on foot. We couldn't get out."

"So we lost communications between the platoons, and my platoon was the fourth platoon. We had lost all communications and at this time the lines—we were encircled—the lines were going back. We were approximately twenty miles behind when we realized we couldn't get back, so we decided that we would try to get back as a group and we were going south and we went through a little ravine or valley and they started firing."

"It was a perfect place for an ambush. The enemy fired from both sides of the hill. A machine gun was in front of us and behind us. There was no escaping. There were forty-three men in the platoon, and after two hours of continuous firing, they killed all of the forty-three but four men. The enemy came down to the group and searched our bodies, took most of the valuables, the shoes, the weapons, and left, thinking that the other four were dead."

"The three and I went into the hills to try to get back at night and, after four days without anything to eat, I was the only one that wasn't wounded, I decided that I would go down into a village and try to get some food. And while I was in that

Korean village to get food, I had lost all caution. I had thrown it away because I was starving and I went down to a Korean farmer and I got some food, and while I was at the house, the North Korean guerrillas or police circled the farmer's house, and when I came out they started firing in the air and up to this time I had seen at least two people with their hands tied behind their back and shot, so I decided that I would shoot myself and I took the pistol I had and tried to do it, but I couldn't shoot myself and I dropped the pistol and one of the guards rushed forward and kicked me, and I fell backward and they beat me."

"Finally, a North Korean officer stopped them from beating me, and right off the bat, he started asking me political questions. What did I think about our president—the president at the time? What did I think about our military headquarters? That's the type questions he asked me. From here, I was taken to a prison in . . . ."

"Was that an officer that questioned you?" Potter interjected.

"It was an officer."

"From here, I was taken to a police station in Taejon. At Taejon they separated the people and started interrogating them one at a time, and they would take us in and they would ask us questions. Why do you fight for the Americans? They ride around in Cadillacs, smoking cigars and everything and having a big time. Questions of that type."

"They would get the colored fellows away and try to turn them against the white fellows."

"How many prisoners were there at that time?"

"Approximately, at Taejon, there were about forty prisoners—forty at this time. At least one-fourth of the forty prisoners were wounded. One fellow had his foot broken off. They had no medical aid, the Koreans, none at all."

"They received no medical attention at all?"

"No."

"Did the guards beat you?"

"Yes, sir, they would beat us. If we did anything at all they thought was wrong, which we couldn't help, we had to go to the latrines and relieve ourselves at times, and when they would catch us downstairs they would beat us with the rifle butts. And the officer in charge at this Taejon camp, he'd beat as much if not more than any of the soldiers. He was in on it too."

"How long were you there, Sergeant?"

"Four days. After four days we left Taejon and we started north. We came into another little town just above Taejon, named Chochowan."

"Had they removed your shoes?"

"They had removed our shoes and most of our clothing. We only had a pair of fatigue pants on. They took us to Chochowan. It seemed they tried to put us in buildings that were conspicuous, that our planes would he sure to hit. They put us in a big building at Chochowan, and our planes, not knowing that it wasn't a military target, not knowing in any way, hit the buildings, and they had wheelbarrows to take out the people that were killed. The only way you knew who was dead was to count who was alive."

"At Chochowan, they didn't question us much about anything. They just kept us out for a short period of time. From Chochowan we went north to Chonan and at Chonan we went with South Korean prisoners. They put us in the same building with South Korean prisoners." (See map on page 63: city northwest of Taejon at top left corner of map.)

"I remember an officer came in one day—he was a colonel: had three big stars, was equivalent to our colonel—and he had a big meal set before him and he had it and we didn't have anything to eat. Our rations up to this time was about one rice ball a day, about the size of a baseball, and he sat down and ate his meal bit by bit and when we were watching him eat the meal he stood up and said, "My God fed me this meal. You ask your God to feed you and see what happens."

"In other words, he meant that the Communist state was providing for him?"

"And we couldn't have anything."

"As to the march that you made, has this been on foot?"

"All the way on foot."

"In your bare feet?"

"Yes, sir. They took all of my clothing and shoes."

"What time of the year was this?"

"This was in the summertime, in July. From Chonan we were taken to Suwon, which is just south of Seoul. At Suwon they kept us about five to six days, and then they took us to Seoul. Seoul was the first any semitype permanent camp we were in. We stayed there about a month and at Seoul they put us in a South Korean school for girls. It had previously been a school for girls—separated groups and started indoctrination. They gave us Communist literature and magazines and they showed us movies that had been taken in Russia."

"Was that the same camp where Mr. Kim was propaganda man?"

"That is the same one."

"Did you ever see the guards shoot?"

"I witnessed two personally. And the junior lieutenant who was in charge from Seoul to Pyongyang did one of the shootings. He was the man in charge of the group."

"It was an officer who did the shooting?"

"Yes, sir."

"See the big difference. Our way of life is based upon the dignity of the man and their man is subjugated to becoming a cog in a diabolic Socialist machine known as communism," the senator asserted.

"That is right."

The senator then began his usual finale asking about Red ideology. "Sergeant, you have seen communism in the cold hard light of the experiences that you went through. Do you have any comments about Communists in the United States who would like to overthrow our form of government and substitute communism?"

"Yes, sir. I think that I know communism just about as good as anybody else. I have lived with it. I have watched their soldiers. I have watched when they were together. When they were by themselves they were talking to you, they were nice people, but when they would get together in groups they were afraid of each other."

"They would inform on each other. That's communism. As far as communistic people in this country, it is inconceivable to me to think how a person can hide behind the flag of a glorious country like ours and still stand for something like happened in Korea. They are far worse in my opinion than the people we were fighting in Korea.

"Is it not true, Sergeant, that Communists in the United States receive the orders from the same sources . . ."

"Yes, sir," Sharpe preempted.

" . . . as the Communists in North Korea that massacred you in Sunchon?"

"That is true."

"Sergeant, I want to extend to you the thanks of the United States Senate and of the American people for appearing here and retelling an experience which I know you would like to forget."

"Yes, sir."

"What I have said for the other men certainly goes for you. You are a great man. You can go through life with your head high, and we salute you."

"Thank you."

"Thank you, Sergeant."

* * *

On the third and last day of the hearings, Makarounis and Locke would be the last to testify. They were also the two who had contributed the most to the *Argosy Magazine* story that was the definitive public—unclassified—account of their POW ordeal.

"Captain, do you swear the testimony that you are about to give will be the truth, the whole truth, and nothing but the truth, so help you God?"

"I do solemnly swear."

"Captain, will you identify yourself for the record, giving your full name and where you are stationed at the present time? I believe you have a prepared statement. Is that true?"

"Yes, I do."

"Feel free to go right ahead and give your statement. I believe it is correct that you have written an article outlining the experience that you have had, so if you care to read from your prepared statement feel free to do so. What is your home address, Captain?"

"My name is Alexander George Makarounis, Captain, Infantry, 058962, United States Army. My home address is 548 Fletcher Street, Lowell, Massachusetts. My military address presently is the Walter Reed Army Hospital, Washington, DC."

"My story as told here is what I personally saw, heard, and suffered along with hundreds of other fellow American soldiers who were captured by the Communist North Korean Army. What I personally did not see or hear I was told from the lips of fellow American prisoners with my group. To allow me to relate my complete story would take hours and thousands upon thousands of words, for there is much to tell. This committee in executive hearings agreed to allow two magazine articles into the record, one of which appeared in

March 1951, in *Argosy*, and again in April 1953, in *Adventure*. This story is titled 'I Survived the Korean Death March.' I have a copy here I would like to show. This was the picture when I was first liberated on October 20, 1950, in Pyongyang, North Korea."

Mr. O'Donnell asked, "Captain, may we have that made a part of the record as an exhibit?"

"Yes."

Senator Potter expanded, "It will be made a part of the record." (The article was marked as Exhibit No. 22 and may be found in the files of the subcommittee.)

"This picture shows a beard of approximately three months. I never knew I had that heavy a beard, but I do now. The second article is in the Roman Columbian Fathers Publication, *The Far East*, published in May of 1951. This story is titled 'I Met Them in Jail.' Namely, three Columbian fathers—missionary priests."

Mr. O'Donnell, again, asked permission, "Could we prevail upon you to let us have that as an exhibit?

"Yes, sir. This story is fact, as told in my own words by me in November 1950 following my liberation as a prisoner. This is the truth, and it is the actual thing as I saw it and told back in 1950. My story tells of the suffering, the wounds, and the courage and guts of our soldiers, officers, and Columbian Father missionaries. It establishes our treatment as captured and wounded American soldiers and Roman Catholic missionaries in the early days of the Korean War. It shows the filth, the brutality, the forced Communist interrogations and propaganda thrust upon us, and the nonexistence of medical care, the lack of food to survive, the forced continuous marches, and the infamous Korean death march from which 33 out of 376 survived and are alive today."

"To corroborate this infamous death march story, a Major William Locke (air force), Lieutenant James Smith, Lieutenant

Douglas Blaylock, Sergeant First Class Sharpe, Sergeant First Class Kumagai, Corporal Arakawa, Private First Class Martin, Mr. Sylvester Volturo, and a small number of others who make up the thirty-three sole survivors from the Korean death march and the Sunchon Tunnel massacre, which is the one and same group that I was prisoner of. I shall read excerpts from this story, which tells in over thirty-one thousand words the numerous details, names, places, conditions, and other facts of evidence."

"The who, when, where, what, how, and many times why is told here. This is actually something instilled in us as basic trainees in the United States Army. I was company commander of I Company, 29th Infantry Regiment, stationed in Okinawa.

In July 1950 we were alerted for duty in Japan following the outbreak of hostilities in Korea. This was changed a few days later to movement to Korea, the place of hostilities. While waiting to go to Korea, I remember the photograph carried in the Far East publication of the *Stars and Stripes* of the first atrocity that was committed in the war by the Communist North Korean Army. It was that of four American soldiers, whom I believe were drivers of jeeps with trailers carrying ammunition to the front, who had their hands tied behind them and were shot through the head and back. This was a violation of the rules of land warfare."

"Having been assigned to duty with German prisoners of war during World War Two, I was extremely familiar with the Geneva Convention rules governing prisoners of war. Being a soldier I am familiar with the rules of land warfare adhered to by all civilized countries of the world. We landed in Pusan, South Korea, on the morning of July 24, 1950. Only two battalions of the 29th Infantry Regiment were committed from Okinawa. They were the 1st and 3rd Battalions. From Pusan, we moved on to Masan . . . . We became attached to the 19th Infantry Regiment at Chinju. On July 25, 1950, my battalion, the 3rd Battalion of the 29th Infantry Regiment, received a mission of moving to the area of a town called Hadong and engaging around two hundred guerillas. Instead of two hundred guerrilla troops, we engaged leading elements of four Communist North Korean divisions moving down to form what we commonly known as the Pusan Perimeter. The 3rd Battalion was practically decimated at Hadong on July 27, 1950. I was shot through the back and taken prisoner." (See with "map on page 61: cities in a horizontal line at bottom of Korean peninsula.)

"The first atrocity I knew and believed beyond any doubt was committed by the Communist North Korean Army was on July 27, 1950. Up to eighteen to twenty-four multiple wounded American soldiers from our battalion were left behind at a road junction approximately two hundred yards from the place of my capture. They were murdered by the Communist army, for I saw them alive. They were piled up one on top of another in a pile. We never saw them again, and their bodies were never found. I believe they are still listed as missing in action by the Defense Department."

"Our battalion had a handful of South Korean soldiers and officers attached to it. Among them was the former South Korean chief of staff of the army who had been relieved following the fall of Seoul. My company, I Company, had three such South Korean soldiers attached to it. These South Korean soldiers, when captured by the Communist army, were murdered by being bayoneted in the rice paddies on the 27th of July 1950. This was following their capture as prisoners. Their number was from five to ten. This was reported to me by fellow American soldier-prisoners from my company who had seen this atrocity committed on the battlefield."

"I estimated approximately 150 American soldiers from our battalion were captured on July 27, 1950. The majority were wounded. The Communists loaded about six of our own captured jeeps and took approximately thirty seriously injured prisoners into the town of Hadong, a distance of four miles. The remainder of the prisoners marched into the city."

"During this ride hundreds of Communist army troops marching on either side of the road of these four North Korean divisions would swing their rifles at we prisoners on the jeeps striking many of the prisoners, who were wounded. The one and only time we received medical care during my captivity was on the evening of July 27, 1950. Four North Korean Communists army medical first-aid men applied some sulfanilamide, some iodine with a strip of gauze to approximately thirty of the captured seriously wounded American prisoners. None of us could walk or crawl but a short distance."

"For example, one soldier was shot in both legs by small-arms fire, both legs being broken. Another, seventeen years of age from California, had a hole in the base of his spine approximately four inches long and three inches wide."

"On July 28, 1950, approximately one hundred prisoners of war, American, started a march from Hadong to Seoul, South Korea, under Communist army guards. On the thirty-first of July 1950, two other soldiers and I escaped from Hadong, all three of us having been wounded on the twenty-seventh of July 1950. The corporal who escaped with me was shot in the kneecap. The private first class was shot through the thigh, and I was shot through the back."

"I would like to add here about the one and only time that we had food during our first four days of capture. About food, there wasn't a great deal. On the third evening, at least I think it was the third evening, they, the North Korean Army guards, brought us the water pail filled with rice, and there were flies all over it. Some of the men ate it, flies and all, and I tried putting mine on a piece of paper and maybe took one or two bites. By the time we finished, three-fourths of the pail was still full of the stuff, and that was all the food they ever gave us until I made my first escape."

I was a bit delirious at this time and felt sure I would die in Hadong. Being a soldier, I felt sure I would not die in Communist hands. Five days later following my first escape, I was recaptured with my two fellow American soldiers in a small Korean village where we were in a so-called doctor's office. We had found some soiled bandages and sulfanilamide powder, and we proceeded to redress our wounds. I believe we were all suffering from shock."

"Following our recapture by the North Korean Communist army we were transferred from village to village and finally to the city jail in Kwangju, South Korea. All these jails to which we were committed until we reached Taejon also had civilian prisoners. This was a violation of the Geneva Convention in handling prisoners of war." (See map on the last page of the book: southwest on Korean peninsula.)

"In Kwangju we met three Roman Catholic Columbian missionaries who had also been taken prisoners in the port city, Mokpo. Among the three missionaries was an American monsignor and two missionary priests from Ireland. I will never forget these three Columbian missionaries, for we were put in the cell with them in the early morning hours. The first morning that I awoke and turned over, opening my eyes, they were looking at me kind of smiling, three Roman Catholic priests."

"I have entered their names here, but they are still missing. One was a monsignor from America—Chicago—and the other two were from Ireland. Two of the priests, the monsignor and one from Ireland, were formerly prisoners of the Japanese during World War II. The monsignor was a prisoner of the Japanese for six months, and was repatriated on the *Gripsholm* back to the United States, where he entered the United States Army as a chaplain."

"The other priest from Ireland was a captive of the Japanese for three years in Korea. This is where he learned to speak, read, and write Korean fluently, for in the years 1905 to 1945 the teaching of the national tongue of Korean was prohibited by the Japanese, as he explained to me."

"All three of them were missionaries, and they had been arrested about a week after the war started. They, all three, expected to be shot, but it didn't seem to bother them. If it did, they didn't let on. I mean by that the monsignor was always cheering us up. Once we heard a bird chirping outside the window, and he said, 'That's a good sign, lad, that's an omen of hope.' He said exactly that. I remember the words."

"One of the missionaries from Ireland would sing, mostly Irish songs, and once he danced the jig, and one other time I will not likely forget he sang 'Faraway Places,' and we cried like babies, all six of us."

Senator Potter inserted, "In other words, they had a greater faith than communism."

"They certainly did, sir. From Kwanju to Taejon, our hands were handcuffed with hand irons, and the hands of the priests were tied with rope. I might say before we moved out from Kwanju we were told that we would be going to Seoul. Generally at this time we were happy. We really were. We got onto a truck, thirty-two of us. There were two other American soldier prisoners who were in the jail, but in separate cells from us. They joined us. But, like I said, we were quite happy. I mean by that we had been told there were lots of American prisoners in Seoul and also that there was good food and the Red Cross was there, and we figured we could write letters and get letters and that our folks would find out we were all right. So we were generally encouraged."

"I hope nobody will take offense if I say here that most of the Koreans I met reminded me of lawyers. You know, you ask a lawyer a question, and he'll give you all the points

The Major

for and all the points against, but you'll never get anything definite out of him. The North Koreans were just like that, except when you did get a definite answer it was almost always a lie. I don't mean that is necessarily true of lawyers, of course. I mention that because there was no Red Cross. There was nothing of what they had promised us in Seoul when we finally arrived."

"Anyway, we started off, and I remember two things especially. First, these handcuffs were the kind that get tighter as you struggle. Well, with the fast driving and going over these bad mountain roads we jerked all the time. You couldn't help it, and the cuffs would tighten. It was very painful. Also, about the guards on the truck, we judged them to be frontline troops who maybe had been given a break, and they hated us. You could tell that right away. As we rode along, they would point their guns at the hills and shoot and then laugh and sing, and if we moved an inch, they jabbed their guns in our ribs and laughed. I figured this was just more of the good old Korean sense of humor. We were on the truck for three nights straight. We would drive all night, and every morning, we would be thrown into a jail cell and given a rice ball. Then at dusk, off we'd go again. It was cold too. Even though our bodies were huddled close together, we always seemed to be shivering, and our teeth chattered."

"All of us, including the missionaries, went through constant interrogation through my captivity until I reached Taejon in late August or early September 1950. It was constant interrogation and yelling at us by English-speaking North Korean officers. They kept asking us over and over why we had come to Korea. They told us we were invaders, and they continuously blamed Truman, MacArthur, and the Wall Street capitalists as responsible for the war."

"During all these interrogations and questionings on many occasions, the communist North Korean army officers would take their pistols and revolvers, cock the pieces, point them at our heads, and demand that we admit that we were there as invaders. That Truman, MacArthur, and the Wall Street capitalists were responsible for the war, and to sign papers to this effect. To my knowledge, none of us signed."

"I might add that up to this point our food had consisted of two rice balls or two barley balls per day. There was no medical care of any kind whatsoever. The shoes of all other poor soldiers were taken away from them by the Communist army guards. All our movement up to Taejon and from there to Seoul was done at night. It was at Taejon that the three Columbian missionaries and we split never to see each other again. I shall always remember what the monsignor told me when we first met. He repeated many times, 'Everything will come out all right in the end if you trust in God.'"

"It was at Taejon that I met my first large group of American prisoners of war. There were approximately ninety-one of us. As soon as I arrived at one of the two prisoner rooms, I was instructed by an American master sergeant prisoner to disfigure my fatigue clothing and cut up my shoes. Otherwise, they would be taken from me by the Communist guards as they had done to the majority of the ninety-one other prisoners."

"In the room I was in, a big room about forty by sixty feet, I guess there were maybe sixty GIs. In one just like it next door were thirty or so more Americans, plus a lot of South Korean prisoners. In my room were two young lads who each had a limb amputated by a Korean doctor. One had lost his arm almost up to his shoulder, and the other had his foot removed right above the ankle. They were supposed to be recuperating in this room. That is what they had been told. The stench in the room could not be described, and the floor was covered with filth because we American GI prisoners could not relieve ourselves by getting out. Only at certain times of the day would the guards let us go out to the latrine downstairs."

"The many details of our lack of medical care, striking, and maltreatment of the American prisoners by the Communist guards are given in the two magazine articles which are being admitted into the record."

"From Taejon, sixty prisoners were forced to march to Seoul, Korea, by rail and by foot. A brief distance of this was by rail at night. I learned two words while a prisoner: They are *habe, habe*, meaning faster and faster, and *skoche, skoche*, meaning a long distance. We continuously all through our captivity kept hearing these words from our Communist guards."

"During the march from Taejon to Seoul we were continuously receiving the bayonets of the guards across our backs for we were not moving fast enough. A majority of the eighty prisoners had no shoes, had no outer clothing, and had bleeding diarrhea. The majority of the prisoners were also wounded. We received but two rice balls of food each day. There was no medical attention."

"On September 11, 1950, in the morning we entered Seoul, Korea, on our march. Something happened just before that just as we were entering the city. I didn't see it myself, but I was told by a fellow prisoner. A man whose name I cannot remember just fell down on the ground in the vicinity of the airport at Seoul. A couple of GIs carried him a little distance but he was just dead weight. They couldn't take him any farther. So they put him down by the side of the road in a kind of field like."

"About then a column of North Korean wounded came along. There was a North Korean officer in charge. One GI was standing right there beside this man who had fallen. He stated this officer kicked the GI who had fallen in the face several times. The man standing tried to revive the man on the ground. This officer who kicked this GI on the ground left for approximately a minute and came back with a submachine gun. He leveled the gun at this GI on the ground and sprayed him, and that was the end of him. He also walked on laughing."

"They made a public spectacle of us by marching us all through the main streets of the city at a very fast rate of speed. This was at a time during a United Nations air raid on the city by B-29 bombers. It was in Seoul that we first met our first large group of American prisoners of war. There were approximately four hundred, including ten officers. From about the fifteenth of September 1950 or so, the air raids by the United Nations on Seoul became intense, and there were many jets and fighters hitting the city on the outskirts. We were told we would be going to Pyongyang, which was north of the 38th parallel, and we were supposed to be going to the main prison camp in Korea. We were also told that General Dean was in this camp. I do not believe any of us had any idea that we would be making the infamous Korean death march."

"This is as good a place as any to mention the three Japanese-American boys. I am not sure how to spell their names, but Sergeant First Class Kumagai, and Corporal Arakawa, and a sergeant whom I cannot mention, they acted as interpreters for us and they were very popular with all of us, for they were always willing to interpret and sometimes they didn't get any sleep at all in a full day. Besides, if it wasn't for Sergeant Kumagai, I wouldn't be here today, and neither would Major Locke."

"During this march our food consisted of rice balls, North Korean army crackers, dried fish containing all kinds of maggots and worms, and besides not being sufficient in quantity, they would only often give us one rice ball each day."

"The Communist guards never shared the same food that they doled out to us. As we would go through villages, they would go off into the village and get chickens, for example, and corn. They would bring this back and eat it with relish right in front of us, offering us none of it."

Senator Potter interjected, "I think, Captain, we will have to recess for lunch. The committee will be in recess until two o'clock."

* * *

"The committee will come to order," Senator Potter declared. "This is the last session of the hearings. I would like to announce that I will hold a press conference immediately after the hearings here in this room. I want to extend my appreciation to the chairman of the committee, of the Permanent Subcommittee on Investigations, Senator McCarthy, for his interest in the hearings that we are now holding. He has turned over a considerable number of his staff to work on the problem that we are now discussing."

"As I mentioned this morning, I am particularly pleased with the work of our special counsel, Don O'Donnell, who is here on my left. Don has done most of the work in preparation for the hearings that we are holding. Also, Frank Carr, the executive director of the committee, and my right-hand man from my own office, Bob Jones who is on my right. I also wish to extend my appreciation to the army for the splendid cooperation they have given us, and to Colonel Wolfe, who has been with us all during the hearings . . . ."

"I believe we left off this morning with Captain Makarounis. Captain, if you can pick up from where you left off, you may begin your testimony."

Following our escape on October 14, 1950, assisted by three Korean underground schoolteachers, we remained in hiding for six days and six nights, being given water and a little food daily by one of the underground teachers. On

October 20, 1950, the city of Pyongyang fell to United Nations troops, and we were liberated. All three underground teachers were turned over by us to Task Force Indian Head. I have in my possession at home a letter from one of the Korean teachers who helped us escape, stating that the other two teachers who had helped us were branded Communists by the Counter Intelligence Corps, who had first handled these three teachers when we turned them over on the twentieth of October 1950."

"It imbedded in my mind that the Communist plan is really detailed in planning for future operations. Here we were, three of us, helped by three of them, and I am told by this one Korean who personally wrote me a letter—I still maintain correspondence with him—that the other two teachers were branded Communists by our CIC . . . ."

"Captain, when did you get back to the States?"

"I returned the first part of November 1950, sir."

"Were you liberated, or did you escape?"

"I escaped and was liberated when the city of Pyongyang fell to the United Nations troops."

"Did you require hospitalization after you came back?"

"My back had healed by the course of nature, sir. I did not require hospitalization. I was suffering from malnutrition."

Raising a hand, Mr. O'Donnell had one question, "The ranking officer in your group was a Major, as I understand it?

"He was, sir."

"Not to mention his name, because he did not return, do you have any comments as to his particular operations?"

"I might say here that the Major, a West Point officer, the S-3 of the 34th Regiment, was one of the most courageous men that you will ever find in the United States Army, one of the most courageous men I have ever met. Continuously during the march from Seoul to Pyongyang, he would always head

The Major

the column, trying to keep the pace slow. He would always try to secure, beg, and plead for medical aid and care, more food, oxcarts to carry our prisoners. He was always denied this."

The senator recalled, "This Major then turned down an opportunity to escape in order to stay with his men because he was the ranking officer."

"That is correct, sir."

"Captain, I wish to say to you, as I have to the others, you have gone through a great ordeal and you served as a good officer and I know you can hold your head very high. You are a credit to our army. You are a credit to us as an American. Do you care to comment briefly—you have seen communism at firsthand—on communism as a way of life?"

"There is much that can be said. I have restricted myself to saying this: I personally am afraid of communism, what it stands for, and how it works. I believe it is a sickness that is curable by having a strong, healthy American body and mind. I am proud to say that it is my belief, and my belief only, it has not made a penetration in the ranks of the United States Army, of which I am now a member and proud to be so."

* * *

The fighter pilot would be the last to testify and, as always, Locke would relish in sharing his opinion when asked, especially, anything to do with the Reds.

"Major Locke, will you raise your right hand? Do you swear that the testimony you are about to give this committee will be the truth, the whole truth, and nothing but the truth, so help you God?"

"I do."

"Before you begin, Major, I would like to state that Major Locke is the last witness which will appear before the committee at this time. I think it would be fair to state also that the witnesses that you have heard were not selected because the atrocities they experienced were any more vicious or inhuman than hundreds and thousands of atrocities in the files. They were picked more or less at random, trying to get as good a geographical picture as possible. Major, would you identify yourself for the record?"

"I am Major William D. Locke, United States Air Force, 124558, presently assigned to Headquarters, Tactical Air Command as a staff operations officer, Langley Air Force Base, Virginia."

"What is your home address, Major?"

"I was born and raised in Enfield, North Carolina, sir."

"Will you explain the conditions under which you were captured?"

After describing the crash of his Mustang aircraft, Locke went on, "I was taken up into the hills to a command post, about three or four miles from this place. The place that I bellied in was just a few miles across the Naktong River from Waegwan. This area was full of enemy troops and I spent two days and nights at this place. I was bound hand and foot and tied to a tree both nights, and practically eaten up by mosquitoes. I was not mistreated at this time, except for being slapped in the face and kicked around. My shoes were taken away from me by force at gunpoint. I was interrogated quite a bit at this point regarding the position of our troops and artillery along the old Pusan perimeter there and was threatened with death on numerous occasions because I did not give them the information. In the first place, I didn't have it. I had quite a time convincing these people that I didn't have the information they wanted. After two nights in the hills, I started marching toward Seoul, and the second or third day out, I met a group of thirty-five other American prisoners, all from the army, and about half a dozen South Korean prisoners. Together, we walked to Seoul."

"Did you experience the same type of treatment as has been recorded here by these other men?"

"Yes, sir. I stayed in Seoul for three weeks, and my story is practically the same as Captain Makarounis's. As a matter of fact, I assisted Mr. Merrill Miller in writing that story for Captain Makarounis."

"You were one of the three officers that escaped?"

"Yes, sir."

"Thank you."

"Mr. Chairman?" Senator Welker weighed in. "I am a guest of your committee, but I would like to ask this major a question. You were shot down, as I understand, in an aircraft. I was in a telephone booth, and I missed your preliminary remarks. After they made you a prisoner, was any attempt made to get you to sign statements and make speeches, television, newsreels, and the like, with respect to germ warfare?"

"No, sir."

"You never got in on that?"

"No, sir. That did not take place until quite some time later."

"Thank you very much, Major."

"I had escaped before that program started, thank God."

"My story is practically the same as that written in *Argosy* magazine. The story is not exaggerated in any way. It is the true facts. Out of a group of 376 prisoners, there are now 33 alive, approximately 30 of which survived the massacre in the railroad tunnel just north of Pyongyang. I had made my escape approximately a week before that happened, and anything that I could tell you about the massacre in the railroad tunnel is strictly hearsay, and what I have read and heard in this hearing."

"How long were you in the hands of the enemy?"

"Sixty-five days, sir. I would like to say that I know personally of at least a dozen to fifteen prisoners that were shot by our Korean guards on this march from Seoul to Pyongyang, because they became so weak from malnutrition and pneumonia, dysentery and diarrhea that they could not continue. When they fell by the road, the guards shot them and we marched off and left them. We were not even allowed to bury them. We tried to keep records of every death, and the place of death. However, these records were lost when the ranking officer in the group was presumably massacred in the railroad tunnel. I believe his body has not been recovered and neither have the records."

"That is the Major that was mentioned by Captain Makarounis?" Mr. O'Donnell reinforced.

"Yes, sir. These records were kept unbeknown to our Communist guards. On the road from Seoul to Pyongyang, sometimes we would go as much as two days with no food at all. We were only allowed to have water approximately once every six hours, although there were numerous wells along the road. We were not allowed to stop long enough to get a drink of water. There was plenty of food along the road. They could have fed us very well if they so desired."

"What did you weigh when you were captured, Major?" Potter asked.

"I weighed approximately 165 pounds."

"What did you weigh when you got back to our lines?"

"Approximately 130, sir. I was fairly lucky. I tried to watch my diet. I was not wounded except slightly cut on the head when I crash-landed. I did not require medical attention. I did not contract diarrhea. The weight that I lost was strictly from lack of food. We passed by numerous cornfields that had fresh corn that we would have been glad to eat. Potatoes were being harvested. Apple orchards were loaded with apples and we begged for this food and they would not give it to us because they said the farmers under the communistic way of life were responsible for their harvests, and so much was expected to be turned in to the government, and it was not for us to have."

"In other words, it belonged to the state rather than the people."

"It belonged to the state."

Senator Welker inserted a question. "So much for the government and so much in the form of taxes, is that correct?"

"Yes, sir; as I understood it. Anyway, they would not give it to us. We received a little soup and a few dried fish and millet balls, and once in a while a handful of rice."

Senator Potter picked up, "Major, I know that Captain Makarounis has explained how the escape took place, but I wonder if you would review that briefly, how you escaped."

"The first I heard of a plan to escape was the ranking officer, the Major that we have talked about, came to me and asked me if I would care to attempt an escape. I said I certainly would, if there was any hope of surviving. I knew that we were going to be marched from Pyongyang on up to North Korean border of Manchuria, and we didn't know at that time but what we would not be taken into Manchuria. It was beginning to get cold at night, actually pretty close to freezing temperatures in October, and I said that I knew none of us could survive to march another 150 miles. He told me that he had been contacted by North Korean civilian sympathizers that would arrange an escape for three of us, and they wanted him to go. And Sergeant Kumagai had all the details."

"Actually, the contact had been made with Sergeant Kumagai because he spoke fluently the Japanese language. The Major told me that as much as he would like to escape, he felt that as the ranking officer it was his duty to remain with the troops. We knew that the American forces, the UN forces, had already crossed the parallel and were in hot pursuit of the retreating North Korean Army. He felt like, sooner or later, we would all be rescued."

"The Major absolutely refused to escape, but gave his blessings to any attempt that we might make at escaping. We shook hands and wished each other the best of luck."

"Senator Welker, do you have any questions?"

"Yes. Major Locke, were you born in Guilford County, North Carolina?"

"No, sir. I was born in Halifax County."

"Where is High Point?"

"That is Guilford County, the hometown of my wife."

"You were a graduate of High Point College?"

"Yes, sir."

"I know the chairman will bring this out, but since your experience with communism, would it surprise you to know that in a committee that I head, at Chapel Hill, North Carolina, the residence and domicile of the great University of North Carolina, our committee discovered in the back end of the Intimate Bookstore, right across the street from the entrance to the University of North Carolina, we discovered and brought forth to the American people the fact that there was an underground printing press operating in the back end of the Intimate Bookstore, which spewed out its propaganda, Communist propaganda, to all of the southern people and to all of the world? They printed the *Southern Worker* and other Communist publications there. I would like your observations with respect to that sort of activity going on right in the area where you were born and raised. And I might say further to you, that my people came from Guilford County. My mother, father, and five brothers were born there. It shocked me, as I am sure it will shock you, to know that here near one of our greatest educational institutions, that Communist propaganda originated and came from that business, the Intimate

Bookstore, located, as I say, so close to the University of North Carolina."

"Do you feel that sort of propaganda, coming from your own home county, is any different propaganda than you received, and other of your veteran colleagues received in Korea?"

"Sir, I believe it is even worse. I am surprised that things of that nature are going on near our institutions of higher learning and among the young people of this country. But to me that is no more shocking than what we read about in the papers about Communists actually managing to get jobs in our federal government. I think it is even worse, this is strictly a personal opinion, I think it is even worse, such things as that going on in this great country of ours, than it is in foreign countries, because to me communism is a way of life that has been sold by a bunch of power-hungry individuals to a group of young people, mostly, in these countries that have been poor and downtrodden."

"Actually, in a lot of cases I don't believe these people know any better. They are actually groping for a better way of life than they have been used to, and sad to say, communism is not the answer. But in a lot of cases they don't know any better. Whereas in our own country it is hard for me to visualize any American citizen taking part or even joining any organization that advocates the overthrow of the democratic way of life that me have in this country."

Senator Welker went on, "And from Chapel Hill, I went over to North Carolina State, from North Carolina State I went down to Duke University, and at Duke University, the chairman of the board of Duke University was our very great senator that the Lord took away from us a few months ago, Senator Willis Smith. We found that Communists tried to work on students of these institutions. I only have this observation,

Mr. Chairman, and you, Major, that if you people could go out and talk to these young people who are being misled or attempted to be misled by the Communist propaganda, we would do more to save this country than all the congressional hearings, all the hearings we can possibly present from this table or other tables."

"Yes, sir. I thoroughly agree."

"Thank you very much."

Senator Potter then added, "I just want to endorse what Senator Welker has said. Major, I want to say to you, you are the only airman, I believe, that we have had before this committee. You know as well as I do that there are many others that we could have called. When I speak to you I am speaking to all of our airmen. It wasn't limited just to our infantrymen who were captured who received the mistreatment, the inhuman torture that has been received. It was universal to all that were captured.

I am proud of our military establishments. I am proud of the men that make it up, that our Military Establishment is made up of men. The uniform of our country has never shown any brighter, it has never looked any neater, than in the past three days. When I think of men who have never even served their country, men who could no more go through the tortures, that you men have, trying to destroy and overthrow the government and the country that you fought for, I know my blood increases in temperature by ten degrees. I wish that the statements that you and the others have made will be drummed into the ears of the American people day after day after day. If that were done, communism would not be an issue in 1954 or an issue tomorrow.

Americanism is the issue—Americanism that you boys exemplify. Thank you."

"Thank you, sir."

THE MAJOR

The senator then brought the three-day hearing to a close with these words. "I would like to indulge in one piece of vanity. We have had before us, I think, some of the bravest men that this country has ever sent to war. All the men who testified before this committee who experienced these atrocities, if you would come up here, I would like to have my picture taken with you men. It will be my honor. The committee is now adjourned."

* * *

As General MacArthur once famously said, "There is no substitute for victory." For without victory, there are no vanquished to be tried, judged, and punished. So while Congress did rail against the Reds who committed war crimes in Korea, the perpetrators of the atrocities against POWs in Korea and their political and military masters would never stand trial and receive justice.

Unlike WWII's Nuremberg Trials and the Tokyo War Crimes Tribunal after the Allies had achieved total victory—unconditional surrender—the Red war criminals in the Korean War would escape retribution. Those held in captivity by the Allies—such as Junior Lieutenant Lee Hae Do, POW #114963—were exchanged for Allied POWs.[3] (See Appendix 5.) And other war criminals, like Mr. Kim, could avoid any incarceration as long as they remained in North Korea.

In war, like sports, everyone detests a tie after a hard-fought human contest. In the case of Korea, the war was, indisputably, a prodigiously lethal contest. And its culmination in an international stalemate could never mitigate the colossal losses in blood and treasure and only perpetuated a vacuous, indefinite finish to be endured by all the warring nations, even to this day.

Chapter Eleven

Rites: Second and Last (1954 to 1955)

> *When the inhumanity of man to man is gone from this earth. When the brotherhood of man comes in its place. When the children are free to walk in a world of peace, let the whole world remember him. For this is a man, an American, the kind of man who gives millions faith in a better day, a better world.*
> —**Gabriel Heatters's 1950 broadcast summary on Major McDaniel**

Helen opened the apartment door. She laughed. She knew better. It was no way to greet a would-be suitor, especially one rated by the local ladies as the second best-looking man in town. But Dick Mahone stood there in the doorway with a sheepish grin and took in his first impression of her, weighing Helen's inaugural display of impudence.

She did not mean to laugh. Dick was only one of many men who had rung her doorbell. Her colleagues at the Williamsburg Craft House and other friends in town were often sending eligible bachelors her way. And most would not call beforehand, the men would just show up, usually after dinner, on her doormat—perfect strangers, curious, and/or lonely.

Although she was not expecting Dick, she knew at first glance who he was. And for sure, her friends had not exaggerated his good looks. In fact, she could not imagine how the gentleman, who was touted as the best looking, could possibly be more handsome. Dick was Helen's age, thirty-three years old, over six feet tall with a forty-eight-inch chest, yet he was lean. But then he still was an extraordinary athlete.

He had almost signed a contract with the Pittsburg Pirates when he was at his physical peak and was considered the best third baseman in Virginia. But WWII got in the way, and as an enlisted soldier, Dick ended up fighting in the Battle of the Bulge with the 84th ID, the "Railsplitters," wheeling a BAR and earning a Bronze Star and a Purple Heart.

After the war, he tried many vocations—lumberjack, owner of a dry cleaning business, etc. But he eventually found his niche in horticulture and forestry, his double major at North Carolina State, and began working for Colonial Williamsburg. He married once and fathered a daughter, Sarah; but after one year, Dick was divorced. And his former wife took their daughter and moved far away. Now Dick seemed ready again to be more particular about who he dated. He had to be serious when he decided to call on Helen, a widow with two children. Of course, Helen had been taught by her Aunt Hallie to be particular about everything in her life, most notably the men.

* * *

It was four years earlier in May 1950 that Kitty Chalk married her longtime love Lieutenant Stanley Tabor at the Presidio Chapel in San Francisco. And today, 29 March 1954, General Dean would present her a Silver Star and honor her husband at the spot of their nuptial. She knew he had died in captivity, but like so many other POW relatives, her loved one's remains had not been recovered.

Major General Dean Presents Kitty Tabor the Silver Star

The ceremony would be solemn and poignant. After the citation was read and the medal presented, General Dean shared with Kitty the fact that he would not be alive if her husband had not been there to tend to him in those first days after his fall down the mountain. Dean told Kitty, "I wish to express my most sincere admiration for the bravery and selfless devotion to duty which your husband demonstrated while accompanying me."[1]

* * *

The sanctuary at Bruton Parish Church never looked better on 27 November 1954. The arrangement of flowers around the vestibule and altar were magnificent. But, then, it was to be expected by everyone attending the marriage ceremony of Helen and Richard Daley Mahone. After all, Dick was the chief horticulturist for the Colonial Williamsburg Foundation and native born many years before the restoration of the colonial capital. This was his town and his church. He made sure every detail about the wedding was to Helen's liking.

Tom and John were very excited. They already loved being around their soon-to-be father. He was great to roughhouse with and to watch him play baseball in the local casual league. They would never forget the time he was smoking a cigarette in centerfield when a hard-hit line drive came his way. He put the cigarette in his mouth, snagged the ball at full stride, spun, threw the ball with precision to second base, and got the double play. Then Dick took a drag on his cigarette as the small crowd cheered in amazement. Even the other team tipped their hats, acknowledging his God-given talents.

Now that the big day was here, Helen and the boys were more than ready to be a family with a man in the house.

Tom Gazes Up at His New Father Dick Mahone

* * *

It had been over a year since Helen had been to the commissary at Fort Eustis. She, of course, was no longer able to go inside as her marriage to Dick had negated all her military benefits. This day she sat in the car of her friend waiting for the friend to make a quick purchase inside. As she watched, she was amazed. The commissary was filled with Oriental women shopping for food—what an irony. She surmised most of these "foreigners" were soldier's Japanese wives. But the fact that these Orientals, her dead husband's past enemies less than a decade ago, had commissary privileges and she did not, was mind-boggling to Helen.

* * *

As the ascendant voice in the US Army after the war, General Ridgeway proclaimed that, "The training of American soldiers will henceforth be tougher and more efficient for their sake and for their country's honor and security. If any of our men should again be called upon to meet such brutal and diabolic Communist inhumanity, they will be far better prepared, better armed spiritually, and with higher morale than ever before."

To undergird Ridgeway's proclamation, President Dwight D. Eisenhower (USMA 1915) established "The Code of Conduct" with the issuance of Executive Order 10631 on 17 August 1955. Hereafter, all future POWs would now have simple, straightforward guidance on how to behave in battle and in enemy captivity. The code encompassed six articles of faith to be imprinted in the consciousness of every member of the Armed Forces who swears an oath "to defend the Constitution against all enemies, foreign and domestic . . . ." It states:[2]

The Major

I.

I am an American fighting in the forces which guard my country and our way of life. I am prepared to give my life in their defense.

II.

I will never surrender of my own free will. If in command, I will never surrender the members of my command while they still have the means to resist.

III.

If I am captured I will continue to resist by all means available. I will make every effort to escape and aid others to escape. I will accept neither parole nor special favors from the enemy.

IV.

If I become a prisoner of war, I will keep faith with my fellow prisoners. I will give no information or take part in any action which might be harmful to my comrades. If I am senior, I will take command. If not, I will obey the lawful orders of those appointed over me and will back them up in every way.

V.

When questioned, should I become a prisoner of war, I am required to give name, rank, service number, and date of birth. I will evade answering further questions to the utmost of my ability. I will make no oral or written statements disloyal to my country and its allies or harmful to their cause.

VI.

I will never forget that I am an American, fighting for freedom, responsible for my actions, and dedicated to the principles which made my country free. I will trust in my God and in the United States of America.

* * *

On 17 November 1955, Helen answered the door of her home on Capitol Landing Road in Williamsburg. She was surprised to find an army officer and a noncom standing there.

"Ma'am, my name is Captain Sousa. I'm from the Judge Advocate's Office at Fort Eustis, and I'd like to talk to you about your first husband and his time in Korea."

"Please come in. Can I get you some coffee or anything else to drink?"

No, ma'am. We've had enough coffee today."

As the captain and stenographer settled into two chairs, Helen made herself comfortable on the couch in her well-appointed living room. The stenographer got out her notepad for the pending interrogatory. And then the captain began.

"What is your name, please?

"Mrs. R. D. Mahone."

"Did you know a Lieutenant Colonel William T. McDaniel?

"Yes."

"What is your relationship to Lieutenant Colonel William T. McDaniel?

"Wife."

"What information do you have concerning what has happened to Lieutenant Colonel William T. McDaniel?"

"I understand my husband was a prisoner, was taken prisoner . . . on July 20, 1950. He was subsequently shot by the Communists at Sunchon October 20, 1950—at the hands of the Reds."

"Can you tell us something, Mrs. Mahone, concerning the character of Lieutenant Colonel McDaniel?"

"I have never known anyone with so much character—completely selfless."

"How long had you been married to Lieutenant Colonel McDaniel?

"I was married in March 1942.

"Can you tell us something about the Colonel's attitude toward duty, in the performance of duty?"

"It came above everything, and he used to actually . . . . I thought he used to think too much of the military and too much of the duty of it. He never did anything for himself, it was everything for the army."

"Do you think that Lieutenant Colonel McDaniel was the type of officer that would collaborate?"

"I know he wouldn't."

"Why do you say that?"

"He couldn't. It would be against all his principles, and he had such high principles."

"In your relationship with Lieutenant Colonel McDaniel, was there ever any discussion of matters that would lead you to believe he would engage in anti-American activities?"

"Absolutely not."

"Do you have any photographs of Lieutenant Colonel McDaniel taken and sent to you from Korea?"

"No. I have never seen anything from Korea. I had one letter before he ever went to the front."

"Do you know a person by the name of Lieutenant Colonel Paul Liles?"

"I knew him at Fort Benning in 1947, not intimately, but knew him."

How would you say his physical appearance compares with the physical appearance of your late husband, Colonel McDaniel?

"I just remember him vaguely actually, but he is taller, I thought, fairer than my husband and had a scar, I believe, somewhere; I'm not sure of that, but it is vague in my mind. I'd know him if I saw him."

"Mrs. Mahone, can you tell us if you are in possession of information which bear on the conduct of your husband while he was a prisoner in Korea?"

"I have quite a lot of information."

"Will you tell us the type of information you have, from whom—the source of that information?

"I have Don Whitehead's report."

"What is the nature of that report?"

"It was a news story from Korea at the scene of the Sunchon Massacre."

"What else do you have?"

"I have a letter from Corporal Lloyd D. Kreider at Fort Bragg, who had been a prisoner with my husband hoping that they will find him; and he ends his letter saying that Colonel McDaniel thought of everybody else except himself.

"And do you have any other correspondence indicating your husband's character during the period of his internship in Korea?"

"Would you like me to tell about an officer that knows some information about him? A Major William Locke; he was at Langley Field last year. He was a prisoner with him and who escaped in his place. My husband had a chance to escape and he wouldn't take that chance and he says this man could take his place, which the man did escape, and he has information."

"And you have other information besides what you have related?

"General William F. Dean."

"And what information do you have from General Dean?"

"He inscribed his book and sent it to me personally, and spoke of the outstanding ability: 'To Mrs. McDaniel, the wife of the valiant officer who gave his all and his outstanding performance in combat will always serve as an inspiring example to me. Signed William F. Dean, 23 April 1954.'"

"Mrs. Mahone, would you be willing to go to Fort Lewis to testify before some board or other should it be necessary?"

"If it were necessary, I certainly would."[3]

* * *

For Helen, the many years of waiting for definitive proof of her husband's murder would begin to be realized with Operation GLORY. This operation succeeded in retrieving 4,167 United Nations' remains from the North Koreans by the end of October 1954. The possibility of Tom's remains being among those repatriated was, at least, a reason to renew hope for closure. But then more than a year elapsed before a letter of notification from the army, dated 18 November 1955, finally came with the official pronouncement: "Colonel McDaniel was returned to us by the Communists during the mutual exchange of remains."[4]

Her close friend Barbara, the former wife of Lieutenant Colonel Faith, told her that her husband, Colonel Warren K. Bennett, could confirm that the remains were McDaniel's. Colonel Bennett had talked to Graves Registration and had personally examined the details of their identification process.

In short, he believed the laboratories in Camp Kokura, Japan, had ascertained that the bones with the broken wrist from Tom's childhood plus dental evidence left no doubts.

* * *

Investigations of American POWs by the US government had been in the works from almost the time the first Americans were captured. Out of 565 American military POWs—426 army, 52 marines, and 87 air force—that were investigated, McDaniel's West Point classmate Lieutenant Colonel Paul V. Liles was the twelfth and would become the last soldier to be court-martialed on collaboration charges. Three men were acquitted—a major, a lieutenant and a sergeant. Lieutenant Colonel Harry Fleming was convicted and dismissed from the army, and Major Ronald E. Alley was sentenced to ten years in prison. Six enlisted soldiers were also given prison time, ranging from two years to life.

Liles's court-martial convened around Thanksgiving in 1955 at Fort Lewis, Washington. The board was headed by Brigadier General Fred W. Sladen (USMA 1929), a former military tactics teacher at the United States Military Academy. His board consisted of six colonels and five lieutenant colonels. The court proceedings were scheduled to last a month, involving eighty witnesses.

Liles would become only the third army officer to be punished. Specifically, he received a suspension in the privileges of his rank for two years, could not hold a position of command, and could not be reviewed for promotion. He was found guilty of "discrediting the military Services" by making propaganda recordings. In his defense, two witnesses who testified for him were especially helpful in moderating his penalties.

The Major

Lieutenant Commander Edwin C. Moore, who crashed his helicopter in North Korea during a rescue mission, told how in Red captivity it was impossible to abide by navy regulations. The rule to give only name, rank, and serial number almost guaranteed the loss of one's health and was a prescription for death. He had, in fact, resisted in giving any other information and was placed in solitary confinement for three and a half weeks in 1952 and for five and a half weeks in 1953.

Another more compelling witness for the defense—army officer Charles A. Fry—emphasized that early in the war, conditions were far worse for American POWs under the North Koreans than later after the Red Chinese had taken over. At Pyoktong along the Yalu River bordering China, where Liles was imprisoned, hundreds of Americans died of starvation and disease. Under oath, Fry said, "I have never seen human beings come so close to being animals as we were . . . ."

And Liles, during his testimony, admitted, "Yes, we had to buy our food, and the price was to make Communist propaganda."[5]

* * *

Helen stood at graveside. The final resting place for Tom was down the hill from the Custis-Lee Mansion. The grave was at a point where the steps first plateau before descending to three more sets of steps prior to the walk's juncture with the road. She knew being buried so close to the ancestral home of his lifelong ideal of the gentleman soldier would please Tom. And being a Virginian, she was happy he had designated Arlington as his preferred interment location should he be killed. And as a serious student of Virginia history, Helen could almost recall verbatim the words Lee uttered one hundred years earlier: "Arlington" . . . [is] . . ."where my affections and attachments are more strongly placed than at any other place in the world . . . ."[6]

Helen watched from her elevated view as the "Old Guard" platoon came up Sheridan Drive. The formation of marching soldiers followed by the horses, the limber and the caisson carrying Tom's flag draped coffin were magnificent to behold in their solemnity and beauty. She could see the Lincoln and Jefferson Memorials in the distance as the deciduous trees had shed their leaves for winter. She supposed, maybe, she had made a mistake to not bring her sons, especially as she was three and half months pregnant with her new husband's child. After all, Tom Junior was eight years old and John was seven years old. And for a December day the air was crisp, but not cold. But then, with her emotions running helter-skelter, she was conflicted as to what she really felt or would feel as the ceremony progressed.

Old Guard Soldiers, Limber and Caisson with Flag-draped Casket[7]

The grave site was surrounded by Tom's family and friends. Chairs were arranged so family could be seated during the ceremony. Helen would sit on the front row with Papa to her right and George McDaniel to her left. Granny could not make the trip from Georgia, but wanted Papa to accept the flag for her. Since Helen had remarried, protocol dictated the flag go to the parents of the deceased soldier and so it would be.

Everyone stood and watched as the six Old Guard escorts lifted the coffin off the caisson and hoisted it to their waists. Then, with the military chaplain in the lead, the soldiers marched up the fifteen concrete steps on Cutis Walk and sidestepped onto the grass before bringing the coffin to rest over the hole that would receive Tom's remains. The escorts withdrew and the noncommissioned officer in charge (NCOIC) of the platoon proceeded to straighten the flag over the casket, so it was perfectly aligned with the hallowed cist beneath it.

The chaplain seated the family, spoke of Tom's life of service and read several passages from scripture, concluding with a benediction from John 15:13: "Greater love has no man than this, that a man lay down his life for his friends." He then backed away.

The officer in charge stepped forward and bellowed, "Present arms!"

Off to the side some twenty yards away, seven soldiers lifted their rifles in unison and fired a volley skyward. Most of the civilians assembled jumped as the rifles' loud *crack* shattered the tranquility and reverberated across the hilly garden of stones. Three volleys, multiple echoes, and the squad returned to attention.

Then a lone bugler, separated from the others in the platoon, blew Taps—the most mournful melody ever to mesmerize the American soul.

Helen wept.

The six casket team members returned to the coffin and folded the flag widthwise to one-third its original size. Next, they fed the NCOIC, who stood at the end of the coffin, the flag, as he pulled and meticulously folded the American banner thirteen times into a tight equilateral triangle, tucking the end to preclude its unraveling. With the flag secure, the sergeant handed the flag to the OIC.

The Old Guard platoon departed down the hill, leaving only the chaplain and the OIC left at graveside. The OIC walked directly to Papa, kneeled on one knee, handed him the flag, leaned forward, and whispered words meant for only him and Helen, "On behalf of the president of the United States and the people of a grateful nation, may I present this flag as a token of appreciation for the honorable and faithful service your loved one rendered this nation."

Papa took the flag, kissed it, and handed the flag to Helen. She would remain its keeper that day until Papa left Washington. He would bring it back to Albany, Tom's childhood home, and place the flag in Granny's waiting arms.

The ceremony over, those in attendance filed by and paid their respects to the family.

Sometime later, in close proximity to Tom's casket, Helen was standing alone, clutching the flag, when Colonel Jack Norton (USMA 1941)—former first captain at West Point and Tom's close friend—came up to her with his wife. He kissed her on the cheek and gave her a big hug. He was ardent as he put his right hand on Helen's left elbow and the flag and spoke, "What we all admired most about Tom was his perfect sense of duty. He loved his country. And as a POW, his men were all the 'country' he had. He could never forsake them. It was with absolute resolve that Tom chose the only honorable way home. And, Helen, it won't be that long before you and I and Cheyney and his classmates will be at home with him sharing only good times. Don't ever let go of that certainty."

Epilogue

*If you can talk with crowds and keep your virtue,
Or walk with Kings—nor lose the common touch,
If neither foes nor loving friends can hurt you,
If all men count with you, but none too much;
If you can fill the unforgiving minute
With sixty seconds' worth of distance run,
Yours is the Earth and everything that's in it,
And—which is more—you'll be a Man, my son!*

—**Kipling**

For all those American POWs chronicled in this book who were shot at, wounded, imprisoned, abused, and/or killed by the Reds in Korea, much good has come from their extraordinary sacrifices. Today, the Republic of Korea is a vibrant force in the world for the fundamental human rights of "life, liberty, and the pursuit of happiness." The very rights the Americans came to defend in 1950.

The South Korean nation is a modern, functioning constitutional democracy with three branches of government: executive, legislative, and judicial. Christianity is the major religion among the seventy-two million homogenous South Koreans. The market economy ranks fifteenth in the world by nominal Gross Domestic Product and twelfth by purchasing power parity: South Korea is one of the G-20 major economies among nations. Despite having no natural resources beyond their self-developed prodigious human capital, South Korea has refined an export-oriented economic strategy to grow and sustain its wealth. In 2010, South Korea was the sixth largest exporter and tenth largest importer in the world. South Korea's comparative advantage has generated products—under brand names like Hyundai, KIA, Samsung, LG, and Daewoo—that not only allows Koreans to prosper but also has provided Americans a more affordable lifestyle.[1]

Conversely, North Korea—the nuclear-armed "Hermit Kingdom" under the uninterrupted dynasty of Kim Il Sung—remains the pariah of the world. The deceitfully named Democratic People's Republic of Korea persists to this day in threatening its blood kin to the south while starving its own enslaved people, as it did the American POWs, to ensure their submissive subjugation and perennial dependency on the "Great Leader."

In sum, the Americans who gave their lives—wholly or partially—in securing South Korean sovereignty more than half a century ago, and those who loved them dearly, can be encouraged by how this story ends in this the twenty-first century of our Lord.

Helen Accepts DSC from Secretary of the Army with John by Her Side

William T. McDaniel

Distinguished Service Cross—an award second only to the Medal of Honor—is accepted by Helen and bestowed, by law, to the eldest son. This "gift" from Tom Senior to Tom Junior is emblematic of the officer and gentleman the father was and the man the son would strive to become. Secretary of the Army John O. Marsh makes presentation at McDaniel grave site in a ceremony at Arlington National Cemetery. Witnesses include Major General Norman Schwarzkopf (USMA 1956), outgoing commander of the 24th Infantry Division; other government dignitaries; family; and POW survivors—Locke, Smith, Kumagai, and Yeager—with their wives. At the time of the 1985 presentation, the DSC is the highest medal ever given to an army soldier for actions as a POW. Subsequently, McDaniel Hall is built and dedicated at Fort Stewart, Georgia—the home of the 24th ID at that time. (See Appendix 6 for DSC award citation.)

William D. Locke

Retires from the air force as a major while serving as an ROTC instructor at the University of North Carolina. Has a successful second career at Chapel Hill managing the university's extensive parking infrastructure. Battles with PTSD until his death at age eighty-one with his ever-supportive wife Ronda at his side. Makes last request to be buried as close to Lieutenant Colonel McDaniel as possible in Arlington National Cemetery.[2]

James B. Smith

Retires after twenty-four years from the army in the grade of captain. Nurtures, with Florence, three boys to maturity. Becomes deputy director of the Technical Institute of Central Ohio, helping troubled youth. Works part time at Don Scott, the Ohio State University Airport. Serves in the reserves and the Ohio Defense Corps, achieving the rank of colonel.[3]

Takeshi Kumagai

Helps install nuclear power plants in both the Arctic and Antarctica before retiring from the uniformed Service, earning a Legion of Merit. Goes on to become an army civilian electrical engineer with a master's degree in his profession. Receives the Civilian Meritorious Service Award. Dies of cardiac arrest at sixty-seven years and is buried in Arlington National Cemetery with his wife Irene.[4]

Allen J. Gifford

Raises five children with his wife Rose who dies in 2008. Makes a living as a trucker driving "eighteen wheelers" up and down the East Coast. Becomes devoted follower of Jesus Christ in answer to his mother's prayers.[5]

Edward G. Halcomb

Retires after twenty years as a sergeant first class in the army, spending ten years in the medical field and the last ten years in the armor branch. Fathers and parents two boys and two girls. Becomes an entrepreneur, owning a Chevron gas station and Bait & Tackle store. Stops working, fishes for freshwater bass, and settles into a life of leisure in Florida for more than twenty years with Jo Ann, his wife.[6]

Valdor W. John

Stays in the army twenty-six years on medical waivers that had to be renewed every three years. Serves in Vietnam. Marries his drinking partner Linda, whom he met while both were going through a divorce. Attains a business degree and licenses to work on heating and air-conditioning systems. Receives extensive counseling for PTSD and alcoholism. Remains sober for more than two decades before his death in 2009.[7]

Robert L. Sharpe

Makes a career in the army, retiring after twenty-six years as a sergeant major. Marries Kathy, a mother with six children. Deploys to Vietnam after tour was sanctioned by pregnant wife in her eighth month. Serves a second combat tour in Vietnam. Earns two master's degrees and teaches at the college level. Works in corrections and eventually becomes the warden of the Macon state prison. Buries wife at the chosen location for his interment—Andersonville, Georgia, the site of the National POW Museum.[8]

Edward N. Slater

Is discharged from the army in 1956. Works as a salesman for thirty-eight years, switching companies and products after alienating some of his employers. Finds his soul mate Phyllis after two failed marriages. Volunteers at the Veterans Administration, is active in various POW organizations, and becomes the principal organizer of Sunchon Tunnel Massacre Survivor reunions.[9]

James Yeager

Becomes a licensed chiropractor and practitioner of naturopathic medicine. Hampered by PTSD, antisocial behavior becomes the norm. Marries Nadine, adopts her daughter, and has three more children together. Sustains a lifelong strong relationship with family. Commits years of service to PROJECT FREEDOM to find and return the remains of US Armed Forces personnel.[10]

Appendices

1. Silver Star Award Citation

Major WILLIAM T. McDANIEL, 024088, Infantry, United States Army, a member of Headquarters Company, 34th Infantry Regiment, 24th Infantry Division, displayed gallantry in action on 20 July 1950, at Taejon, Korea. After a Battery of 155-millimeter howitzers had been overrun by the enemy and the weapons turned on our own troops, Major McDANIEL was ordered to neutralize the position. He gathered a group of volunteers from headquarters personnel and led the attack on the battery position. Despite intense small-arms and mortar fire, Major McDANIEL succeeded in retaking the howitzers. Going beyond his instructions, he brought up prime movers, coupled the guns, and through a hail of hostile fire, led the convoy out to a position of safety. By his inspirational leadership and outstanding courage, Major McDANIEL not only neutralized the captured battery position but succeeded in restoring to friendly forces the critically needed artillery pieces. His gallantry brought the highest credit to himself and to the military service. Entered the service from Albany, Georgia.

2. Timeline[1]

1945

August 9—Soviet forces invade Manchuria and oust Japanese occupation forces.

August 15—Agreement divides Korea into US and Soviet occupation zones along the 38th Parallel.

September 8—US occupation forces land at Inchon.

1946

January 9—Joint Chiefs of Staff approve General MacArthur's plan for a Korean police force.

1947

November 14—UN resolution proposes removing troops from Korea following supervised national elections.

1948

April 8—President Truman orders US troops to withdraw from Korea.

May 10—Syngman Rhee is elected as chairman, later president of Republic of Korea. Kim Il Sung forms the Democratic People's Republic of Korea.

August 15—US government turns over power to the Republic of Korea.

1949

June 29—Last US troops withdrawn from South Korea.

1950

January 12—Secretary of state Dean Acheson states that the western defense perimeter of the United States stops short of South Korea.

June 25—North Korean People's Army invades South Korea.

June 27—President Truman announces US intervention.

June 27—All non-Korean civilians evacuated from Inchon by air and sea, and from Pusan (women and children only), by sea to Japan.

June 28—B-26 bombers attack the enemy and register the first US fatalities.

June 28—Seoul captured.

July 1—First US troops, Task Force Smith, arrive in Korea.

July 5—Task Force Smith fights North Koreans for the first time.

July 7—UN creates United Nations Command under General MacArthur.

July 10—UN forces gain air and sea supremacy over and around entire Korean peninsula.

July 9 to 18—The 25th Infantry Division arrives in Korea.

July 10 to 12—US forces retreat down the Seoul-Taejon road.

July 13—Lieutenant General Walker appointed to command the ground forces in Korea.

July 13 to 16—North Koreans assault US troops and cross the Kum River.

July 19 to 21—Battle for Taejon, US troops retreat.

July 20 to 21—Battle of Yechon, the US Army's first victory in Korea.

July 25 to 26—North Koreans decimate 3rd Battalion of 29th Regimental Combat Team at Hadong.

July 26—Major McDaniel and PFC Gifford captured in vicinity of Yongdong.

July 27—American field commanders are advised as to the collection and perpetuation of evidence relative to war crimes.

July 27—Battle at Anui.

July 29—General Walker issues "stand or die" order.

August 4—US and Republic of Korea troops establish Pusan Perimeter in southeastern Korea.

August 5 to 19—North Koreans make three crossings of the Naktong River.

August 19—General MacArthur warns Premier Kim Il Sung: "I shall hold you and your commanders criminally accountable under the rules and precedents of war." This for actions in violation of the Geneva Convention.

August 27 to September 15—UN troop strength exceeds that of North Korean People's Army.

September 3 to 5—The 1st Provisional Marine Brigade drives North Korean People's Army back across Naktong River.

September 15—US, British, Australian, New Zealand, Canadian, and Netherlands forces conduct Inchon landing.

September 16 to 18—UN forces begin to break out of the Pusan Perimeter, and North Korean troops begin retreat northward.

September 20—McDaniel POW group leaves Seoul and begins "Death March" through North Korea.

September 19 to 29—UN forces attack and capture Seoul.

September 21 to 26—McDaniel POW group arrives in Kaesong and stays at red-brick schoolhouse bombed by B-29.

September 29—General MacArthur and South Korean president Syngman Rhee enter Seoul.

September 27—General MacArthur gains permission to cross the 38th Parallel into North Korea.

October 8—McDaniel POW group strafed by four US Air Force F-80s.

October 9—UN forces invade North Korea crossing the 38th Parallel.

October 10—McDaniel POW group arrives in Pyongyang.

October 13—Chinese People's Liberation Army regular troops cross Yalu River and enter Korea.

October 15—McDaniel POW group departs Pyongyang on train.

October 15—President Truman and General MacArthur meet on Wake Island.

October 19—UN forces capture Pyongyang.

October 20—First airborne drop of the war at Sukchon and Sunchon ensues to cut off retreating North Koreans and to rescue McDaniel POW group.

October 20—North Koreans massacre members of McDaniel POW group at Sunchon Tunnel.

October 21—US Air Force aircraft hit POW train with rockets.

October 22—North Koreans massacre more members of McDaniel POW group and burn train at Kujang-dong.

October 25—UN forces make contact with the Chinese Communist forces.

November 27 to December 9—Battle of Chosin Reservoir is fought.

1951 and 1952

April 11, 1951—President Truman fires General MacArthur.

July 10, 1951—Truce talks begin at Kaesong, then move to Panmunjom.

July Forward—UN forces battle Communist forces in a stalemate along the 38th Parallel.

December 27, 1951—UN and Communists exchange names of prisoners held.

August 29, 1952—Largest air raid of war: 1,403 UN aircraft bomb Pyongyang.

1953

April to December—"Little Switch" and "Big Switch" POW exchange transpires.

July 27—Armistice signed, officially ending the war.

December 2 to 4—Senate hearings take place on "Korean War Atrocities."

1954

August to December—Operation GLORY repatriates Allied remains from North Korea.

1955

August—President Eisenhower issues "The Code of Conduct."

3. Basic Military Map Symbols[1]

Basic Military Map Symbols

> Symbols within a rectangle indicate a military unit, within a triangle an observation post, and within a circle a supply point.

Military Units—Identification

Antiaircraft Artillery	△
Armored Command	⬭
Army Air Forces	∞
Artillery, except Antiaircraft and Coast Artillery	•
Cavalry, Horse	╱
Cavalry, Mechanized	⌀
Chemical Warfare Service	G
Coast Artillery	⬧
Engineers	E
Infantry	⊠
Medical Corps	⊞
Ordnance Department	♂
Quartermaster Corps	Q
Signal Corps	S
Tank Destroyer	TD
Transportation Corps	⊛
Veterinary Corps	▽

> Airborne units are designated by combining a gull wing symbol with the arm or service symbol:

Airborne Artillery	⌣•
Airborne Infantry	⌣⊠

The Major

Size Symbols

The following symbols placed either in boundary lines or above the rectangle, triangle, or circle inclosing the identifying arm or service symbol indicate the size of military organization:

Squad	•
Section	••
Platoon	•••
Company, troop, battery, Air Force flight	I
Battalion, cavalry squadron, or Air Force squadron	II
Regiment or group; combat team (with abbreviation CT following identifying numeral)	III
Brigade, Combat Command of Armored Division, or Air Force Wing	X
Division or Command of an Air Force	XX
Corps or Air Force	XXX
Army	XXXX
Group of Armies	XXXXX

EXAMPLES

The letter or number to the left of the symbol indicates the unit designation; that to the right, the designation of the parent unit to which it belongs. Letters or numbers above or below boundary lines designate the units separated by the lines:

- Company A, 137th Infantry
- 8th Field Artillery Battalion
- Combat Command A, 1st Armored Division
- Observation Post, 23d Infantry
- Command Post, 5th Infantry Division
- Boundary between 137th and 138th Infantry

Weapons

- Machine gun
- Gun
- Gun battery
- Howitzer or Mortar
- Tank
- Self-propelled gun

341

4. POW Leadership[1]

The Officers

Major William T. McDaniel, 34th Regiment, 24 ID, Georgia.

Captain William D. Locke, 35 Fighter Group, North Carolina.

Captain Frederick B. Wirt, 3rd Engr, 24 ID, Illinois.

First Lieutenant Douglas W. Blaylock, 26th AAA, Florida.

First Lieutenant Crenshaw A. Holt, 34th Inf, 24 ID, New York.

First Lieutenant Alexander Makarounis, 29th Inf, 24 ID, Massachusetts.

First Lieutenant Arthur F. Mulock, 34th Inf, 24 ID, Massachusetts.

First Lieutenant James B. Smith, 24th Inf, 25 ID, Ohio.

First Lieutenant Howard C. Smith, 15th FA, 2 ID, California.

First Lieutenant Stanley E. Tabor, 19th Inf, 24 ID, Texas.

Second Lieutenant James L. Boydston, 3rd Engr, 24 ID, Colorado.

Second Lieutenant Robert B. Miller, 5th Cav Regt, 1st Cav, California.

Second Lieutenant Mitchell Thomas, 29th Inf, 24 ID, Alabama.

The Enlisted

Master Sergeant Marion Michael, 27th Inf, 25 ID, state unknown.

Master Sergeant Edward F. Perry, 34th Inf, 24 ID, state unknown.

Master Sergeant Earl W. Sherman, 34th Inf, 24 ID, Maryland.

Master Sergeant Robert Shinde, 1st Cav, California.

Sergeant First Class Don F. Van Dine, 34th Inf, 24 ID, New Jersey.

Sergeant Robert C. Bomberry, A Btry, 63rd FA Bn, California.

Sergeant Leonard Hines, 24th Inf, 25 ID, Pennsylvania.

Sergeant Takeshi Kumagai, 34th Inf, 24 ID, Hawaii.

Sergeant Robert L. Morris, 29th Inf, 24 ID, Pennsylvania.

Sergeant Louis Rowlette, 29th Inf, 24 ID, Kentucky.

Corporeal Jack C. Arakawa, 19th Inf, 24 ID, Hawaii.

Corporeal Richard L. Wilson, 29th Inf, 24 ID, Indiana.

The Medics

Private John Q. Adams, 29th Inf, 24 ID, Arizona.

Ray L. Allbritton, rank, unit, home state unknown.

Sergeant Junior Catchings, 34th Inf, 24 ID, Michigan.

Private First Class Allen J. Gifford, 21st Inf, 24 ID, New Jersey.

Private First Class Arnold G. Gresser, 5th Cav, 1st Cav, Montana.

Private First Class Edward G. Halcomb, 29th Inf, 24 ID, Ohio.

Private First Class Herbert Harmon, 29th Inf, 24 ID, West Virginia

Private First Class Lloyd D. Kreider, 34th Inf, 24 ID, Pennsylvania

Private Anthony Renneburg, 29th Inf, 24 ID, California

Private First Class Robert L. Sharpe, 19th Inf, 24 ID, North Carolina

5. North Korean Guards Who Executed the Sunchon Tunnel Massacre[1]

Major Chong Myong Sil, Commander, 2nd Bn, 316th Unit, Security Guard Bureau, Home Affairs Ministry.

Junior Lieutenant Lee Hae Do, 3rd Plat, 1st Co, 2nd Bn, 316th Unit, Security Guard Bureau, Home Affairs Ministry.

Junior Lieutenant Moon Myong Ho, NKPA, unit unknown.

Master Sergeant Cho Chang Ho, 2nd Bn, 316th Unit, Security Guard Bureau, Home Affairs Ministry.

Master Sergeant Kang Moon (or Myong) Sik, 1st Co, 2nd Bn, 316th Unit, Security Guard Bureau, Home Affairs Ministry.

Senior Sergeant Kim Bak Ching (or Kim Hak Chin), 2nd Plat, 3rd Co, 316th Unit, Security Guard Bureau, Home Affairs Ministry.

Sergeant Kim Dae Hong, unit unknown.

Private Chae Chang Ho, 2nd Plat, 1st Co, 2nd Bn, 316th Unit, Security Guard Bureau, Home Affairs Ministry.

6. Distinguished Service Cross Award Citation

General Orders 1 HEADQUARTERS DEPARTMENT OF THE ARMY NO. 24j Washington, DC, 7 October 1985

By direction of the President, under the provisions of the Act of Congress, approved 25 July 1963, the Distinguished Service Cross for extraordinary heroism in action against an enemy is awarded posthumously to:

Lieutenant Colonel **William T. McDaniel**, 0-12650, (then Major, United States Army) who was captured by North Korean Army forces at Taejon, **Korea**, on 20 July 1950. During the period 27 August through 19 October 1950, Lieutenant Colonel **McDaniel** was the senior officer in a column of some 370 American prisoners of war being marched from Seoul to Pyongyang, North **Korea**. The prisoners were suffering from wounds, hunger, disease, malnutrition, and the constant brutality of enemy guards. At great personal danger, Lieutenant Colonel **McDaniel** continually interceded with the captors for food, medication, and better treatment of his men. By personal example, and with disregard for retribution which followed his efforts, he organized his fellow prisoners toward assisting the wounded and weak, not allowing them to be left behind. Lieutenant Colonel **McDaniel** inspired the men and restored the will to live and resist among the soldiers in the column. Additionally, he sanctioned and materially aided the prisoners who planned to escape the enemy-held column. Resisting his own instincts for safety and survival, he declined to participate in several successful escape attempts of others because of his unfailing loyalty to, and compassion for, his fellow prisoners. Lieutenant Colonel **McDaniel's** refusal to break under mistreatment by his captors and inspirational leadership at a time when the North Koreans were intent upon breaking the morale and spirit of their captives, finally led to his execution at the hands of the North Koreans at the Sunchon Railway Tunnel. Lieutenant Colonel **McDaniel** s courage and unwavering devotion to duty and his men were in keeping with the most cherished traditions and ideals of military service and reflect great credit on him and the United States Army. (This award is authorized under the provisions of AR 672-5-1, paragraph 1-30.)

Acknowledgments and Sources

Foremost, I want to recognize the courageous men—the former POWs—who shared their individual stories. To do so was often painful, but their candor was always remarkable and humbling to me. Without them, the authenticity of the book would be greatly diminished. These heroes are Al Gifford, Grady Halcomb, Bill Locke, Auvil Parsons, Bob Sharpe, Ed Slater, Walt Whitcomb, and Jim Yeager.

For those departed POWs who could not tell all or parts of their story, I am most grateful to Ronda Locke (Bill's wife), David Smith (JB's son), Hakobu and James Kumagai (Tak's brothers), and Jim Krieger (Stanley Tabor's nephew). They ably filled in the gaps.

As for reference material, Pat Avery's and Joyce Faulkner's *Sunchon Tunnel Massacre Survivors* and David Halberstam's *The Coldest Winter* were inspirational—Avery and Faulkner for the story's particulars and Halberstam for the story's context.

Finally, I want to thank Dr. Mark Gulesian for insisting I write a nonfictional account. And lastly, I must acknowledge my wife Lindy who gave me the book's title—*The Major*. Naming the book was, for me, my toughest task; and I was failing, according to my sons who had read the book. Unsolicited by me, Lindy proffered one title without having read a single page. And I knew in an instant she had nailed it.

* * *

Adjutant General. Letter on finding of presumptive death. 31 December 1953.

Allen, Frank A. "Sworn Statement of Brig. Gen. F. A. Allen Jr." Pyongyang: 26 October 1950.

Appleman, Roy E. Letter to Mrs. Don C. Faith, 9 March 1980.

Appleman, Roy E. *South to the Naktong, North to the Yalu.* Washington DC: Department of the Army, 1961.

Avery, Pat and Faulkner, Joyce. *Sunchon Tunnel Massacre Survivors.* Branson: Red Engine Press, 2008.

Bergin, Wm. Adjutant General's letter on Paul V. Liles. 23 September 1953.

Blair, Clay. *The Forgotten War.* New York: Times Books, 1987.

Carlson, Lewis H. *Remembered Prisoners of a Forgotten War: an Oral history of the Korean War POWs.* New York: St. Martin's Press, 2002.

Chinnery, Philip D. *Korean Atrocity!* Annapolis: Naval Institute Press, 2000.

Dean, William F. *General Dean's Story.* Wesport: Greenwood Press, Publishers, 1954.

Dean, William F. Letter to Mrs. Stanley Tabor informing her of the Silver Star recommendation, undated.

Defense Prisoner of War/Missing Personnel Office, Personnel Missing—Korea (PMKOR), a list of Korean War missing personnel was prepared by the Defense Prisoner of War/Missing Personnel Office (DPMO). Report Prepared: 2005/05/06.

Futrell, Robert F. *The United States Air Force in Korea.* Washington D.C.: U. S. Government Printing Office, reprinted 1996.

Gifford, Allen J. "Statement of PFC Allen J Gifford," Case No. 76. Honshu, Japan, 30 October 1950.

Gifford, Allen J. Telephone interviews, 2010-2011.

Gurney, Gene. *Arlington National Cemetery.* New York: Crown, 1965.

Halberstam, David. *The Coldest Winter.* New York: Hyperion, 2007.

Halcomb, Edward G. "Telephone interviews, 2010 to 2011."

Hanley, James M. "Letter to Commander-In-Chief, United Nations Command, Subject: Trial of War Criminals, Korean War Crime 76 (KWC 76)," 10 July 1951.

Hearing before the Subcommittee on Korean War Atrocities. S. Res. 40, 83rd Congress, 1st Session, Part 1-3. December 2-4, 1953.

"Heroes Given Top Honors." Unknown newspaper, 21 June 1951.

Interim Historical Report. War Crimes Division, Judge Advocate Section, Korean Communications Zone, cumulative to 30 June 1953.

Joint Operating Environment. USJFCOM, 18 February 2010.

John, Valdor. Signed Affidavit of Valdor W. John, Case No. 76. Transcribed on 28 October 1950.

Knox, Donald. *The Korean War: Pusan to Chosin, An Oral History*. San Diego: Harcourt, 1985.

Korean War Atrocities. Senate Report 848 on Korean War Atrocities. S. Res. 40, 83rd Congress, 2nd Session. January 11, 1954.

Krieger File. "Notes and Letters from and to Kitty Tabor." Received by author in June 2011.

Krieger, Jim. Internet posting on Veteran site, titled, "Lt. Tabor's Last Days in Korea," June 8, 2010.

Kreider, Lloyd. "Personal letter to Mrs. McDaniel," 12 September 1953.

Kumagai, Hakobu. Written personal recollections of brother's POW experience, undated and brother's "Military Record," last updated, 1 May 1968.

Kumagai, James. E-mail letter, 5 Jun 2011.

Korea—1950, Washington, D.C.: Office of the Chief of Military History, Department of the Army, 1952.

Lea, Walter. Photo, POWs in truck at Sunchon.

Lech, Raymond B. *Broken Soldiers*. Chicago: University of Illinois Press, 2000.

"Letter of Recommendation, Distinguished Service Cross," sent to Far East Command, General Headquarters, 20 June 1951.

Life Magazine. "Letters to Editors." June 23, 1953.

Life Magazine. "Some GIs not on Exchange List." May 11, 1953.

Life Magazine, "The Captain Talked Back." June 8, 1953.

"LIST American Prisoners of War (Data 1950-51)." List of 510 names (Task Force Russia-3 155-177) from Podolsk military archives provided to Senator Robert Smith (R-NH), Chairman, Senate Select Committee on POW/MIA Affairs, by Russian officials, February 1992.

Locke, Ronda. Taped interview, 1 November 2001.

Locke, Ronda. Telephone interviews, 2010.

Locke, William. Signed Affidavit of William D. Locke, Case No. 76. Transcribed on 1 November 1950.

Locke, William D. Taped interview and notes by author, 1998.

Los Angles Examiner. "Peiping Photo of U. S. Captives Recalls Bataan Death March," identified as a print from China Photo Service in Peiping and described as "a group of American prisoners of war in Korea . . . on their way to a P.O.W. camp in Pyongyang." September 21, 1950.

Mahone, Helen J. Taped interview and notes by author, 2002.

McDaniel, William T. Personal letters, official letters, military records.

Makarounis, Alexander. "I Survived the Korean Death March," as told to Merle Miller. *Argosy*, March 1951.

National Archives, Korean War Atrocities Congressional Files, 1953.

New York Times. "Colonel is tried as Collaborator," November 22, 1955.

New York Times. "Tells of POW Ordeal," December 15, 1955.

"Operation GLORY." Two page Historical Summary of Graves Registration Division Records, Korean Communications Zone, July-December 1954.

Petredis, Paul G. "Anui: Tragic Ambush." *VFW Magazine*, June/July 2010.

POW's Calling. Chinese propaganda pamphlet, Hsinhua News Agency, Peking, 1951.

Quinn, Sadie. Personal letter to Helen McDaniel from Camp Haugen, Japan, dated February 21, 1951.

Register of Graduates. Bicentennial Edition, United States Military Academy, 2002.

Smith, David. Telephone interviews, 2010-2011.

Smith, James B. "Prisoners of the Red Koreans," unpublished manuscript. Yokohama, Japan, 1950 and DSC letter of recommendation, June 1951.

Sharpe, Robert L. "God Saved my Life." *The Saturday Evening Post,* January 13, 1951.

Sharpe, Robert. Telephone interviews, 2010-2011.

Slater, Edward. Telephone interviews, 2010-2011.

Sousa, James J. Disposition taken from Mrs. Helen Mahone by Fort Eustis JAG Office, 17 November 1955

"Task Force Russia (POW/MIA)." Biweekly Report 6-19 February 1993, 15th Report to the US Delegation, US-Russia Joint Commission on POW/MIAs, 26 February 1993.

The News and Observer. "Liberated Tar Heel In Korean Celebration." October 24, 1950.

The Officer's Guide. Harrisburg: The Military Service Publishing Company, 1943.

Thompson, Annis G. *The Greatest Airlift: The Story of Combat Cargo.* Tokyo: Dai-Nippon, 1954.

Todd, Jack R. and Wolf, Cladius O. "Historical Report for period ending 31 December 1952." War Crimes Division, Judge Advocate Section, Korean Communications Zone.

Toland, John. *In Mortal Combat Korea, 1950-53.* New York: Quill, 1991.

Tunner, William H. *Over the Hump.* Washington DC: US Government Printing Office, 1998.

Turbak, Gary. "Kum River to Taejon," *VFW Magazine*, June/July 2000.

"Unclassified Working Papers," Korean War Crime # 75 and # 76, References to POW Camps and Sites, Part 3.7b2, May 2002.

Veterans Administration. Letters on benefits. 5 February 1954.

VFW. "War in Korea," June/July 2000.

Whitcomb, John. Signed Affidavit of Walter R. Whitcomb, Case No. 76. Transcribed on 21 November 1950.

Whitcomb, Walt. Telephone interviews, 2010-2011.

Whitehead, Don. AP news transcript. Sunchon, North Korea, 22 October, 1955.

Whitehead, Don. "Heroic Major's Wife Awaits Word of His Fate in Korea." *The Evening Star,* September 10, 1953.

Yeager, James. Telephone interviews, 2010-2011.

Yenne, Bill. *"Black '41."* New York: John Wiley and Sons, 1991.

Young Sik Kim. *Eyewitness: A North Korean Remembers,* 1995.

Zeiszler, Earnst E., Lt. Colonel. "Memorandum for Record: Review and Determination of Status under the Missing Persons Act; AGPS-D 201 McDaniel, William T., 0 24 088, 27 April 1953.

Endnotes

Prologue

1. Blair, pp. 28-29.

Chapter One

1. McDaniel; The Officer's Guide, p. 166; Register of Graduates, p. 4-228.
2. Locke, Ronda.
3. Smith, David.
4. Kumagai, Hakobu; Kumagai, James.
5. Gifford.
6. Halcomb.
7. Carlson, pp. 101-105; Avery, pp. 24-25.
8. Sharpe, Telephone.
9. Slater.
10. Yeager.

Chapter Two

1. Quinn; Appleman letter.
2. Young
3. *Korea—1950*, p. 44.
4. Blair, p. 89.
5. Appleman, p. 601.
6. *Korea—1950*, pp. 13-14.
7. AP Photo, 5 July near Osan
8. *Korea—1950*, pp. 13-20; Blair, pp. 92-93; Avery, pp. 12-15.

9. Blair, p. 151.
10. Blair, p. 152.
11. Toland, p. 109; Blair, pp. 152-153.
12. AP wire photo.
13. Appleman, p. 147; Blair, p. 132.
14. Toland, p. 103.
15. Appleman, map attached to back book cover.
16. Blair, p. 137.
17. *Korea—1950*, p.57.
18. Appleman, p. 168.
19. Appleman, p. 169.
20. US Army photo.
21. Appleman, map attached to back book cover.
22. Appleman, p. 179.
23. AP Photo, Jim Pringle, 30 September 1950.

Chapter Three

1. Knox, p. 57.
2. Appleman, p. 170.
3. Photo from National Archives, Truman
4. Gifford.
5. Dean, pp. 39-54.
6. Kumagai.
7. Yeager.
8. Makarounis, pp. 32-35, 54; Appleman, pp. 214-221.
9. File photo South Korean refugees fleeing Taejon, July 1950.
10. Avery, p. 57; Gifford.
11. Halcomb; Appleman, pp. 222-224; Blair, p. 166; Petredis, p. 40.
12. Avery, p. 76.
13. Carlson, p. 100.
14. Gifford.
15. Whitcomb.

16. This US Army photo, once classified "top secret", is one of a series depicting the summary execution of 1,800 South Korean political prisoners by the North Korean military at Taejon, South Korea, over three days in July 1950. (AP Photo/National Archives, Major Abbott/US Army)
17. Avery, pp.76-88.
18. Photo of F-51 in Korea, unknown source
19. Locke, William; Locke, Ronda.
20. Carlson, p. 100.
21. Slater.

Chapter Four

1. Smith, p. 33; Makarounis, p. 64.
2. *Hearing,* p. 31.
3. Slater.
4. Makarounis, p. 64.
5. Yenne, p. 21.
6. Halcomb.
7. Gifford.
8. *Life,* May 11, 1953.
9. Halcomb.
10. Yeager.
11. *POW's Calling,* p. 40, first page of photo section.
12. *POW's Calling,* p. 40, first page of photo section.
13. *Life,* May 11, 1953.
14. Makarounis, p. 64; Avery, p. 89.
15. Whitcomb.
16. Makarounis, p. 64; "Unclassified Working Papers," p. 17; Locke, Affidavit.
17. *Life,* May 11, 1953.
18. *Life,* June 8, 1953.
19. Halcomb.

Chapter Five

1. *Los Angles Examiner,* p. 1.
2. *Korea—1050,* p. 95.
3. Makarounis, p. 65; Locke, William.
4. AP photo, Max Desfor.
5. Halcomb; "Unclassified Working Papers," p. 17.
6. Makarounis, p. 66; Gifford; Smith, James, p. 41.
7. B-29 photo, internet, source unknown
8. Kumagai.
9. Smith, James, p. 44; Halcomb; "Unclassified Working Papers," p. 15.
10. C-47 photo, internet, source unknown.
11. Halcomb.
12. Yeager.
13. Sharpe, Telephone.
14. Slater; Sharpe, Telephone.
15. Smith, James, letter; Avery, pp. 236-238.
16. *Hearing,* p. 136.
17. *Korea—1950,* p. 103.
18. Locke, William; Locke, Affidavit.
19. Krieger File.
20. Makarounis, p. 68; Locke, Affidavit.
21. Futrell, p. 198; Makarounis, p. 68.

Chapter Six

1. Makarounis, p.69; Locke, William; Smith, James, pp. 47, 50; Avery, p. 221.
2. Makarounis, pp.69-70.
3. Smith, James, p. 51; "Unclassified Working Papers."
4. Makarounis, p. 70.
5. *Korea—1950,* p. 199.

6. Halcomb.
7. *Life,* June 23, 1953; Makarounis, pp. 71-72.
8. *The News and Observer,* p. 1.
9. Halcomb.

Chapter Seven

1. *Hearing,* p. 37.
2. "Unclassified Working Papers," pp. 2, 15, 24; Avery, p. 126.
3. Sharpe, Telephone; Gifford.
4. Avery, p. 127.
5. Appleman, p. 665; Zeiszler, pp. 2, 9.

Chapter Eight

1. Thompson, p. 23.
2. Thompson, p. 23.
3. Tunner, pp. 238-241; Appleman, p. 661; Thompson, p. 22.
4. *Korean War History Photo, 20 October.*
5. Sharpe, Telephone; Slater; Avery, pp. 130-135; *Hearing,* pp. 37-38.
6. Whitehead; Slater; Whitcomb.
7. National Archives.
8. *Hearing,* p. 52; Todd, Exhibits C2-C3.
9. Lea.
10. Carlson, p. 104; Appleman, p. 662; Whitehead.
11. *Korean War Atrocities,* p. 27.
12. Chinnery, p. 73; "Task Force Russia," pp. 27, 35; Whitcomb; Slater.
13. Appleman, p. 662.
14. *Toland,* p. 247.
15. *VFW,* p. 15.

Chapter Nine

1. Mahone.
2. Smith, David.
3. AP Wirephoto, Raleigh, NC, October 23, 1950.
4. Mahone.
5. Dispatch Photo News Service, New York, October 30, 1950.
6. Halcomb.
7. Yeager.
8. AP Wirephoto, October, 1950.
9. Sharpe, Telephone; Sharpe, "God."
10. John, pp. 23-27.
11. Halcomb.
12. Whitcomb, Signed affidavit, pp. 21-27.
13. Gifford.
14. Slater.
15. Halcomb.
16. Sharpe, Telephone.
17. Photo by Harry Saltzman.
18. U. S. Army Photo taken at Valley Forge Army Hospital, 1951.
19. Gifford; Unknown newspaper article, 1951.
20. Smith, James, pp. 40; "Letter of Recommendation"
21. Slater.
22. "Heroes;" Blair, p. 462.
23. Special Order No. 135, p. 7.
24. Carlson, pp. 102-105.
25. Sharpe, Telephone; Sharpe, "God."
26. Yeager.
27. Mahone.
28. Blair, p. 975.
29. "Bataan Death March," Wikipedia internet site on 1 April 2011.
30. Whitehead, "Heroic."

31. Kreider.
32. Lech, pp. 1, 2, 74, 150, 280.
33. Bergin.
34. Adjutant General; Veterans Administration.

Chapter Ten

1. Joint Operating Environment, p. 11.
2. *Korean War Atrocities*, pp. 1-2; *Hearing*, pp. 1-228. The dialogue—every word within quotation marks—from the hearings is verbatim from the official transcript. Each witness is presented in the order they were called to testify. Some witnesses and testimony were excluded from this book because they were not relevant or were redundant to the story already told in earlier chapters. As for the testimonies that are included in this chapter, any factual inconsistencies between witnesses have been retained, since each witness spoke the truth as he knew it. However, any factual incongruity between Chapter Ten and the other chapters should be superseded by the facts in the other chapters. The other chapters are based on the most recent evidence available to the historical record.
3. Todd, pp. 8, 11.

Chapter Eleven

1. Photo by Ken Hilmer, 6th Army Central Photo Lab, Presidio; Dean letter.
2. "The Code of Conduct" was established with the issuance of Executive Order 10631 by President Dwight D. Eisenhower on 17 August 1955, after the Korean War. It has been modified twice—once in 1977 by President Jimmy Carter in Executive Order 12017, and most recently in President Ronald Reagan's Executive Order 12633 of March 1988, which amended the code to make it gender-neutral.

3. Sousa.
4. "Operation GLORY," pp. 1-2.
5. *New York Times*; November 22; December 15; December 22, 1955.
6. Gurney, p. 89.
7. *VFW,* p.56.

Appendix 2

1. *VFW,* pp.13-17.

Appendix 3

1. Appleman, pp. 783-784; "Unclassified Working Papers," p. 20. The "POW Leadership" list in this appendix is undoubtedly incomplete. This list of leaders was based on the accounts of the survivors and rank played no part in determining "The Enlisted" or "The Medics" list. The list of "The Officers" included all those in the McDaniel POW group because no survivor related any evidence that an officer failed to do his duty. The degree of their leadership, however, is reflected in the quality and quantity of coverage each officer has in the book, recognizing that some officers spent much less time than others in the group and many survivors did not know all the officers' names and often were confused about which officer did what.

Appendix 4

1. Avery, pp. 223-239

Appendix 5

[1] Todd, pp. 8-9.

Map of Korea—1950

[1] *Korea—1950*, Map 7 inside back cover.

Index

A

Allen, Frank A., Jr., 180, 183, 186-87, 251, 260-63
Anui, battle at, 86-87
Arakawa, Jack, 130, 154-55, 158, 165, 214, 292, 300
Argosy (magazine), 290-91, 305
Arlington National Cemetery, 323, 329-30
Associated Press (AP), 261
Ayres, Harold "Red" B., 50, 59, 190

B

Baltimore Sun, 180, 261
Bataan Death March, 226, 353, 364
Beauchamp, Charles E., 55, 59-60, 86
Bennett, Warren K., 321
Biggs, Bradley, 54
Bussey, Charles, 53

C

Choi Yung Kun, 46
Church, John H., 46
Clark, Arthur M., 68-70
Code of Conduct, 11, 316, 339, 365

D

Dean, William F., 48, 51, 55-57, 59-61, 64-66, 68-73, 300, 313-14, 350, 365
Division (US)
  1st Cavalry, 48, 57, 159, 161, 251, 260
  24th Infantry, 39, 48-49, 51, 60, 70, 91, 329
  25th Infantry, 26, 52, 54
Dunn, John J., 56

E

Eisenhower, Dwight D., 316, 339, 365
equipment
  2.36-inch bazooka, 50

369

3.5-inch bazooka, 59, 70
4.2-inch mortar, 50
105-mm howitzer, 50
155-mm howitzer, 61
B-29, 129-31, 147, 300
C-47, 133, 169-70, 172
C-54, 49, 196
C-119, 169
F-51, 94
F-80, 94, 141
   PPsh-417.62x25 mm (burp gun), 47, 81, 87, 96, 110, 136, 174, 271
   T-34 (Soviet tank), 47, 55-56, 59

F

Faith, Barbara, 44-45, 216-17, 321
Faith, Don C., Jr., 44-45
Fentriss (US ship), 74
Fleming, Harry, 229, 322
Floyd, Rothwell, 230

G

Gallagher, James, 230
Gifford, Allen James, 28, 55, 67, 82, 84-85, 90, 107, 129, 166-67, 174, 204, 210-11, 330, 336, 344, 351

H

Hadong, battle at, 76-78, 82, 86, 293-95
Halcomb, Edward "Grady" G., 30, 32, 85-87, 104, 108, 117, 120-21, 126, 133, 139, 150, 154-55, 158, 196-97, 206-7, 330
Herbert, Robert, 56-58
Hope, Bob, 199

I

In Min Gun, 56, 72, 100, 131. See also North Korean People's Army (NKPA)

J

John, Valdor W., 33-34, 91, 174, 180, 201-2, 219-20
Johnson, Maurice A., Jr., 177-79
judge advocate general (JAG), 103, 179, 201, 220, 251

K

Kean, William "Bill," 54
Kim (Communist propaganda officer), 98, 100-102, 105-7, 109-10, 113, 115-17, 119,

122, 126-28, 135, 246, 278, 288, 311
Kim Il Sung, 92, 102, 140, 161, 256, 328
Kreider, Lloyd D., 177, 228, 252, 257, 320
Kumagai, Takeshi "Tak," 26-27, 73, 130, 138-39, 144, 149-54, 156, 165, 214, 221, 292, 300, 307, 329-30
Kum River, 46, 55, 68, 131, 285

L

Lambert, Tom, 54, 161
Lee, Robert E., 14-15
Liles, Paul V., 229, 231-32, 320, 322-23
Locke, Ronda, 22-23, 94, 143, 194-95, 208, 222, 329
Locke, William D., 21-24, 94-96, 99, 103-6, 112-13, 117, 122-25, 128-30, 139-44, 149-54, 156-57, 164-65, 207, 290-91, 303-4, 329
Loveless, Jay, 55

M

MacArthur, Douglas, 147, 170, 193-94, 297-98, 311, 334-35, 337-39
Mahone, Richard D., 312, 314

Makarounis, Alexander, 75-82, 114-17, 120-24, 133, 139, 144-46, 149-54, 156, 159-60, 165, 213, 215, 290
Marsh, John O., 329
Martin, John E., 175, 240-41
Martin, Robert, 55
McCarthy, Joseph R., 235-36, 301
McDaniel, Helen, 17-18, 20, 44-45, 191-92, 195-96, 209-10, 216-19, 224-25, 227, 231-33, 252, 312-16, 318, 321, 323-26, 354-55
McDaniel, William T., 14-15, 18, 59-62, 66-67, 82-85, 99, 104-6, 113, 136-40, 143-44, 148-50, 152-53, 168, 227-28, 231-32, 329
McGrail, Thomas M., 56, 59
Medal of Honor, 17, 213, 216, 329
Morris, Robert L., 128, 149, 155, 158, 165, 197, 214, 343

N

Nininger, Alex "Sandy" R., Jr., 17-18
North Korean People's Army (NKPA) (*see also In Min Gun*), 46-47, 50, 54, 60, 65, 70, 86-87, 122-24, 157, 160
Norton, Jack, 326

O

Office of the Adjutant General, 231, 350, 365
Operation Big Switch, 226-27, 231, 339
Operation GLORY, 321, 339, 354, 366
Operation Little Switch, 226, 339
Owens, Jesse, 25, 138

P

Parsons, Auvil, 90, 105, 120, 167
Pierce, Samuel, Jr., 54
Potter, Charles E., 235-38, 240, 243, 246, 250, 252, 258-60, 263, 277, 280, 283-84, 286, 291, 296, 301, 306-7
Pyongyang, 46, 124, 147, 156-57, 159, 214

Q

Quinn, William W., 45

R

Raibl, Tony J., 74
Regiments (US)
19th Infantry, 64, 77, 86, 285, 293
21st Infantry, 39, 49-51, 60, 344
24th Infantry, 26, 52-53, 137
29th Infantry, 74-75, 85-86, 292-93
187th RCT, 169, 171, 173, 177, 180, 183, 202
Rhee, Syngman, 46
Ridgeway, Matthew, 45, 236, 238, 316
Roberts, Paul V., 53
Rowlette, Louis, 120, 146, 149, 168

S

Schwarzkopf, Norman, 329
Seoul, 39, 45, 88, 92, 97-98, 296, 300
Sharpe, Robert L., 34-35, 91, 93-94, 135-36, 166, 173, 199-200, 220, 284, 289, 292, 331
Shinde, Robert, 130, 136, 149, 168, 214
Shtykov, Terenti, 47
Sladen, Fred W., 322
Slater, Edward N., 37-38, 51, 91, 93-94, 97, 102, 136, 166, 175, 184-87, 199, 204-5, 215, 331
Smith, Charles "Brad," 49

Smith, Florence, 25, 193-94, 329
Smith, Howard C., 149, 166
Smith, Jack, 59-60
Smith, James "JB" B., 24-26, 54, 103, 105, 149, 154, 212, 263-84, 329
Stratemeyer, George, 170
Subcommittee on Korean War Atrocities, 235
Sultan, Daniel I., 18

T

Tabor, Stanley, 68, 71-73, 112, 117, 120, 122, 131, 140, 143, 145, 313-14, 342, 349-50, 352
Taejon, battle at, 51, 55-57, 59-60, 62, 64-66, 68, 211, 227
Takasago Maru (US ship), 74
Task Force Indian Head, 302
Task Force Rogers, 169, 180, 261
Task Force Smith, 49-50, 335
38th Parallel, 39, 123-24, 129
Toney, John, 41, 74-75, 109-10, 135, 175, 199, 223
Tucker, Richard, 180, 261
Tunner, William H., 169-72, 356, 363
Tuskegee Institute, 25

V

Van de Voort, L. D., 177-80

W

Wadlington, Robert L., 55, 60-61, 66
Walker, Walton H., 45, 52, 336
Whitcomb, Walt, 91, 115-16, 176, 184-87, 203, 349, 356, 360-61, 363-64
White, Horton V., 53-54
Whitehead, Don, 180, 182-83, 196, 227-28, 261-62, 320
Wirt, Frederick B., 105, 112, 117, 122, 131, 140-42
Wolfe, Claudius O., 238-39

Y

Yeager, James, 40, 74-75, 109-10, 135, 165, 175, 182-83, 198-99, 223, 329, 332
Yechon, battle at, 52-54, 336

Z

Zeiszler, Earnest E., 231, 357, 363

Glossary

AAA—American Automobile Association
AP—Associated Press
ASAP—as soon as possible
AWOL—absent without leave
BAR—Browning automatic rifle.
BCT—Battalion Combat Team
Bn—battalion
Btry—battery
CIC—Counterintelligence Corps
CINC—Commander-in-Chief
CO—commanding officer
Co—company
Comm—communications
DPRK—Democratic People's Republic of Korea
DSC—Distinguished Service Cross
Engr—engineer
ETO—European Theater of Operations
Exec—Executive Officer
FA—field artillery
FBI—Federal Bureau of Investigation
GI—enlisted person (Government Issue)
Hq—headquarters
ID—infantry division
Inf—Infantry
JAG—Judge Advocate General
KWC—Korean War Crime
Lt—Lieutenant
MIA—missing in action **mm**—millimeters
MP—military police
NCO—noncommissioned officer
NCOIC—noncommissioned officer in charge
NKPA—North Korean People's Army

Noncom—noncommissioned officer
OIC—officer in charge
PFC—Private First Class
PLA—People's Liberation Army
Plat—platoon
PTSD—post traumatic stress disorder
RCT—Regimental Combat Team
Regt—Regiment
ROK—Republic of Korea, a military person serving in South Korean Armed Forces
ROTC—Reserve Officer's Training Corps
R&R—rest and recuperation
S-3—Plans Officer
SFC—Sergeant First Class
UN—United Nations
US—United States
USMA—Untied States Military Academy
USSR—Union of Soviet Socialist Republics
VA—Veterans Administration
VFR—visual flight rules
VIP—very important person

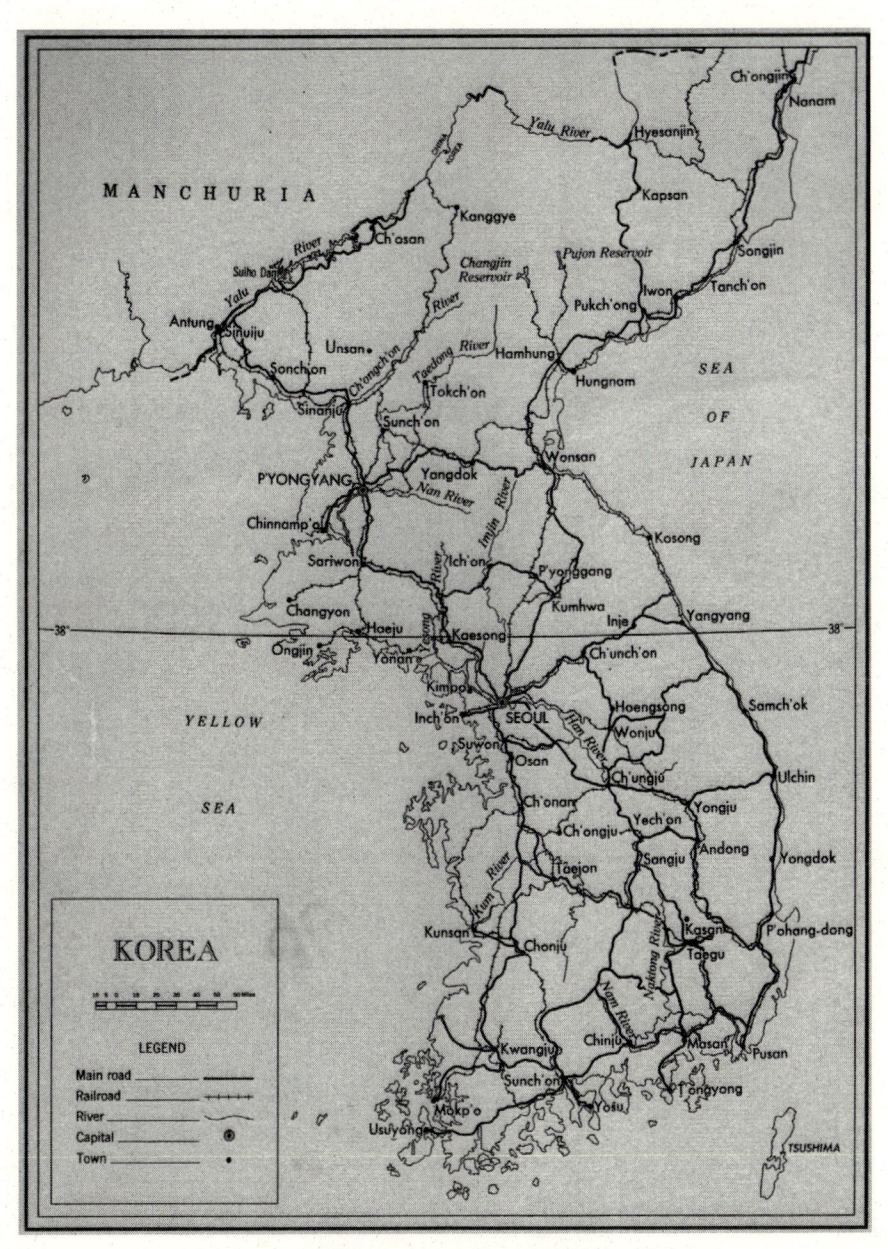

Map of Korea—1950[1]

Edwards Brothers, Inc.
Thorofare, NJ USA
August 23, 2011